THE BUSINESS OF MEDICINE

Private Health Care in Britain

JOAN HIGGINS

**MACMILLAN
EDUCATION**

First published 1988

Published by
MACMILLAN EDUCATION LTD
Houndmills, Basingstoke, Hampshire RG21 2XS
and London
Companies and representatives
throughout the world

Printed in Hong Kong

ISBN 0–333–45829–X (hardcover)
ISBN 0–333–45830–3 (paperback)

Contents

Tables

Acknowledgements

This book would never have reached completion without the support of a number of organisations and individuals.

I am particularly indebted to the Economic and Social Research Council for awarding me a Personal Research Grant (G 00 24 2023) in 1985–6, and to my colleagues at the University of Southampton who enabled me to take a year's leave to write the book. The Department of Sociology and Social Administration also provided me with financial support which was much appreciated. This enabled me to employ two research assistants, Fiona Bower and Mary Thomas, to help with the bibliographical work and piles of press cuttings. Linda Hull also gave me valuable help.

I am grateful to the many people in the private sector who so readily showed me their facilities and talked about their work. John Randle of the Association of Independent Hospitals was especially helpful in supplying statistics on changes in the private market.

Numerous other people, including Barbara Castle, MEP, discussed a wide range of relevant topics which filled gaps in my knowledge or allowed me to check ideas with their experience.

I have benefited greatly from the critical comments of colleagues on the occasions when I have talked about sections of the book and from those of anonymous readers who saw a draft of the manuscript. Steven Kennedy from Macmillan gave constructive editorial advice.

Special thanks go to Tony Rees and John Martin who read the manuscript very carefully and made detailed suggestions. I am sure the finished product – with all its flaws – is an improvement on the original, as a result of their advice. John Martin encouraged me in the research from the beginning and I am very grateful for his support.

The typing services provided by Veronica Jones Associates

ACKNOWLEDGEMENTS ix

were extremely fast and efficient and a good advertisement for private enterprise!

My final acknowledgement is also a sort of dedication and a wish for the future. I have always felt a profound commitment to the National Health Service and to the values it represents. I was born just 21 days before it came into being and was one of its first customers for 'free' services. My parents both worked in it all their lives. I share the view of Richard Titmuss that its creation was 'the most unsordid act of British social policy in the twentieth century' (1973, p. 254). This book is written for all the people who have worked in the NHS (especially my parents and friends) and all who have benefited from its services. I trust that the developments described in these pages will never weaken the principles upon which the Service was founded and that the generation which saw its flowering will not see its demise.

JOAN HIGGINS

Introduction

When the National Health Service came into existence in 1946 it was expected to divorce the care of health from questions of personal means and ability to pay. However, the notion of a health service completely free at the point of need, and paid for out of general taxation, never became a complete reality and the purity of the socialist conception of health care was flawed from the beginning. After 1948 NHS doctors were permitted to continue in private practice and charges were introduced for drugs and appliances, dentures and spectacles. For thirty years, however, the private sector in Britain was more of a 'cottage industry' than big business. The NHS played a dominant role in the supply, control and financing of health services, and the British system of health care stood in contrast to those of North America and Western Europe where there was a much greater private input to the mix of health services.

In the 1970s this picture began to change. Between 1979 and 1985, in the United Kingdom as a whole, there was a 35 per cent increase in the number of private acute hospitals and a 54 per cent increase in the number of private acute beds outside the NHS. At the same time the number of people covered by private health insurance more than doubled. The traditional dominance of two British companies, British United Provident Association (BUPA), which provided health insurance, and Nuffield Hospitals (providing in-patient treatment), was shaken when new aggressive American corporations moved into the market. In 1979 the Americans owned just 3 hospitals with 366 beds. By 1986 they owned 31 hospitals, with 2239 beds, and controlled almost one quarter of the private market. The smaller, charitable and religious-owned nursing homes were either taken over or swept aside in this expansion, and within just seven years the for-profit groups and multinational corporations had come to dominate a market once controlled by the Church, the small entrepreneur and the British businessman. The consequences of these changes may be far-reaching, especially in their impact upon the National Health Service.

Definitions

This book looks at the growth of profit-seeking in medicine and at changes in private health care in Britain since the inception of the NHS. It is specifically concerned with the acute sector and not with long-stay residential care nor with other contemporary issues such as the 'privatisation' of ancillary services in the NHS. As the Royal Commission on the National Health Service discovered in 1979, defining 'private practice' or 'private health care' is not a simple task. This book is concerned with four main areas of activity: private practice by hospital doctors and general practitioners; charges for health care within the NHS; private acute hospital provision outside the NHS; and private health insurance. It will become clear that the private sector itself is not a unified whole and there are many differences in aims, style and outlook, especially between the for-profit corporations and the not-for-profit groups. What unites these different organisations and practitioners is that access to the care they provide is governed primarily by the ability to pay and not medical need.

Themes

This book explores a number of themes and questions. Why was the public/private mix which preceded the creation of the NHS regarded as unsatisfactory? What were the goals of the architects of the new service and why was private practice allowed to continue? Why did the controversies about NHS pay beds and charges remain a running sore in the post-war decades? Why was there such a tremendous boom in private health insurance and hospital and nursing home care in the

late 1970s? Why do patients 'go private' and who has benefited from the expansion of private health care?

One of the most important sections of the book looks at the
part played by American health care providers, both at home
and in the British market. The growth of for-profit facilities in
Britain has been a by-product of American attempts to control
rising costs and maintain profitability in the USA. It is
essential to see these developments in a broader international
context, where there have been significant changes in the ways
in which the burden of health care provision and financing have
been shared between employers, individuals and the State.

The International Context

It was once the case that Britain and America sat far apart, at
different ends of a spectrum of public and private financing
and supply of health care. However, in the past twenty years
both have moved closer to the centre of the spectrum and
other European countries have vied with Britain for the title of
the 'purest' public system. As the private market in Britain
has expanded, so the public contribution to health care in
Western Europe and North America has grown. The arguments which were once made about the distinctive qualities,
which set the NHS apart from the 'mixed' systems of Europe,
are now no longer valid. As Gordon Forsyth has remarked:

> If 'socialized medicine' means the collective protection of
> families and individuals against the costs of illness, requir-
> ing people to pay while they are well and working, for
> services they will want when they are ill and not able to
> work, with the State or State-regulated agencies acting as
> the fund holder, then the European systems are just as
> 'socialist' as the NHS. (Forsyth, 1982, p. 77)

The real debate, however, is whether Britain has become 'less
socialist' as other countries of Western Europe have become
'more socialist' and – many critics would add – whether the
NHS is now 'socialist' enough. Has the increasing emphasis on

profits in medicine and the rebirth of the 'wallet-conscious' doctor meant that the NHS patient has been neglected or kept waiting? Has the private sector drawn resources away from the NHS or has it added to the total pool of available resources? Has the business ethic in medicine led to the abandonment of a commitment to equality of access and fairness in the distribution of health services?

Culyer and Jönsson (1986, p. 3) have shown that in the OECD countries the public share in health care financing has gone up from just 60 per cent in 1960 to nearly 80 per cent in the early 1980s. In the UK the public share grew by just 3.2 per cent between 1960 and 1983 (to 88.4 per cent) while in the USA it increased by 17.2 per cent (to 41.9 per cent). In Belgium, Ireland and Sweden the expansion of public financing has been even more rapid and, in each case in 1983, public sector payment for medical care was greater than in the UK (Poullier, 1986, p. 13). However, public *financing* of health services does not necessarily coincide with public *provision* of health services and countries such as France and West Germany have relied heavily upon the private sector to provide institutional care and other facilities.

Cross-national comparisons underline two important points: first, that every Western industrialised nation has a complex mix of public and private health services and, second, that the assault upon the 'purity' of the British National Health Service which has been particularly evident since 1979 is not new. For two decades at least the British system has not been as 'socialist' as it was painted just as the American system has not been totally dominated by private enterprise. Even though the two systems remain far apart each has elements to be found in the other. Nevertheless, the contrasts and comparisons which can be made are invaluable in highlighting the characteristic features of public health services and private market provision.

A Personal View

The developments described in these pages have aroused strong feelings and there are few people in Britain who have no views about the virtues or disadvantages of private medicine. I began this book because of a deep commitment to the fundamental principle upon which the NHS was based, that access to health care should not be based upon the ability to pay the costs of treatment, especially during periods of sickness. This was accompanied by a growing anxiety that changes in the private sector since 1979 had undermined that principle. Most of what I have seen and heard in the research for the book has confirmed that view, although the private sector is responsible for only a small share of the health care market. At the same time I have met and interviewed many people in the private sector who are doing an honest job out of honourable motives and nothing which follows is intended as a condemnation of them or of the patients who seek treatment privately.

At the end of the day, however, the test of a good health service must be how well and how quickly it treats the sickest and poorest groups in society. It will be for the reader to judge what mixture of public and private health services can meet the requirements of dignity, humanity and compassion, as well as the high standards of professional expertise which patients are entitled to expect from their doctors.

1. Public and Private Medicine in the 1940s

Many histories of the National Health Service have been written and the chronological details are well known. The purpose of this chapter is to look at the transition from a largely 'private' system of self-help, voluntary activity and commercial endeavour to a public health service. It examines the arguments in favour of a service provided on the basis of need rather than ability to pay and at the vestiges of private medicine which remained when the NHS came into being.

Health Services in the Early Twentieth Century

The movement towards a 'nationalised' and a public health service began well before 1948 and when the White Paper, *A National Health Service*, was issued in 1944 a substantial sector of the population had access to free or subsidised hospital care and was covered by some form of health insurance. The national health insurance scheme for general practitioner care was introduced by Lloyd George in 1911 and covered 21 million people. Others were members of private schemes and hospital savings associations. Nevertheless, there were large (and vulnerable) groups of the population excluded from the national scheme and without the means to insure themselves privately. Despite the gradual extension of insurance cover from 1911, at the outbreak of World War II women and dependent children were still excluded from the scheme, as were the unemployed and the self-employed and those whose annual incomes exceeded £250 (this was later increased to £420). Even those who were covered had very limited benefits. They were entitled to GP care and to drugs and medicines as well as to sickness benefits, but the sums paid out were very

6

small. Hospital services were originally excluded but were gradually covered and by 1939 around half the population was entitled to hospital care through one scheme or another.

The hospitals themselves varied enormously. Many of the beds were in voluntary hospitals which ranged from the large, prestigious London teaching hospitals to small cottage hospitals run by general practitioners. When war broke out there were more than 1000 voluntary hospitals in England and Wales with some 77 000 beds. Of these hospitals 700 were general hospitals dealing with a variety of cases, while more than 230 specialised in particular diseases such as eye conditions, ear, nose and throat problems or diseases of the nervous system. Only 75 of the hospitals had more than 200 beds while 250 had less than 30 beds and many more had less than 100. They depended for their income upon charity and philanthropy, upon subscriptions, donations and endowments, charges to patients, flag days and all manner of fund-raising techniques.

The other main providers of hospital beds were the local authorities. There had been a long tradition of free health care for the poor in the workhouses of the nineteenth century. The poor law infirmaries, with their low standards, appalling conditions and stigma, were gradually improved and in the pre-war years many had become the responsibility of the local authorities. They provided care and treatment primarily for the chronic sick, the elderly and the mentally ill. By 1939 the local authorities in England and Wales provided nearly 70 000 beds in 140 general hospitals and there were almost 60 000 more in 400 poor law institutions. Again, the provision varied greatly from 'sick wards' in institutions for the elderly, to modern, well-equipped general hospitals. Patients were expected to pay for their treatment, either directly or through an insurance scheme, except where they were suffering from an infectious disease or where they had little or no income.

In addition to these general hospital beds there were many more provided for patients suffering from infectious diseases or from tuberculosis. In the former case there were 38 000 beds in 810 small isolation hospitals scattered across the country. TB sanatoria provided 28 000 beds, some of them in local authority hospitals, and some were provided by other agencies. Many more beds were provided for the mentally ill, for maternity care and for cancer patients. Mental hospitals were very large – often with 1000 or more patients – but other hospitals were small and often isolated. The Emergency Hospital Service, established to deal with wartime demands, added a further 50 000 beds to the increasingly complex picture.

The first forty years of the twentieth century had seen the gradual acceptance of public responsibility for the health care of the nation. But the result was a tangled web of services which varied dramatically in quality and was badly organised. There was little or no effective planning of health services. Some areas were over-doctored, with an excess of hospital beds and duplication of facilities, while others were relative deserts with few hospitals and fewer doctors. It was a matter of chance whether the incidence of disease coincided with adequate provision (and often it did not). The White Paper put it mildly when it talked of:

a complicated patch-work pattern of health resources, a mass of particular and individual services evolved at intervals over a century or more . . . and for the most part coming into being one by one to meet particular problems, to provide for particular diseases or particular aspects of health or particular sections of the community. (Ministry of Health, 1944 p. 53)

Money and Medicine

If geography was one of the key determinants of access to pre-war health services money was the other. The significance of wealth and pattern of provision, however, were complex. In some cases having no money was as much a guarantor of receiving treatment as having a great deal of money. From the beginning of the century a series of measures had been introduced which sought to provide free or low-cost care for those groups who could not purchase treatment. Public hospitals were obliged by law to take in anyone requiring attention, and, although means-testing was in use, those who could not make a financial contribution were entitled to free treatment. Out-patient departments were used extensively by low-income patients as their first point of access to medical care, especially where they had no insurance cover for GP services.

The voluntary hospitals, which had been established as charitable institutions in the eighteenth and nineteenth centuries, also provided treatment free of charge to those who could not afford the fees. As far as physical access to these hospitals was concerned, the poor, especially the London poor, indeed sometimes had an advantage over their richer neighbours in the suburbs or the country. The voluntary hospitals had been built in the centres of population and often, as Eckstein points out, in the most unsalubrious settings:

> In London for example, Guy's is located in what must be about the grimiest and noisiest of waterfront districts, it is in the midst of warehouses, power stations, factories, river and land traffic, and there is usually an appalling amount of din and smoke. . . A London hospital which permitted grouse shooting in its grounds in the eighteenth century was in the midst of industrial hubbub in the nineteenth, and a large provincial hospital which was a landmark in the countryside at its founding is now bounded by railway yards on two sides and factories on others. (Eckstein, 1958, pp. 39–40)

So, while some voluntary hospitals had been deliberately built amongst the industrial working classes they were designed to serve, others had become 'urban' as the population and industrial development had engulfed them. Although the location of the voluntary hospitals might have seemed less than ideal in some respects, it did mean that they were within walking distance for many of the poor. What is more, they attracted some of the finest medical staff in the country. In these respects they made a significant contribution to the medical care of the working man and his family. Indeed, as Eckstein argued: 'The urban poor . . . enjoyed almost every conceivable advantage over the rest of the population in access to good hospitals and specialists – and this includes Mayfair no less than Surbiton' (ibid., p. 40).

Apart from receiving free hospital care in certain circumstances, the poor were also enabled to pay for treatment through a variety of schemes. National health insurance steadily extended its cover but for those who were not eligible for benefits there were friendly societies, provident associations, doctors' 'clubs' and so on. In return for weekly contributions individuals could purchase medical treatment and the services of a GP.

Despite these advances there were many gaps in provision, for poor and rich alike. Insurance coverage was limited. The benefits paid out by most schemes offered minimal protection against the financial insecurities of ill health. However low the weekly contributions to private schemes, some of the poor could not afford them. Conditions in both local authority and voluntary hospitals were very variable and sometimes crude. There was a heavy concentration of voluntary hospitals, teaching hospitals and medical staff in London and one or two other urban centres. Low income families elsewhere had fewer chances of decent hospital care.

What of those for whom money was no barrier to purchasing medical care? Ironically, they were little better off. The rich were reluctant to seek treatment in the public hospitals and even, to a degree, in the voluntary hospitals. The stigma of the Poor Law and charity were unpalatable to them, as were the rumours of rough and ill-educated nursing staff (and patients). Some of the voluntary hospitals had private rooms or private wings where the rich could remain separate and secure from the rest of the inhabitants. Most, however, preferred to be treated at home or in smaller nursing homes where they could be with a better class of patient. The standard of care they received there was inevitably limited (because of the size of the institution and its resources) and much less good than they might have received in a public or voluntary hospital.

Thus, the relationship between money and medicine in pre-war health services was complex. Having no money sometimes ensured a higher standard of treatment and readier access to hospital care than having a great deal of money. But it would be wrong to exaggerate the benefits to the poor. Much depended upon geography and luck. There were many low-income families outside London, without insurance cover, without the means to purchase medical care and without access to in-patient treatment. Even so a number of writers (Eckstein, 1958; Watkin, 1978) have argued that it was the middle classes (rather than the rich or poor) who fared worst in the pre-war health system.

Doctors in the voluntary hospitals generally had honorary contracts and worked free of charge. Their association with these hospitals was a matter of prestige and the subject of considerable competition. They made their incomes from private practice and from fees charged to their better-off patients in their clinics and consulting rooms. The fee-paying patients, in what amounted to a system of 'forced medical charity' (Eckstein, 1958 p. 38),therefore, provided very heavy subsidies to the voluntary hospitals and their patients. Watkin argues that doctors worked informally on the 'Robin Hood' principle, 'charging their middle-class patients more than the economic rate for their services so as to offset the losses they incurred in caring for the poor at reduced fees or no fees at all' (Watkin, 1978, p. 10). Middle-income groups were also disadvantaged in the insurance market. They were excluded from the National Health Insurance scheme because their incomes were too high and were thrown onto the provident associations and friendly societies where high premiums did not always guarantee generous benefits.

If money was a problem for patients it was also a problem for doctors and hospitals too. The voluntary hospitals, in particular, were in an almost constant state of crisis in the years preceding the war. The increasing demands they faced could not easily be met from charitable donations and there was little, if any, surplus in many hospitals for necessary equipment or for the development of new treatments and techniques. As far as the doctors were concerned, only a minority earned a high income, with many more struggling hard and working long hours to earn a meagre living. Their problems were exacerbated by their dependence on fee-paying patients and the frequent necessity to hire debt collectors to pursue bad payers. The organisation of the financial and administrative aspects of medical care was often rather poor, especially in the GP's surgery. Eckstein attributes this not just to the constant pressure of work but also to a distaste for anything that smacked of 'trade': 'To the professional middle class', he suggests, 'trade even now, is perhaps little more than a useful evil, the sort of thing one prefers to leave to others' (1958, p. 81). It is a persisting anomaly, he argues, that the British medical profession should 'couple a considerable appetite for fees with an aversion for certain much less critical aspects of the commercial role' (ibid., p. 81).

If the GPs found the collection of money distasteful, how much more distressing was it for patients? Lena Jeger, in a letter to the *Guardian* in 1964, for example, described the indignity and misery her mother experienced when sitting on the edge of a chair in the consulting room 'opening and shutting her purse', waiting to pay over her half-crown: 'She never knew whether to just slide it across the desk, which she said might make the doctor feel like a waiter, or to actually put it in his hand and make him feel as if he worked in a shop. Sometimes we dropped the money and that was the least dignified of all, especially if the fat doctor let my mother pick it up' (quoted in Forsyth, 1966, p. 26).

In the pre-war health service, then, each social group or class was disadvantaged in some way by the close relationship between money and medicine. The poor, although provided for in the public and voluntary hospitals and under national insurance, had an unhealthy and insecure existence. The spectre of illness was a major threat and there were many gaps in the system designed to satisfy their needs. The middle classes were the major sources of finance in the system and paid more than their fair share of doctors' fees and hospital bills. The rich, despite their money, voluntarily excluded themselves from some of the best hospital care, preferring instead the small, private hospital or nursing home with sometimes poor facilities and inadequately trained staff.

The aim of the NHS, therefore, was not simply to ensure that the poor received medical care as and when they needed it but, much more generally, to break the cash nexus between sickness and medicine. The White Paper in 1944 explained that:

it is still not true to say that everyone can get all the kinds of medical and hospital service which he or she may require. Whether people can do so still depends too much upon circumstances, upon where they happen to live or work, to what group (e.g. of age, or vocation) they happen to belong, or what happens to be the matter with them. Nor is the care of health yet wholly divorced from ability to pay for it, although great progress has already been made in eliminating the financial barrier to obtaining more of the essential services. There is not yet, in short, a comprehensive cover for health provided for all people alike. That is what is now the Government's intention to provide. (Ministry of Health, 1944, p. 6).

Not only was health care not 'wholly divorced' from the ability to pay for it, but the White Paper, in fact, goes on to say that for 'something like half the population' securing the services of a general practitioner depended upon 'what private arrangements any particular person can manage to make' (ibid., p. 7).

It was not only Aneurin Bevan who argued that 'money ought not to be permitted to stand in the way of obtaining an efficient health service' (*Hansard*, 30 April 1946, col. 43). Many of his opponents agreed. It was the way in which this aim should be realised which was the subject of such disagreement and debate.

Reform and the White Paper

The pre-war health services suited no one's need perfectly and the prospect of reform was generally welcomed. A series of reports, from the 1930s onwards, had paved the way for the White Paper, *A National Health Service*, in 1944. The White Paper itself had three broad aims:

1. To ensure that everyone in the country 'irrespective of means, age, sex or occupation' should have equal opportunities in securing the medical care they needed.
2. To provide a comprehensive health service covering all aspects of preventive and curative medicine.
3. To divorce the care of health from questions of personal

means' and to provide the service free of charge (apart from certain possible charges in respect of appliances). (Ministry of Health, 1944, p. 47)

Considerable emphasis was placed upon the need to ensure that lack of money was not a barrier to the receipt of essential services and treatment. The service was not, of course, to be literally free of charge but the method of payment was to be changed so that resources for medical care came from general taxation and from insurance rather than from direct cash payments when people were ill.

The White Paper saw a single, comprehensive service for all as the 'natural, next development' (p. 5). It argued 'at this stage of social development' (p. 6) the care of personal health should be the concern of a publicly organised and financed service. What is more, it emphasised the desirability of preventive care and positive health programmes. 'Personal health', it argued, 'still tends to be regarded as something to be treated when at fault, or perhaps to be preserved from getting at fault, but seldom as something to be positively improved and promoted and made full and robust' (p. 8).

The goal of a free, comprehensive service, which included preventive as well as curative medicine was to be achieved in a number of ways. The two key areas of change were to lie within the hospital and consultant services and the GP services. The White Paper was generally cautious in its comments about the hospitals, especially the voluntary hospitals, and was encouraging rather than threatening. It was not, at this stage, proposed to 'nationalise' the voluntary hospitals. They were to remain independent and would receive payments from central funds for services rendered. It was expected that they would still attract voluntary donations. They were, however, required to observe national wage rates and conditions of service and to conform to a common method of appointing senior medical staff. The White Paper was similarly reticent in its discussion of GP services, though it was made clear that there would be overall public control. If services were to be accessible to all and free to all, the argument ran, the doctors themselves would naturally seek remuneration from public funds. If taxpayers' money was to be spent in this way, it continued, general practitioners must be in a contractual relationship with public authorities and accountable to them.

The White Paper did not express the intention of abolishing private practice or fee-for-service medicine, though the effects of its proposals would be to reduce their scope and appeal. Indeed, it fought shy of compulsion in many areas. It emphasised the continuing freedom of patients to choose their doctors and the freedom of doctors to practise their professional skills both inside and outside the new health service. Similarly, it claimed that there would be 'no compulsion into the new service, either for patient or doctor' and 'no interference with the making of private arrangements at private cost' (p. 47).

Not everyone was convinced, however. The *British Medical Journal*, for example, in a leader compained that 'it is difficult to see how . . . private practice as we know it today can survive as much more than a shadow of itself' (1944, vol.1, p. 295), while the British Medical Association, it is alleged, 'tried frantically to discredit it, finding sinister implications of bureaucratic control lurking everywhere under the idealistic promises' and keeping up 'an unedifying racket until the very eve of the new service's creation' (Calder, 1969, p. 540).

If the doctors were generally anxious about the White Paper and suspicious of its implications, they were also divided on a number of key issues. While the BMA leadership was hostile to the proposals, many of the 'rank and file' doctors proved to be supportive of many parts of the plan, not least the idea of a 'free' and comprehensive service. As Eckstein points out, however, there were different vested interests at work, especially among the GPs. These he divides into four categories: 'working-class, Mayfair, suburban and resort practitioners' (1958, p. 153). The working-class doctor had much to gain from a free, salaried service as did the Mayfair doctor (as long as private practice was allowed). The other two groups stood to lose. The same point is made of hospital doctors where specialists in lucrative areas, such as obstetrics and gynaecology, feared a levelling down of their incomes, while other groups without large private practices (ENT surgeons and physicians) had little to lose.

The reaction of the medical profession to a free, comprehensive service was, therefore, far from uniform and different interest groups within it perceived different benefits. On the other hand, the general public, without such concerns, were enthusiastic and positive about the scheme and especially welcomed the idea of a service free at the point of use.

Although some commentators see the White Paper as the culmination of a long process of reform in public health care, it was really only the beginning of a protracted and bitter debate. A key feature of this debate centred upon the role of private practice in the new health service. As Pater has indicated, it was a matter of concern to all interest groups of all political persuasions (Pater, 1981, p. 81). The conservatives were fearful of losing their lucrative private practice in a comprehensive and free health service and the radicals were concerned that to allow private practice would be to undermine the new public service.

The White Paper which had been issued on 17 February, 1944 was the subject of considerable discussion right through 1944 and into the first half of 1945. When a Labour government swept to victory in the General Election of July 1945 the resolution of the debate was just one of a number or urgent priorities. Many of the groups involved in the debate thus far, especially the doctors, were apprehensive about what was in store. Some factions within the Labour Party were known to favour the abolition of private practice, the nationalisation of voluntary hospitals and a full-time salaried service. Aneurin Bevan, the new Minister of Health, had a reputation for radicalism and toughness which went before him.

Bevan and the Bill

Discussions in Cabinet and elsewhere in the Autumn of 1945, about the content of the proposed Bill on the national health service, revealed a number of divisions in the Labour ranks. Bevan himself favoured much firmer, centralised control of the voluntary hospitals than had been envisaged in the White Paper. If they were to receive 80–90 per cent of their funds from public sources, he argued, then they could not remain under independent management. Although many of his colleagues concurred with this view, some (especially Herbert

Morrison) felt strongly that the hospitals should be under the control of local authorities and not the central government. On the other hand Bevan, somewhat to the surprise of friend and foe, recommended the retention of pay beds in public hospitals and a degree of private practice. His argument was that these concessions were necessary as a way of ensuring the commitment of hospital consultants to the new service, that priority would be given to NHS patients and that tight controls would exist to limit the extent of private practice and the use of pay beds.

Although all these matters had not been resolved they had been thoroughly debated within the Government itself and by interested parties, and on 20 March 1946 the National Health Service Bill was published. As far as private practice was concerned it proposed that consultants would either have full-time contracts with the NHS or part-time contracts which would enable them to undertake private work. The Government hoped to discourage them from treating private patients in nursing homes and they were to be allowed to see fee-paying patients in NHS hospitals. At the same time, patients were to be allowed to buy some privileges (including privacy) in these hospitals, either in amenity beds (where they would pay a fee for accomodation only) or in private beds (where they would pay both for their treatment and for their accommodation). The Bill set out its intention to establish maximum fees which specialists could charge patients in these 'pay beds'. The White Paper summarising the Bill emphasised, however, that these provisions were 'subject always to the requirements of patients who need such accomodation on medical grounds' and that such patients 'will be able to have it without payment (Ministry of Health, 1946, p. 8).

Although it was intended that the health service would be entirely free of charge a number of important exceptions were built into the Bill:

1. Patients would be required to pay for the repair or renewal of spectacles, dentures and other appliances.
2. There would be means-tested charges for domestic help, supplementary foods and blankets.
3. Patients would not be required, but would be permitted,

to pay for 'additional amenities within the arrangements of the service', such as articles or appliances of a higher cost than those which would normally be available, and for private rooms in hospitals (p. 4).

Aneurin Bevan, explaining this provision later to the House of Commons argued that:

> If people wish to pay for additional amenities or something to which they attach value, like privacy in a single ward, we ought to aim at providing such facilities for everyone who wants them. . . it inevitably happens that some people will want to buy something more than the general health service is providing, (*Hansard*, 30 April 1946, col. 57)

Bevan claimed that he was reluctant to make this concession and to allow private practice to continue. However, it was the only way, he suggested, to ensure the co-operation of hospital specialists with the scheme. It was intended to encourage them to undertake their private practice within the NHS and not in small, unsuitable nursing homes around the country.

> If we do not permit fees in hospitals, we will lose many specialists from the public hospitals because they will go to nursing homes. I believe that nursing homes ought to be discouraged. They cannot provide general hospital fa- cilities. (ibid., p. 57)

Similar concessions were to be made to GPs. Taking part in the service, the White Paper suggested, would 'not debar them from also continuing to make private arrangements for treat- ing such people as still wish to be treated outside the service' (Ministry of Health, 1946, p. 10). The only constraint here was to be that GPs could not accept as private patients individuals who were already on their list (or that of their partners) as NHS patients.

The goal of eliminating all fee-for-service medicine from the new service was modified, therefore, at a relatively early stage in the deliberations and these key concessions to the doctors formed part of the Bill. While the provisions related specifi-

cally to England and Wales a separate Bill for Scotland made
exactly the same points on private practice.

The Government was rather more determined (and successful) in its handling of the voluntary hospitals. Here it was made clear that the majority of them would be taken into public ownership, compulsorily if necessary. This transfer of ownership was also to apply to mental hospitals and mental deficiency institutions but teaching hospitals were treated separately and were to be managed by boards of governors. Although exceptions would be allowed in certain circumstances, it was expected that the voluntary hospitals would lose their independence and autonomy and become the responsibility of the Ministry of Health.

One more well-established tradition was threatened by the Bill. This was the sale of GP practices, which had been going on for many years. The 1944 White Paper had been guarded on this issue and it was argued, at that stage, that the success of a national health scheme was not contingent upon the elimination of this practice and that a resolution to this question could wait until a later date. The Bill in 1946, however, took a different line – maintaining that the sale of practices was inconsistent with many of the principles of a health service under national control. It foresaw difficulties in directing GPs to under-doctored areas if the custom continued and consequently proposed to prohibit the sale of practices (and pay suitable compensation) as soon as was practically possible.

Reactions to the Bill

The first reading of the National Health Service Bill took place on 19 March 1946. When it was given a second reading on 30 April 1946 there had already been six weeks of speculation, lobbying and criticism.

The Lancet (23 March 1946) argued that 'We should perhaps be thankful that Mr. Bevan, in storming the Bastille of the hospitals, shows no inclination to proclaim the complete revolution in medical organisation which logic or his own convictions might dictate'(p. 422). It described the proposal to retain private practice as 'remarkable' (p. 423) and was plainly impressed by the Bill as a whole. It was pleasantly surprised to find it was not the 'doctrinaire Socialist programme that was deemed inevitable' (p. 423) and it had many positive features. *The Lancet* commented, in conclusion, that 'It is easy to be too much afraid. We should ask ourselves whether, with all its risks, the Service contemplated does not give us opportunities' (p. 423). The proposals, it claimed, 'do not call for wholesale condemnation or irreconcilable opposition' (p. 424) and, on the whole, it gave them warm and enthusiastic support.

Less sanguine views were reflected in the letters column of subsequent editions with vociferous opposition from Dr Charles Hill of the BMA and Sir Bernard Docker of the British Hospitals Association, amongst others. The latter took a highly critical line and described the Bill as advocating the 'mass murder of the hospitals' (*The Lancet*, 30 March 1946). The *Manchester Guardian* also had serious reservations, but for different reasons. It saw grave dangers in retaining fee-for-service medicine of any kind.

Poor patients [it suggested] will claim their rights and be convinced that they are getting an inferior service: rich patients – and many others who cannot really afford it – will insist on paying fees in the expectation of preferential treatment, and will go elsewhere if they do not get what they are paying for. This, in short, is a false freedom that can only survive to the extent that it is abused. It must inevitably poison the doctor-patient relationship. It is the reef on which this splendid venture, with all its prospects for development, might founder at the outset. (*Manchester Guardian*, 22 March 1946)

Although reactions to the Bill were very mixed, the vast majority of commentators saw many encouraging and positive aspects to the proposals and when it was read for a second time there was much excited anticipation.

In introducing the Bill at its Second Reading in the House of Commons on 30 April 1946, Aneurin Bevan enumerated five key reasons for wishing to create a national health service, three of which related to money.

First, it had become the 'firm conclusion of all parties', he argued, 'that money ought not to be permitted to stand in the way of obtaining an efficient health service' (*Hansard*, 30 April 1946, col. 43). He went on:

> It is cardinal to a proper health organisation that a person ought not to be financially deterred from seeking medical assistance at the earliest possible stage. It is one of the evils of having to buy medical advice that, in addition to the natural anxiety that may arise because people do not like to hear unpleasant things about themselves, and therefore tend to postpone consultation as long as possible, there is the financial anxiety caused by having to pay doctors' bills.

Second, there was the problem of the inadequate coverage of the national health insurance scheme. Approximately half the population was covered by that time but half was not and these were often vulnerable and needy people. Those without cover often had no access to a doctor when they were ill and 'in an overwhelming number of cases', Bevan claimed, the services of a consultant or specialist were unavailable to poor people (ibid., col. 44). In short, he argued, 'no matter how ill you are, if you cease to be insured you cease to have free doctoring' (ibid., col. 44).

The third area where financial barriers restricted access to health care was in dentistry. Many people were deterred from seeking dental care because of the cost of treatment, with the result that the condition of peoples' teeth in 1946 was 'a national reproach' (ibid., col. 44). Similarly large numbers were unable to afford to have eyesight tests and spectacles and little was being done to provide cheap hearing aids.

Fourth, the hospitals and services which did exist across the country were not part of a plan or system and the best facilities were often located where they were least needed. Many of the hospitals, Bevan maintained, were too small to operate safely and effectively as general hospitals. More than 70 per cent of them had less than 100 beds and 50 per cent had less than 30 beds. Some people sought to defend the small hospitals on the grounds of 'localism and intimacy' but this sentiment was probably misplaced because the hospitals could not provide the kinds of specialised services which were really required. Bevan himself concluded that: 'Although I am not a devotee of bigness for bigness' sake, I would rather be kept alive in the efficient if cold altruism of a large hospital than expire in a gush of warm sympathy in a small one' (ibid., col. 44). Bevan suggested that many cottage hospitals were trying, or claiming, to provide services they could not actually provide and that the interests of patients were being sacrificed to the 'vaulting ambitions' of those in charge (ibid., col. 48). In his view, only a hospital with 1000 beds could offer the range of general and specialist services required by the population and provide them to an adequate standard.

The final reason for wishing to establish a national health service was to draw in the mental illness services which had previously been isolated. Bevan wished to see the mentally ill have access to general hospitals instead of being shut away in remote institutions.

An essential element in the Bill was the 'nationalisation' of the voluntary hospitals. Bevan said that he found it 'repugnant to a civilised community for hospitals to have to rely upon private charity' (ibid., col. 47) and declared his intention to abolish voluntary fund-raising 'entirely'. 'I have always felt a shudder of repulsion', he said, 'when I have seen nurses and sisters who ought to be at their work, going about the streets collecting money for hospitals' (ibid., col. 47). It was, in any case, a 'travesty', he maintained, to call the hospitals 'voluntary', as so many of them were actually sustained by weekly contributions made by industrial workers. They were not required to pay by law but were well aware that it was their only chance of getting hospital treatment if and when they needed it.

The Debate on the Bill

The debate on the Bill, which followed, centred on a number of issues. The Opposition were concerned about the proposal to nationalise the voluntary hospitals, interference with the clinical freedom of doctors and the plan to abolish the sale of practices. Labour Members were divided on the issue of retaining private practice and regretted the loss of local authority hospitals.

Viscountess Davidson, for the Opposition, claimed that the management of the voluntary hospitals would be too bureaucratic and remote from the people they served. Everyone would, she complained, became impersonal cogs in the 'machine of the State' (*Hansard*, 30 April 1946, col. 89). The 'spirit of service' would be lost and the community would cease to take a pride in its hospitals. State control would also mean that clinical freedom would be lost and doctors would become 'salaried servants of the State, bound hand and foot' (ibid., col. 86). Patients would have no choice of doctor and they would simply be allocated one by the bureaucracy. She defended the buying and selling of practices, arguing that the doctor was simply selling his goodwill and not his patients. The ambitious and enthusiastic doctor would now be driven overseas. The Health Services Bill, she concluded, would kill off the 'spirit of enterprise and of individual attainment' and 'saps the very foundations on which our national character has been built' (ibid., col. 9).

Bevan did not escape the censure of his Labour colleagues either. Many of them spoke out against the proposal to retain private practice. Dr Comyns, for example, said that he deprecated the fact that doctors would still provide two standards of care – one for those who could pay and one for those who could not. If everyone was entitled to the new service free of charge, he argued, people would only wish to have private treatment if they thought they were buying something better. He asked for the Minister's assurance that the existence of the private sector would not be detrimental to the public service. He also took up the point about freedom of choice. How well informed were the general public about their doctors, he asked, and how often – in practice – did they (and were they able to) exercise free choice? Before the war, he went on, a patient tended to assess the medical skill of his doctor 'by the year and make of his car, or, on occasions, by the number of new hats which his wife was seen to be wearing' (ibid., col.

84). Dr Comyns believed that 'free choice, when applied to medicine, is simply a catch phrase which will not bear serious analysis' (ibid., col. 85). The real argument, he felt, should be about standards of care rather than about choice. There was little real evidence that patients cared a great deal about choosing their doctor or that they exercised choice when it was available to them.

These sentiments were echoed by a number of speakers from the government benches. Miss Bacon, representing Leeds, feared that consultants might refuse to take patients on their public list while agreeing to see them privately. She was also concerned that those who could not pay would feel they were getting an inferior service. Mr Sargood, of Bermondsey, regretted that private mental institutions, run for profit, were excluded from the Bill. He described the tendency of proprietors to treat patients longer than may have been necessary, in order to retain the income. Finally, Mr Anthony Greenwood, of Heywood and Radcliffe (making his maiden speech), welcomed the Bill as a 'great measure of social advancement' (ibid., col. 119), but was concerned about the implications of earlier statements. Some of them reflected badly upon the medical profession. It would seem that doctors would do more work if paid more money and that a surgeon would perform an operation better for 20 guineas than for 5 (ibid., col. 121). He hoped that this was not so and that doctors were more concerned with service and with helping their fellow men than with money.

Despite these criticisms many Members, on both sides of the House, warmly welcomed the Bill and saw it as a great step forward. Although some felt the issues raised above were of fundamental importance and greatly weakened the Bill, many others regarded them as matters of detail. The Government won the vote with ease.

From the Bill to the Act

As the National Health Service Bill progressed through its further stages (in Committee, a 3rd Reading in the House of Commons and a 2nd Reading in the Lords), it became clear

that there was a growing division between the hospital doctors, who were represented by the Royal Colleges and the GPs
who were the majority of members of the BMA. This latter
group felt very threatened by the proposals and were much
more hostile to the Bill than the hospital doctors. There was
widespread antipathy to the notion of a State-run service,
suspicion that the Government intended to introduce an
entirely salaried service and resistance to the idea that the
Ministry would direct GPs to under-doctored areas. There
was also some dispute about private practice, the sale of
practices and other issues raised in the Second Reading of the
Bill in the Commons. Hospital doctors felt there were too
many constraints upon how and where fee-for-service work
might take place and sought a relaxation of the regulations
outlined in the Bill. The BMA and general practitioners were
incensed at the proposal to abolish the sale of practices and
tried to persuade (or bully) the Government into reconsider-
ing its position.

Although Bevan was open to constructive suggestions he
was unwilling to concede any major principles and, despite
the enormous controversy and hostility which followed the
Second Reading in some quarters, he made few concessions to
his opponents. Most of the major amendments proposed in
the House of Lords, with its predominance of Opposition
supporters, were defeated in the House of Commons where
the Government had a large majority.

In November 1946, the BMA held a ballot of all doctors on
the medical register asking whether it should negotiate on the
regulations authorised by the National Health Service Act.
Fifty four per cent (most of them GPs) voted 'No' and agreed
to play no part in the new service if it came into being.
Nevertheless, the Bill became law in December 1946 with the
expectation that it would come into force in January 1948
(later changed to July of that year).

The division which had become apparent between the
hospital doctors and the GPs widened in the months after the
passage of the Act. Many of the interest groups (including a
significant proportion of the hospital doctors) had been mol-
lified by the concessions made in the run-up to the legislation
and had become resigned to participating in the new service.

Some were even enthusiastic and were increasingly impatient with the BMA's insistence that it spoke for all the profession in opposing the Act. The Royal Colleges and the BMA reiterated their concerns about control, salaries and private practice and Bevan reiterated his view that, although amendments were still possible, he was not prepared to move on basic principles. Private practice *would* continue, he repeated. Doctors could choose whether to work full-time for the NHS or whether to work part-time and supplement their incomes with private work. They could undertake their private practice in pay beds within NHS hospitals if they so desired. He did, however, change his position on one point. He agreed that there could be a number of 'no-ceiling' pay beds where consultants were free to set whatever fee they wished.

The BMA still maintained that its members would not take part in the service unless the Minister acquiesced to their demands. The GPs and sections of the medical press condemned Bevan for his intransigence and in early 1948 the question of securing participation seemed further from resolution than ever before. When, in February 1948, the BMA conducted a plebiscite, the results showed that the profession opposed the NHS Act by eight to one. A 'fighting fund' was set up to support the profession in the event of strike action (but only 6000 doctors contributed). The possibility of actually introducing the service on the Appointed Day, 5 July 1948, seemed increasingly remote. However, the Government continued with its plans (determined that the wishes of Parliament would not be overturned by the doctors) and issued publicity about the new service and its benefits, avoiding (with a few exceptions) overt confrontation with the profession. The strategy evidently paid off. When a second plebiscite was held some months later it indicated a lessening of opposition. A large majority still voted against the Act but it was a smaller majority than the BMA had anticipated and it was agreed that the Association would enter into negotiations with the Minister. Various consolatory messages were exchanged and when the NHS finally came into effect in July 1948 the vast majority of the medical profession had agreed to take part.

After the Act

The 'disclaimed' hospitals

When the legislation eventually came into force not all hospitals were taken into public ownership. Although 3118 hospitals and clinics (with 388 000 staffed and 57 000 unstaffed beds) did become the responsibility of the Minister another 230 hospitals were left outside the NHS and were 'disclaimed' (Pater, 1981, p. 148). Originally 277 hospitals and clinics had applied to be 'disclaimed' from the provisions of the Act but 47 were unsuccessful and were taken into public ownership (*Hansard*, 31 May 1949). These hospitals formed the core of private sector provision for some years after the war until the Nuffield Nursing Homes Trust was established in 1957 and began to provide new purpose-built accommodation.

According to a Ministry of Health memo, *Disclaimed Hospitals*, the 230 which were to remain outside the new arrangements were 'not required to enable the Minister to fulfill his statutory obligations' (Watkin, 1978, p. 23). Many of them were small hospitals run by religious orders, such as the Hospital of St John and St Elizabeth or by trade unions, such as the Manor House Hospital. Not all trade union facilities remained independent, however. Watkin comments that the Great Western Railway Welfare Society 'handed over to the Minister a substantial health centre building and a small hospital in Swindon which had been provided for railwaymen and their dependants [sic]' (ibid, p. 23). Several of the excluded institutions were hospices, nursing homes and convalescent homes which provided care for disabled servicemen. Others were run by the Ancient Order of Foresters Friendly Society for its members. The Royal Masonic Hospital, which provided acute care for freemasons, their wives and dependent children was disclaimed as were two large and well-established private psychiatric hospitals, the Retreat in York and St Andrew's in Northampton. The Retreat had been founded in 1792 by William Tuke, a Yorkshire Quaker, and was managed by the Society of Friends. St Andrew's was established in 1838 and run as an independent charity.

Hospitals run by Catholic orders received special dispensation to remain outside the scheme as a result of an agreement between Bevan and Cardinal Griffin.

Some of the other hospitals were disused buildings which had once been smallpox or 'isolation' hospitals. Overall the beds in these 230 hospitals formed a very small proportion of total bed numbers. In 1949 the Association of Independent Hospitals and Kindred organisations was established to represent the interests of those institutions which remained outside the NHS and it continued to perform that function until 1987.

Private practice

Despite the apparent opposition of many doctors, especially general practitioners, to the NHS, the vast majority had agreed to take part by the Appointed Day. As Lindsey remarked (of general practitioners), by the early 1950s their 'private patients all but disappeared' (Lindsey, 1962, p. 203). Although hospital doctors continued to do a significant amount of private practice, enthusiasm amongst general practitioners had waned considerably. Many of them claimed it was 'more trouble than it was worth' (ibid., p. 203) and the Government Social Survey, in 1952 showed that only 1.5 per cent of the population used private GPs exclusively and another 2 per cent were NHS patients but also on the list of a private practitioner. Doctors who complained that private practice was 'too much bother' disliked having to make a fuss of private patients and give them preferential treatment, as well as the purely practical problems of dealing with money and pursuing debtors. As one of them remarked: 'I should dread a return to the old days of accounting, unpaid bills, self-dispensing and the extra time and "fussing" private patients expect as their right' (quoted in Lindsey, 1962, p. 204).

Doctors who favoured private practice argued that it was a means of preserving good standards of care, it created a good relationship between the doctor and patient and it offered a challenge. Private patients themselves seemed to be a heterogeneous group ranging from gypsies who did not wish to register with a GP to low-income families who could barely afford the fee, and patients who simply stayed with their doctor out of loyalty. There was no real evidence to show that they did, in fact, receive different or better care than NHS patients (ibid., pp. 204–5).

Hospital doctors, on the other hand, continued to engage in private practice on an extensive scale. Jewkes and Jewkes (1961) argued that although private practice was difficult to quantify there seemed to be 'a good deal of it' (p. 68). They estimated that in 1955–6 part-time consultants working a maximum number of sessions with the NHS derived one-seventh of their total earnings from private work and consultants doing fewer NHS sessions were earning substantially more. Access to private medicine, however, remained much as it had been in the pre-war years, with a heavy concentration of private practice and private beds in the more affluent South. They argued:

'It is very difficult to escape the conclusion that a very large part of it is found in London. The nursing homes, private clinics and consultants there enjoy outstanding reputations. A survey carried out in 1953 showed that the number of persons per available private bed (either in hospitals or in nursing homes) was 924 for the County of London, 1030 for an area corresponding roughly to the Metropolitan area and 2230 for the remainder of England and Wales (ibid., p. 68).

They also concluded that around half of all subscribers to private health insurance lived in the London area.

Private health insurance and hospitals

Meanwhile, what of the insurance companies, provident associations and other groups established in the 1920s and 30s to help the middle classes pay for hospital care? Each of the three largest companies operating today (British United Provident Association, Private Patients' Plan [then London Association for Hospital Services] and Western Provident Association) had its origins in this period. The coming of the NHS was clearly a threat to their livelihood and, indeed, challenged their very existence. The promise of a free and comprehensive service meant that pre-payment schemes were no longer necessary. All who needed medical care would receive it regardless of means. Critics, however, felt that, while this was indeed beneficial for the working man, the middle classes might be disadvantaged by having their access to private medicine limited. As Sir Arthur Bryant said, in his history of BUPA: 'the Act pressed hard on the professional and formerly well-to-do classes who were accustomed and conditioned by their upbringing to pay in sickness for the best that the medical profession could offer' (Bryant, 1968, p. 12). The provident associations, then, saw provision for this group as a means of ensuring their own survival.

A number of influential figures in the existing associations, with the financial help and encouragement of Lord Nuffield (whom Bryant describes as that 'great apostle of self-help and independence' [ibid., p. 13]) concluded that the only way to secure a future for any of them was in combination. In 1946 a conference, sponsored by Nuffield and attended by 89 different organisations, agreed to form a national association to incorporate all the schemes then in existence. The outcome, in April 1947, was the establishment of the British United Provident Association. BUPA went in to 1948 with a membership of 38 000 but, as the NHS came into being, this dropped to less than 34 000 in the following year. In the first financial year the organisation made a loss but this became a comfortable surplus in its second year. The supporters of BUPA were confident that it would flourish, despite the NHS, because patients preferred to be treated in familiar and congenial surroundings by their own doctor. Although membership did not begin to grow significantly until the 1950s the income of the Association increased, to leave it in a relatively secure financial state. By 1951–2 registrations had gone up to 71 000 and these continued to rise by between 30 000 and 50 000 each year until the 1970s. The Chairman claimed that:

The underlying reason for this expansion is the increasing recognition that, in its present stage of development, the National Health Service is too often unable to provide the prompt treatment and care so much desired by people who take their family responsibilities seriously. (quoted in Bryant, 1968, p. 25)

One of the problems now facing the provident associations was that, as their membership rose, the number of private beds in which the privately insured might receive their treatment was declining. BUPA responded in 1953 by setting up its own hospital company, the Nuffield Homes Charitable Trust (whose development is described more fully in the next chapter). Eventually it became the largest single provider of private acute beds in the country.

Costs and charges in the NHS

Meanwhile, as Bryant implied, the new NHS was, indeed, having its teething troubles. Estimates of the cost of the service, in England and Wales, had increased from £132 million in the 1944 White Paper to £152 million in 1946 to £230 million before the service was due to start in 1948 (Watkin, 1978, pp. 28–9). In the event, expenditure in the first full year (1949–50) was £305.2 million and it continued to grow rapidly. So too did the demand for the service, not least for spectacles, dentures and prescriptions. In 1949–50 the number of prescriptions dispensed had increased to 200 million – a three-fold increase since 1947. Not surprisingly these escalating demands and costs provoked considerable alarm and a demand that charges should be introduced for certain items, both as a means of raising revenue and of reducing demand. In 1949 the Government passed an amendment to the Act which would have allowed it to impose a prescription charge of one shilling per item. This was expected to raise around £10 million per annum. Bevan fiercely opposed health charges and they were not actually imposed until three years later when Hugh Gaitskell became Chancellor of the Exchequer and Bevan had moved to the Ministry of Labour. In April 1951 the Government declared its intention to introduce charges for spectacles and dentures and Bevan and Harold Wilson resigned from the Cabinet in protest.

In his letter of resignation to Attlee, Bevan described the introduction of health service charges as 'the beginning of the destruction of those social services in which Labour has taken a special pride and which were giving to Britain the moral leadership of the world' (quoted in Foot, 1975, p. 329). On 23 April, in the House of Commons, he accused the Labour Party of 'polluting the stream', arguing that it would be charges for dentures and spectacles this year, prescriptions and 'hotel' charges the next, until the Health Service was 'like Lavinia – all the limbs cut off and eventually her tongue cut out too' (*Hansard*, vol. 487, col. 34). On this occasion his eloquence won him few friends, especially amongst members of his own party who felt angry and betrayed.

The resignation of Bevan marked the end of one era in the story of private medicine and the beginning of another. Although a number of concessions had been made since 1945 permitting the retention of private practice, some charges for certain items under the NHS, the independence of private hospitals and the existence of 'pay beds' in the NHS, the introduction of health charges seemed – to some critical observers – to undermine the basic principle of free access to the service, in a way which was qualitatively different.

The Lessons of History

Many of the issues which surfaced in the 1940s are of continuing significance today in understanding the conflicts and tensions surrounding private medicine in this country. Although the themes coming out of this historical review are diverse and wide-ranging they may, for the sake of convenience, be grouped under four headings. First, there were a range of planning and organisational problems. Second, there were many issues relating to money. Third, there was the relationship between the public and private sectors and the images which were formed of the NHS. Fourth, there were interest group conflicts and party political disputes.

○ *Organisational problems in the pre-war health services*

○ It was generally agreed that one of the greatest weaknesses of pre-war health care was its unplanned, *laissez-faire* character.

There were gross distributional problems relating both to hospital beds and to the location of doctors and it was generally the case that the best facilities existed where they were needed least. There were some exceptions, with the urban poor in large cities such as London having relatively easy access to good voluntary hospitals and teaching hospitals. However, there were few controls on hospital building or on hospital doctors and GPs. Hospital doctors, with honorary appointments in voluntary hospitals, established practices in affluent areas where they could make an income from private patient fees. GPs were often constrained by similar pressures, though fewer of them were entirely dependent upon fee-paying patients. In many senses, then, the only logic which prevailed in pre-war medicine was that between cash and service. Those who had the money could buy the service. Those who had no money might or might not receive the service – depending upon their individual circumstances and where they lived. As Brian Abel-Smith remarked, 'The pattern of provision depended on the donations of the living and the legacies of the dead, rather than on any ascertained need for hospital services' (Abel-Smith, 1964, p. 405). No agency had overall responsibility for planning health care and it was left to individual entrepreneurs to pursue their interests.

Similarly, there were few effective controls on standards of care. Although the Nursing Homes Registration Act, 1927, was designed to enforce minimum standards in the private sector, it was a rather weak instrument and did little to ensure good quality health services around the country. Many proprietors evaded the regulations by becoming 'convalescent homes' and some authorities were reluctant to pursue proprietors even where serious abuse was suspected. Standards in the public sector were often no better and, when the Ministry of Health took responsibility for the Emergency Medical Service during the war, Ministers and civil servants were shocked by the poor conditions in many hospitals. Many of the medical staff too, on war-time service, were working in surroundings which they never imagined existed. Indeed, the fact that doctors and articulate middle-class patients found themselves, for the first time, in inadequate voluntary hospitals and poor local authority premises was a significant factor in the pressure for reform after the war. The war had exposed them to conditions they had never seen before and they were determined to change them.

The Hospital Surveys, which took place in all regions in the early 1940s, revealed the full extent of the problems then facing the hospital service. They found that many buildings were 'out of date and fall short of modern requirements' (HMSO, 1947, p. 69). They spoke of 'cramped space' and hospitals which were 'gloomy and depressing'. The municipal hospitals had a 'public assistance atmosphere' and were attempting to perform functions 'for which they were not designed and are not suited' (ibid., p. 69). Hospitals housing the chronic sick were the worst of all and one report (which was regarded as typical) argued that the care of the chronic sick required 'complete and revolutionary change if these people are to be adequately cared for and looked after in a reasonably humanitarian and social sense' (ibid., p. 70). It spoke of long wards with beds placed end to end, where the windows were so high that patients could see nothing but sky, and day rooms which had only hard wooden chairs around the walls. The facilities in these institutions did not even compare with the simplest and poorest family home and were frequently described as 'Dickensian'.

Another important issue, which Bevan had identified in his speech during the Second Reading of the NHS Bill, was the problem of small hospitals. There is no doubt that standards in many small hospitals were poor – and inevitably so. Many of them were isolated, not only geographically but also in terms of professional development. Their staffs were often isolated from mainstream professional thinking and practice. A large number were heavily dependent upon local GPs who were often untrained for, and inexperienced in, the complex tasks they were expected to perform. A survey by Nuffield Provincial Hospitals Trust in 1946 found that GPs were prepared to undertake surgery which was beyond their competence and, indeed, that some were 'entirely self-taught' (quoted in Abel-Smith, 1964, p. 406). Small hospitals did not have the range of specialities, equipment or support services to provide satisfactory care or adequate back-up facilities for the surgical work which they frequently attempted.

In this particular concern Bevan set a marker for the future and raised a question about small hospitals (both public and private) which has become a recurring theme in health policy and planning.

Fee-for-service medicine

It is a striking fact that one of the issues uniting many individuals across all political parties was their abhorrence of fee-for-service medicine. This sentiment was as clear in the Coalition Government's White Paper of 1944 as it was in Bevan's National Health Service Act in 1946. Antipathy towards the practice in pre-war Britain focused not so much upon the doctors who provided medicine for money (although some were criticised for their acquisitive tendencies) but upon a system which allowed money to be the key determinant of access. Indeed, some private practitioners, especially doctors in the voluntary hospitals, had enviable reputations. It was perhaps the experience of war – the 'pooling and sharing' and the decreasing relevance of inequalities of status and prestige – which highlighted the injustices and inadequacies of contemporary practice. It became less and less acceptable that many people should be deterred from seeking medical help because they could not afford to pay for it. The Emergency Medical Service established a pattern and precedents for the post-war service and it would be easy to conclude that, after the war, there could be no going back and no return to the pre-war situation. However, there was nothing inevitable about the changes which occurred and Britain alone, among the countries involved in the war, opted for a free and comprehensive national health service.

Klein has argued that so much of the debate about the legislation centred on administrative details rather than matters of principle precisely because there was so much common ground between different interest groups. 'Nothing is more remarkable', he concludes, 'than the shared asssumption that the health service should be both free and comprehensive – and that it should be based on the principle of the collective provision of services and the pooling of financial risks through the public financing of the service' (Klein, 1983, pp. 26–7).

However, Michael Foot takes a different view. He suggests that there was ready acceptance of some of the proposals, at least initially, because none of the parties involved had understood or fully thought through the consequences. The willingness of the BMA, for example, to accept the so-called '100 per cent principle' was, in Foot's eyes, 'hard to fathom' (1975, p. 111). The effect of the principle, which meant a comprehensive service for all the population, would be that there would be little or no demand for private medicine. Foot claims that neither Willink (the Conservative Minister for Health who proposed it) nor the BMA had really understood the implications of a 100 per cent service and it subsequently became clear that, while they were committed to the ideal, they did not support any of the measures designed to secure it. Similarly, on the proposal to introduce a free service, Foot suggests that any show of unanimity was very superficial: 'Critics of the measure, both in the Tory Opposition and the medical profession, pretended to accept this purpose without demur. Bevan's constant retort was that they did not accept its implications. They dared not oppose the end but they strove to sabotage the means (ibid., p. 129).

It is not clear, then, how far some of the parties to the discussion were genuinely committed to a free service, but there is no question that money (or the lack of it) was a problem for doctors and patients alike before 1948. Although some doctors lived well off flourishing private practices, others barely managed to scrape a living. As Forsyth points out, 'Medicine was a lucrative profession but not for all doctors and the spread of earnings was very wide' (Forsyth, 1966, p. 25). Junior hospital doctors were very badly paid, receiving board and lodgings and an annual salary of £50 'if they were lucky' (ibid., p. 25). Those who aspired to rich pickings in the upper echelons of surgery served a long and impoverished apprenticeship. GPs were usually better off than low-ranking hospital doctors though they had to rely on several sources of income. Even so, a quarter of them earned less than £1000 per annum (and two thirds less than £1300) while only 9 per cent of them earned more than £2000 per annum (ibid., p. 25). Many of them opposed the introduction of a national health scheme because they feared the imposition of a salaried service but, in fact, they stood to gain a stable and secure income. The Spens Committee, for example, recommended that after 1948 three-quarters of all GPs should earn over £1000 per annum (at 1939 prices), one quarter should earn over £1600 and a small number at least £2500. Although the scales seemed generous they compared unfavourably with those of senior hospital doctors where consultants in their middle years were expected to earn £2500 (as against the GPs' £1300).

As Michael Foot has commented, it was ironic that doctors – many of whom lived such a precarious financial existence – should be so hostile to the notion of a regular income from the State: 'the cri-de-coeur of the doctors against the menace of State action came strangely from a profession the majority of whose members had to perform their work in primitive facilities for shockingly low salaries' (Foot, 1975, p. 102). Spokesmen for the medical profession and their political backers, he argued, 'never seemed ready to acknowledge the vast advantages for the medical profession itself' of the proposed service (ibid., p. 129).

The voluntary hospitals raised different issues, in relation to money, patients and medicine, from those involving commercial for-profit activities. Nevertheless the kind of fund-raising measures which they used to maintain their viability were distasteful to some people. Eckstein's description of the scene may be salutary, in relation to both public and private medicine in the 1980s. Many people, he writes:

found the voluntary hospital system morally obnoxious, particularly due to the repellent practices used in the latter days of the system to extract money from the public: stunt appeals, bridge tournaments, flag days, midnight matinees, and soap sales and, not least, the sale of advertising space on hospital walls to patent medicine manufacturers. (Eckstein, 1958, p. 178)

A further issue was the question of charges for health care. There was some support, in the war-time Cabinet, for 'hotel charges' in hospitals. Although this idea did not, in the end, form part of the legislation, a number of minor charges for repairs and appliances did survive the passage of the Act. It would be true to say that even after 1948 the health service was never entirely free of charge at the point of need and this became even more true after the introduction of charges for dentures, spectacles and prescriptions in the 1950s. It was a Labour Government which introduced charges for dentures and spectacles in 1951 and a Conservative Government which, in 1952, introduced the one shilling prescription charge as well as charges for dental treatment, day nurseries and surgical appliances. Although these charges raised a certain amount of income, their principal purpose was that of deterrence, on the (largely untested) assumption that many people were abusing the free service (Martin and Williams, 1959, pp.36–39). The technique of rationing by charges has become an increasingly important feature in the post-war NHS and the arguments advanced in its favour are substantially the same as those in the 1940s.

The 'image' of the public service

It is clear from the debate at the inception of the NHS that public services generally – and local authority services and Poor Law hospitals in particular – had a very bad image. There was some justification for this view. Although some of the Poor Law hospitals had pioneered the provision of medical treatment to low income groups, conditions within them were often appalling and nurses and nursing standards had a bad reputation. The fear of the workhouse and the stigma of the Poor Law persist to this day. Poor conditions were not, however, the preserve of the public services and standards in private nursing homes were often as bad, if not worse. Nevertheless, a number of interest groups played upon this image of the public sector (and exaggerated it) as means to their own ends. The doctors especially issued dire warnings about the future of medicine if it were to be controlled by Town Hall bureaucrats and they fought tenaciously to remain beyond the grasp of the local authorities. The dispute between the Government and the doctors was bitter and damaging and had far-reaching effects. As Sir Robert Platt observed in 1963, 'A generation of doctors had been taught to disparage British medicine, to regard the Ministry of Health as its enemy, and to speak of the Health Service in terms of contempt. The profession had been brought down to the mentality of strike action' (Platt, 1963, p. 56).

This did not augur well for the public service, where some of these disaffected doctors would inevitably work. It gave a lift to the private sector, private practice and the hospitals remaining outside the NHS and it did not enhance the possibility of fruitful co-operation between the public and private sectors in the future. Indeed, some of the private insurance companies sought to foster the distinction (rather than to heal the rift) in order to promote their own images. They also emphasised the class distinctiveness of post-war private medicine. Sir Arthur Bryant, for example, in his history of BUPA remarks that, 'If a citizen of a democratic country prefers to spend his money on buying specialised medical care for himself and his dear ones instead of a drink, motoring, travel, sport, pop music or gambling he has every right to do so' (Bryant, 1968, p. 53). In his view the subscriber to private insurance, therefore, was sober, industrious and responsible – unlike the hedonistic, extravagant wastrels who used the public services. And, in a similar vein, he continues:

> though the majority feel no need for them, preferring the gregariousness and cheerful noise of a general ward, privacy and quiet have a great therapeutic value for many. A sensitive man or woman, accustomed to privacy and contemplation, can suffer in illness from unwanted noise, inconveniences and nervous strains unfelt by those to whom a more communal form of life is habitual and even indispensable to happiness (ibid., p. 55).

So it was to be a large, noisy NHS ward for the masses who knew no better (and even preferred it that way) and a quiet, private room for those used to more refinement. Different images of the public and private services (and their clientele) were deliberately cultivated for professional and economic reasons and persist to this day.

But it was not only the doctors and the private hospital and insurance companies which emphasised the distinction between public and private. A survey by the Welsh Regional Hospital Board in 1949 suggested that the image of 'ordinary wards' in public hospitals was, for some patients, so alarming that they would either refuse to go into them or 'would be so unhappy in them that the chances of deriving benefit would be greatly impaired' (quoted in Ryan, 1975, p. 167). Ryan argues that the Ministry of Health may have calculated that one way to persuade patients otherwise was to allow amenity beds and private beds within NHS hospitals. Fee-paying patients could then see for themselves that public wards were not as bad as they had feared.

> Bevan and his advisers may well have judged that if better-off patients were allowed to buy privacy at a modest charge they would prefer an amenity bed to a private bed in a state hospital or in a private nursing home. The public image of the Service would then be enhanced and the demand for private medical care reduced pro-tanto. (Ryan, 1975, pp. 167–8)

It is difficult to know whether this was, indeed, part of Bevan's calculations in retaining pay beds. It is probably true that the image of the public service gradually improved after 1948 but this, in itself, did not reduce the demand for private medicine.

Interest group conflicts

Finally, although there was surprisingly little conflict over some of the fundamental principles underlying the National Health Service, there were certainly differences of opinion *within* interest groups (as well as between them) about the best way forward. The two key intra-group distinctions were within the medical profession and within the two major political parties.

Discussions about public and private medicine in the 1940s revealed increasingly large divisions between hospital doctors and GPs. There were other differences too, between junior hospital doctors and some of their senior colleagues and between members of the Socialist Medical Association and more conservative thinkers in the profession. These differences of perspective significantly affected the shape of the new service – not least in the retention of private practice. Throughout the negotiations Bevan sought to establish good relations with the hospital doctors in particular. The agreement to retain private practice and pay beds was reached at an early stage and although some commentators have referred to Bevan's off-quoted comment that he 'stuffed their mouths with gold', by way of explanation, it is clear that other – more subtle – issues were at stake. Bevan's primary concerns, it appears, were to get rid of the small nursing homes where standards were dangerously low and to secure the commitment of hospital doctors to the new service. The price of that commitment, as he saw it, was to retain an element of fee-for-service medicine and to permit private practice within NHS hospitals.

Bevan was clearly uncomfortable in this decision. It was inconsistent with his passionate belief that money should not be a factor in determining access to medical care and he commented, in Committee, that 'this Subsection, and the principle itself, has given me more anxious thought than any other part of the Bill' (House of Commons, Standing Committee, May–July 1946, col. 1154). His critics saw (and feared) the potential for a two-class service, with poor standards in the public sector. Nevertheless, he felt able to justify his position. Although he had felt compelled to concede on the issue of retaining private practice, in order to draw doctors into the new service, he argued that a flourishing and comprehensive national service would encompass so many doctors and patients that the scope for private medicine would be very limited.

It is interesting, also, that Bevan did not take the opportunity, after 1948, to close down the private nursing homes which had concerned him. The 'disclaimed' hospitals and nursing homes were allowed to get on with business as usual and no attempt was made, other than through minimal legislative measures, to control their activities. This *laissez-faire* attitude to the "disclaimed" hospitals was, in all probability, a placatory gesture too – regarded as inevitable by a reluctant

Ministry. A number of interest groups were at work here including the Catholic Church, the Freemasons and some trades unions.

Although the hospital doctors were courted assiduously the GPs were relatively neglected in the negotiations about the NHS. There was, in any case, a widening gap between the Royal Colleges and the BMA, exacerbated partly by different interests and by a touch of snobbery on the part of the hospital doctors. The proposed changes were also to modify, in very significant ways, the relationship between, and interdependence of, hospital doctors and general practitioners. As Abel-Smith commented, 'No longer would the consultant curry favour with all general practitioners in the hope of receiving private referred cases. The practitioner without private patients to bestow would not be treated with the same courtesy' (Abel-Smith, 1964, p. 485).

As the *British Medical Journal* put it, GPs would see a 'change from the usual "kind regards" and "Christmas cards"' (quoted in Abel-Smith, 1964, p. 485). In many senses the power relationship between consultants and GPs was reversed and the GPs now needed the hospital consultants more than the consultants needed them. Abel-Smith argues that the GPs were right to be concerned that they would lose prestige under the new system and that their work would become 'less general and more trivial' (ibid., p. 486). Bevan had decided, however, where his loyalties must lie in devising a national health service and he is judged to have been quite realistic in deciding 'whom to woo and whom to fight' (ibid., p. 486).

> He could continue to hold out against the general practitioners and the British Medical Association, because he knew that his proposals had won support, or at least acceptance, in the most influential part of the hospital world. . . . It was no concern of his which individual general practitioners joined the service and which did not, and he knew that many who opposed the service would be carried into it by pressure from their own patients. But the participation of the top hospital doctors was essential to the prestige and therefore 'universality' of the service. (Ibid., p. 486)

Bevan, therefore, took advantage of the disagreements between different groups of doctors and, some would argue,
deliberately drove a wedge between them in order to persuade
the most influential to support his case.

If the disagreement between the doctors was eventually
patched up, rather than resolved, the same was true of disputes in the Conservative and Labour parties. Debates in the
House of Commons revealed distinct differences of opinion
along the Conservative benches with some Members giving ⟁
the legislation unqualified support while others condemned it
out of hand. Although the majority of Conservative Members
welcomed the Bill they still disagreed on important details.
Divisions on the Labour benches, however, were also in
evidence. There was little outright opposition to Bevan's
proposals but there was considerable disquiet, in some quarters, about the proposal to retain private practice – and
especially to retain it *within* the NHS. Bevan's insistence that
this was the only way to involve the doctors was regarded as a
serious breach of principle by some of his colleagues and was
fiercely contested. As Michael Ryan comments:

> opposition to pay beds became virtually an article of faith
> for many Labour Party members – more especially left-
> wingers. The issue of pay beds may have attracted rather
> less attention than that of Health Service charges but it has
> occupied a not dissimilar place in the annals of political
> rhetoric. (Ryan, 1975, p. 169)

A number of critics, then and later (e.g. Navarro, 1978), ○
complained that Bevan's proposals were not sufficiently radical and that they strengthened class divisions and professional
dominance rather than eradicating them. They could not
envisage a combination of public and private medicine which
would not disadvantage the NHS patient. Attlee himself
feared that: 'There would be a danger that some doctors would
devote their energies to maintaining their private practice at
the expense of public patients' (quoted in Klein, 1983, p. 15).
This view was echoed by many of his colleagues, not least
those who were members of the Socialist Medical Association.

In the event, Bevan's Labour opponents fell away or were temporarily silenced – perhaps in the interest of Party unity and the safe passage of the Bill. Sir Frederick Messer, MP, one of his critics, explained that Bevan 'applied an anaesthetic' to his opponents in the Labour Party 'making them believe in things that they had opposed almost all their lives' (quoted in Foot, 1975, p. 155). In the end, however, the anaesthetic wore off and the differences and disputes about private medicine were still there, to surface on other occasions, as we shall see in later chapters.

2. Paying for Medicine Inside and Outside the NHS: 1948–78

Each of the issues relating to private medicine which had caused dissension in the 1940s continued to be the subject of controversy right through to the 1970s even if they were not always prominent on the political agenda. Two of them, however, assumed particular significance. First, there was the continuing debate about health service charges and their place in the predominantly 'free' and comprehensive health service. Second, the dispute about pay beds, which had been simmering since the 1920s, finally came to the boil and provoked conflict, bitterness and strike action. This chapter focuses especially upon these two issues but begins with a review of developments in private medicine outside the NHS. It covers the period from 1948 to 1978.

Outside the NHS

The creation of the NHS in 1948 gave rise, for the first time, to an important distinction between fee-for-service medicine outside and inside the public service. While much of the controversy about private medicine was concerned with developments inside the NHS, those private and voluntary organisations which had survived outside the NHS continued to build on their strengths. Private health insurance, for example, which had suffered a body-blow with the introduction of free medical care for all began, after a slow start, to develop a role for itself which acquired considerable significance by the late 1970s. Similarly, the radical change which had taken place in the hospital sector gradually gave rise to modest but steady growth in private provision outside the NHS.

The insurance companies

Although BUPA expressed confidence that there would always be a demand for private health care outside the NHS it was by no means self-evident in 1948 that this was actually so. The alternative view was that people would not be willing to pay for something they could now get for nothing. However, despite modest beginnings private health insurance did gradually extend its coverage and BUPA's optimism proved to be justified. During the three decades after the establishment of the NHS three insurance companies dominated the market with around 98 per cent of all business. Of these BUPA was by far the largest, covering three-quarters of the market. Private Patients Plan (PPP) had most of the remaining share with the Western Provident Association (WPA) making a very small contribution. In 1950 these three companies had a total of 56 000 subscribers (which, including dependents, meant an insured population of 120 000). By 1955 the figures had increased respectively to 274 000 (and 585 000) and by 1960 to 467 000 (and 995 000). Throughout the 1960s the subscriber population went up by around 50 000 each year. After 1971 the rate of growth decreased and between 1975 and 1977 the companies actually lost subscribers overall (see Table 2.1).

The explanations for this turnaround in the fortunes of the insurance companies will be explored later but, in brief, they may be said to relate to the bitter dispute about pay beds in the NHS as well as to rising unemployment and economic decline. The tremendous boom in the private insurance market which followed hard upon these losses, in the late 1970s, will also be discussed elsewhere.

The subscriber population changed significantly in this thirty-year period. Most of the original subscribers were individuals whom Michael Lee described as 'reacting . . . to the concept of the NHS' (M. Lee, 1980, p. 18). Between 1965 and 1975, although the numbers of individual subscribers continued to grow steadily, it was group schemes where the

Table 2.1   *The provident population: persons insured, number of subscribers and net change (BUPA, PPP and WPA), 1950–77*

Year	Persons insured (thousands)	Subscribers (thousands)	Annual net change (thousands)
1950	120	56	7
1955	585	274	52
1960	995	467	48
1965	1445	680	48
1966	1565	735	55
1967	1670	784	49
1968	1770	831	47
1969	1887	886	55
1970	1982	930	44
1971	2102	986	56
1972	2176	1021	35
1973	2265	1064	43
1974	2334	1096	32
1975	2315	1087	− 9
1976	2251	1057	−30
1977	2254	1057	0

Annual rate of change (%)

1966–71	6.9	6.8	–
1971–6	1.4	1.4	–
1977	0.0	0.0	–

SOURCE: *UK Private Medical Care. Provident Scheme Statistics*, Lee Donaldson Associates, 1977.

greatest expansion took place. Two kinds of group schemes emerged. There were the occupational schemes (sometimes known as voluntary group or employee purchase) where individuals paid their own premiums but took part in schemes organised by their employers or professions. Discounts were normally available and contributions would be less than those paid by individual subscribers. Second, there were company group (or company purchase) schemes where the employer paid the contributions and an insurance package was offered as one of the 'fringe benefits' of the job. The number of subscribers in group schemes almost doubled in the ten years from 1965, with 403 000 subscribers in that year and 793 000 in 1975. By 1979 the numbers had increased to 940 000. The number of individual subscribers who were not part of either type of group scheme totalled 277 000 in 1965 and reached 328 000 in 1972 before going into a steady decline. By the end of the 1970s more than three-quarters of all subscribers belonged to group schemes.

Apart from the 'big three' insurance companies a number of smaller organisations survived the creation of the NHS. Most of them were friendly societies and provident associations which had a particular geographical or professional responsibility, such as the Bristol Contributory Welfare Association and the Revenue Provident Association (linked to the Inland Revenue). Each of these bodies was a non-profit making association. In addition there were several hospital contributory schemes around the country, united under the British Hospital Contributory Schemes Association. These paid cash benefits to subscribers requiring hospital care and again operated on a non-profit basis. They provided primarily for a working-class population, in contrast to organisations such as BUPA, which dealt mainly with professional groups. Subscriptions were usually two or three pennies a week and the individuals covered (and often their dependents) were entitled to use convalescent facilities or to receive grants for spectacles and dentures, as well as maternity grants. The role of commercial organisations in private health insurance was very limited in the early part of this period and there were few apparent attractions to for-profit companies. However, as the market began to change in the 1970s a number of commercial companies, such as Crusader Insurance, began to take a small share of the business.

The changes which took place in private health insurance after 1948 did not occur in a vacuum. They were a reflection of much broader social and economic developments. To an extent they reflected public attitudes to the NHS but they were also a reflection of adjustments in the economy and in patterns of employment. The increase in group schemes and relative decline in the number of individual subscribers was part of an expansion in the 1960s and 70s of fringe benefits for senior managers, professional employees and for some blue-collar workers. Michael Lee suggests that those individual subscribers who had once paid their own premiums now became drawn into group schemes, so that although the nature of the subscriber population may appear to have changed markedly, many of the individuals involved were the same. The rise of mass unemployment and movement of the employed population between available jobs contributed to the volatility of the market in the 1970s. In the end, Lee argued: 'demand is not solely an expression of individual consumer preference, it is more a reflection of arrangements made by industry for key employees' (Lee, 1978, p. 11). Mencher had earlier made similar remarks adding that the emphasis on the benefits to industry of private health insurance schemes was not only an effective selling point but it also got round the 'controversial issue of individual preference'. 'By placing the onus on the firm's needs', he argued, 'private insurance becomes the hand-maiden of efficiency and higher productivity and enhances social rather than individual goals' (Mencher, 1967, p. 30).

The associations themselves claimed that the advantages of private insurance (both to employer and employee) were that the patient could be hospitalised at their mutual convenience and without undue delay. Emphasis was also placed upon privacy and on treating people in congenial surroundings appropriate to their social status and way of life.

Despite the existence of a free health service, then, a surprisingly wide variety of friendly societies, provident associations, hospital contributory schemes, commercial organisations and trade unions continued to provide private insurance or cash benefits to their members after 1948. Although there were quite a number of them their activities and their budgets (with the exception of BUPA, PPP and WPA) were very modest. Together they accounted for only a small percentage of total health care expenditure. Their existence, however, sometimes provoked a reaction out of all proportion to their size. In the 1960s, for example, companies like BUPA were held up by conservative economists as attractive models of health financing which could provide major alternatives to the NHS (e.g. Lees, 1961). In the 1970s they were criticised by a Labour administration for enabling private practice, which it sought to eliminate or reduce, to expand significantly. BUPA themselves have complained that although their aim was simply to provide a 'warm and human service' their activities have often been criticised and sometimes 'reviled' (Robb and Brown, 1984, pp. 5–7). The steady expansion of health insurance outside the NHS after 1948 was not therefore without its critics but the activities of these various groups were not, on the whole, hampered by government and their existence was tolerated, if not encouraged. This picture began to change, however, in the mid-1970s.

Private beds

Meanwhile changes were taking place in the provision of private beds outside the NHS. In 1953, BUPA conducted a survey of pay beds, private hospitals and nursing homes available to its subscribers. If found that there were 8045 NHS pay beds and 29 115 private beds in nursing homes (a reduction from 1921 when there were 40 000). Many of these beds were designated for particular types of care, such as convalescent, geriatric and maternity care, with only 18 000 available for general medicine and surgery (Bryant, 1968, p. 42). It was also clear from the survey that there were insufficient beds in institutions with standards high enough to satisfy BUPA's requirements and the company determined both to improve existing facilities and to build new accomodation. So it was that the Nuffield Homes Charitable Trust (named after Lord Nuffield – a strong supporter of voluntary initiatives in health care) came into being in 1957 with an initial grant of £100 000 from BUPA. Its purpose was to purchase and upgrade hospitals where there was potential for improvement and expansion and by 1967 it had acquired 6 existing hospitals and had built 7 new ones. The Trust aimed to build hospitals where acute care could be provided, with all the facilities of modern medicine, and in surroundings which were comfortable but not ostentatiously luxurious. BUPA continued to provide a good deal of the finance for all these developments but it was expected that wherever a hospital was built there would be 'community' support (usually from local businesses) in the form of financial assistance, amounting to 50 per cent of the total cost. This community support is acknowledged in a visible way, with plaques on room doors bearing the name of local donors. By 1970 the now re-named Nuffield Nursing Homes Trust had 17 hospitals, with 493 beds, and in that year it treated 16 213 patients. During the 1970s, the Trust expanded its activities significantly so that in 1976 it had 26 hospitals (with 831 beds) and had more than doubled the number of patients seen to 36 344 (Lee, 1978, p. 16). It had become the largest single provider of private hospital beds in Britain.

Information about the other hospitals 'disclaimed' in the National Health Service Act in 1946 is very sketchy. Although they had been required to register with health authorities under various Nursing Homes Acts since 1927, very little hard data about facilities and standards was actually collected or disseminated. Lee estimated that, in the early 1960s in England and Wales, there were 1200 private nursing homes with 23 731 beds. The numbers of homes fell steadily throughout the 1960s although bed numbers remained more or less the same (Lee, 1978, p. 15). The majority of these 'nursing homes' provided long stay care for chronically sick and elderly patients and few provided facilities for acute surgery or medicine. After 1948 and until the 1970s, when more detailed information was available on private sector provision, there were probably between 100 and 150 'homes' functioning as acute hospitals with very varied facilities and bed numbers. Many of them were run by religious organisations and were limited in their scope.

Private practice

One of the interesting questions in this period is what became of the doctors (especially the GPs) who had been determined to continue with their private practice despite the NHS and who wished to have no part in the public service? Mencher estimated that, in 1952, there were at most only 2.3 per cent of GPs working entirely in private practice. Four-fifths of GPs had less than 20 private patients and the average GP had just 'a handful'. His income from private practice was very low. A survey in the same year concluded that 97.7 per cent of the population of England and Wales were registered as NHS patients and received free GP care. Only 1.5 per cent of the sample used private practitioners exclusively. A further survey in 1964 showed that almost one third of all GPs had no private patients, over three-quarters had less than 20 patients and only 4 per cent had more than 100 private patients. Various sources concluded that, after 1948, private practice by GPs was on a very small scale and growing smaller (Mencher, 1967, pp. 16–18). There was also a decline in private practice amongst hospital doctors although the numbers involved were much larger. In 1949 the proportion of consultants in England and Wales with part-time NHS contracts (and assumed to be doing private work) was 76 per cent. This declined to 73 per cent in 1959 and to 69 per cent in 1964 (ibid., p. 18). By 1976, according to the Royal Commission on the National Health Service, and for the UK as a whole, the figure was down to 42.8 per cent (Royal Commission on the National Health Service, 1979, p. 287).

Overall, then, the scope of the private sector outside the NHS was distinctly limited. The numbers of beds in private nursing homes decreased but the activities of some groups, particularly the Nuffield Nursing Homes Trust, were extended. Nuffield became the undisputed leader in the private acute market and generally provided a good standard of care at moderate cost. Similarly, the private insurance market expanded steadily with Nuffield's 'parent' company BUPA playing a key role. On the whole, because of the limited impact of these developments, there was relatively little debate about private acute care outside the NHS until the 1970s.

It was private practice and fee-for-service medicine *within* the NHS which gave rise to great controversy and dispute. Two issues dominated that scene: health charges and pay beds.

Charges, Pay Beds and the NHS

Health service charges

The debate about health service charges has had a long and bitter history. The possibility of introducing 'hotel' charges for the food and accommodation elements in hospital care preceded the creation of the NHS and has been raised periodically since then by Ministers in successive governments. No government, however, has ever agreed to introduce them – largely for administrative reasons. The same has not been true of charges for prescriptions, dentures and spectacles, surgical appliances and 'pay beds'. Proposals to charge for these goods and services have become a running sore in the history of public provision, especially for members of the Labour Party and its parliamentary representatives. Charges have represented both a symbolic and a real threat to free access to medical care and, as such, have been vigorously opposed by many socialists. Klein argues that the Labour Party, in most of its election campaigns, has treated the issue of health service charges 'rather like a mediaeval army carrying the embalmed body of a saint into battle' (Klein, 1983, p. 62). Certainly charges have taken on an ideological as well as a practical significance.

The principle of a free health service was breached, in a rather minimal way, in the 1946 National Health Service Act with the proposal to charge for certain items such as the repair or renewal of dentures and spectacles, domestic help and supplementary foods and blankets. The real debate, however, began in 1949 with the passage of an Amendment Act to the 1946 legislation. Amongst other provisions this allowed for charges to be made for pharmaceutical services and could require payment by overseas patients for any treatment they received in Britain. The aim of the legislation was to discourage excessive use and abuse of the Health Service and to raise revenue in a situation where the costs of financing the service had been grossly underestimated. Although responsible for the Amendment Act, many members of the Labour Government hoped not to have implement it. Bevan himself was fiercely opposed to charges and went along with the recommendations extremely reluctantly. Jennie Lee, his widow, claims that the proposal was carried in Cabinet against his 'strenuous opposition' but that he expected it would go no further because he did not believe that the majority of his colleagues would 'defy the clearly expressed views of both Labour and trade union conferences, not just isolated rank and file members' (J. Lee, 1980, p. 186). Although the proposal to introduce prescription charges was not, in fact, implemented at this stage the Labour Government did introduce a further Amendment Act two years later, in 1951, which heralded the introduction of charges for dentures and spectacles. Despite the profound hostility to the legislation of many Labour MPs the legislation received Parliamentary approval and was passed.

After the Conservative Government came to power in October 1951 further legislation was introduced to push through charges for prescriptions, appliances and dental treatment. A number of important exemptions were proposed and the young, the elderly and expectant mothers were not normally expected to pay. The lobby against charges was strong and powerful, led by the BMA (who opposed the prescription charge) and the British Dental Association (opposing charges for dental treatment). Many members of the general public also complained that charges breached the principle of easy access to the health service and free treatment. When the issue was debated in the House of Commons it came under very considerable attack from the Labour Party (who were now categorically opposed to health service charges) but was eventually passed – albeit by a small majority. The shilling-a-form charge was introduced in June 1952.

The controversy about charges continued right through the 1950s and 60s. The Guillebaud Committee which had been set up to examine the use of resources in the NHS concluded in 1956 that allegations of widespread extravagance in the service were unfounded but that, on the other hand, charges for dentures and spectacles did appear to act as a deterrent. The same did not seem to be true, they argued, of prescriptions charges. Indeed, despite a decrease in the number of prescriptions when charges were first introduced, by 1956 their numbers had reached 229 million per annum – an increase of 13 per cent since 1949 (Lindsey, 1962, p. 108). In 1956 a further change in the provisions was made which allowed the Exchequer to charge one shilling *per item* rather than one shilling per prescription form. It was feared that this charge would fall particularly heavily upon patients with chronic conditions who routinely required several items each week. It was resented and criticised by doctor and patient alike. Although it did result in a substantial fall in the number of prescriptions issued, the income from charges continued to represent only a small proportion of the real cost of drugs to the NHS and never reached the 20 per cent level which the Government anticipated. By 1959 the number of prescriptions began to increase again sharply. The Committee on the Cost of Prescribing, reviewing the matter in that same year, argued that prescription charges had not worked as deterrents but that doctors and patients regarded them as a 'tax on illness and old age'. The Committee concluded that prescription charges led to inefficiency and waste and that they should be abolished as soon as practicable (ibid., pp. 109–110). The Government did not follow this advice and in 1961 increased the prescription charge to two shillings as well as increasing charges for dentures, welfare foods and other services.

In 1964, when a Labour Government was returned to office after 13 years of Conservative rule, the issue of charges proved problematic and caused considerable embarrassment and agitation. Given the Labour Party's intense opposition to the charges introduced by the Conservatives it is not surprising that they chose, at an early stage (but against firm advice from the Treasury), to dispense with them. As Richard Crossman remarked in his Diaries: 'our package wouldn't impress anybody if we failed to abolish them right at the beginning' (Howard, 1979, p. 32). He added later, however, that the incoming Labour Government had an 'extraordinary innocence' and made a number of 'instantaneous decisions' which subsequently proved to have been 'ill-judged' (ibid., p. 61). Abolition of prescription charges, in his view, was one of them. The effect of this measure was to reduce the contribution of charges to the NHS budget from 5.4 per cent in 1963–4 (a proportion which had remained steady for some years) to 2.3 per cent in 1967–8 (Klein, 1983, p. 72). It quickly became apparent that the Government could ill afford this loss and, to its dismay, it felt obliged to reintroduce the charge in 1968. On January 16 the Prime Minister announced in the House that the Government proposed to introduce a prescription charge of two shillings and sixpence per item and dental charges were to increase by 50 per cent to £1.10s. Although 60 per cent of the population was to be exempt from paying the new charges the Government faced considerable criticism from its backbenchers, and was roundly condemned for having gone back on its principles.

The following year when Crossman (now Secretary of State for Social Services) introduced a proposal to relate charges for dentures and spectacles to their actual cost (what he described as a 'trivial regularisation') he found his colleagues outraged. Not only was he proposing a 25 per cent increase in charges but he was doing it only days before crucial local elections were to be held. The Parliamentary Party, he comments, regarded it as 'another breach of faith' and when he went into the lobby to vote he found that feelings were running very high. 'The wolves', he said, 'were howling and spitting round me.' He was unsuccessful in convincing his colleagues that no change in principle was involved and that this was simply an up-rating. Every time he went through the lobby that day, he recalls, he was 'spat at, shouted at and whispered at behind the scenes' (Crossman, 1977, p. 476). The whole episode, he argued later, was a 'muck up' and a 'balls up' and left him 'a broken idol, smashed' (Howard, 1979, pp. 611–15).

The other main area of provision where there had been some dispute about fees and charges had been the care of overseas patients. The Amendment Act of 1949 did give the Minister the power to charge overseas visitors for their treatment but he did not, at that time, choose to exercise it. It proved difficult to calculate the number of people visiting Britain in order to receive free health care but in London alone it was probably several thousand a year. Even so, it was calculated that the cost to the Service was less than one-twentieth of one per cent (Lindsey, 1962, p. 189) and successive Ministers were prepared to tolerate this cost as a measure of good will. Immigration officials, however, were instructed to detain individuals who appeared to be visiting Britain for the purpose of free treatment. They were not always easy to identify! According to Lindsey one Minister of Health did give a helpful illustration: 'If they saw a lady pushing a pram, and it would appear the pram was empty and soon might be filled, they would refuse that particular lady permission to land' (Lindsey, 1962, p. 189). Despite quite strenuous opposition to free treatment for foreigners, Ministers resisted the pressure to introduce charges until many years later.

The continuing and bitter debates about health service charges, from 1948 on, indicate that for many people – especially the Parliamentary Labour Party – a genuinely free health service had become an article of faith. Memories of pre-war charges and fears of deterrent effects endowed the issue with a tremendous symbolic significance which has never really gone away. The same arguments in favour of charges (raising revenue, preventing excessive use and/ or abuse of the service) continued throughout the 1970s and the same arguments against them (inefficiency, administrative expense, injustice and deterrence) were made too. The Royal Commission on the National Health Service in 1979 lent its voice to the debate. It examined a proposal to increase pre-scription charges to 50p, to introduce 'hotel' charges of £20 per week, an accident and emergency visit fee of £5 and a GP consultation fee of £2. The total revenue which would be raised from these charges was estimated at £423 million (or 8 per cent of NHS expenditure) for 1975–6 (Royal Commission on the National Health Service, 1979, p. 339). The Com-mission concluded, however, that such charges would be impractical and unreasonable – and unnecessary if their object was to deter abuse: 'If we could see that the charges which exist now made for better doctoring or discouraged frivolous use of the NHS by the public, then we should applaud them. But we do not see them in that light' (ibid., p. 342). It was not, it confessed, enthusiastic about charges and, indeed, recommended their gradual abolition.

The 'pay beds' issue

The debate about charges provoked bitterness and contro-versy in many quarters but it was the 'pay beds' issue which had the most profound and far-reaching effects upon the relationship between public and private medicine and which came to a head in the 1970s.

As we saw in Chapter 1, the issue first arose in the 1940s when Bevan agreed, during negotiations with the doctors about the proposed NHS, that 'pay beds' would be retained within public hospitals. 'Pay beds' had existed in most of the voluntary hospitals since the middle of the nineteenth century and consultants had grown accustomed to treating fee-paying patients in these beds. Although Bevan was reluctant to see pay beds in the new service, he calculated that this was the only way to win the commitment of the hospital doctors. The number of beds available in 1948 was actually quite small (1.3 per cent of all beds in England and Wales) and decreased by more than 1000 to 5628 in 1960. For most of this period the occupancy of these beds by fee-paying patients was less than 50 per cent and NHS patients occupied them for the remainder of the time (Lindsey, 1962, pp. 276–7). A similar number of amenity beds was available with, if anything, rather lower levels of occupancy.

During the 1950s and 60s the pay beds issue attracted relatively little public attention. As Butcher and Randall put it, these were the 'quiet years' in the lengthy saga (1981, p. 273). The Conservative Government did not seek to increase the number of pay beds and the Labour Opposition expressed only passing interest in the question. There were periodic outbursts of concern and allegations about queue-jumping and abuse. Bevan himself, for instance, complained in 1953 that: 'A great deal of evidence is now coming in from different parts of the country that patients who are well-to-do are able to buy their way to a hospital bed, frequently ahead of patients who are more seriously sick but have not got the means' (quoted in Ryan, 1975, p. 169). Similarly, in 1958, he told the House of Commons that he received letters every week from people decribing instances where paying patients were jumping the queue for hospital care. He recognised that the practice was not universal and although it did not, in his view, impair the service it did cause 'great grief' (*Hansard*, vol. 592, col. 1404). The debates at successive Party conferences in the 1950s and 60s when Labour was out of office reflected this concern about possible abuse and the 1963 Conference voted in favour of a gradual run-down of pay beds and measures to combat queue-jumping. Nevertheless, Opposition views on paying patients were remarkably muted and when a Labour Government came to power in 1964 it took a very cautious line on the abolition of pay beds. A number of party members felt, as Bevan had done in the 1940s, that to call for their immediate abolition would antagonise the medical profession and lead them to leave the Service for full-time private practice. The strategy adopted by Kenneth Robinson, the Minister of Health, in 1966 was to call for a review of pay beds and levels of occupancy (which were still low). At the same time (and as a 'sweetener' for the doctors) he proposed the abolition of the upper limit for fees which hospital doctors could charge fee-paying patients in pay beds. He also recommended that specific pay beds in separate blocks and wings should cease to exist and that, within an agreed total, pay beds could be located anywhere in the hospital, on a flexible basis to suit the patient's medical needs. The outcome of the review in 1967 was that the number of pay beds was to be reduced by 24 per cent. Because a deal had been struck with the medical profession and because existing beds were so clearly underused, the decision provoked little controversy.

The return of a Conservative Government to power in June 1970 marked a significant change in attitudes – and increasing political polarisation – on the pay beds issue. The Labour left became more and more vocal in their demand to have private practice separated off from the NHS, if not abolished entirely. A number of factors in early 1971 brought the problem to a head and led to firm calls for action. One incident was the publication of an open letter from the Junior Hospital Doctors to the Secretary of State, Sir Keith Joseph, asking for a public enquiry into the abuse of NHS facilities by 'unscrupulous consultants' engaged in private practice. The letter attracted considerable media attention and was followed shortly after by a claim from Leslie Huckfield, Labour MP for Nuneaton, that unauthorised admissions of private patients to the new Walsgrave Hospital in Coventry were taking place (Butcher and Randall, 1981, p. 276). In Spring 1971 the House of Commons Expenditure Committee embarked upon the most thorough and detailed investigation of private practice in the NHS ever undertaken. Its Report, published in March 1972, ran to 475 pages and reflected very wide-ranging views and evidence.

The Fourth Report from the Expenditure Committee, 'National Health Service Facilities for Private Patients'

The Expenditure Committee's brief was to examine the way in which legislation permitting private beds in the NHS was actually working although, in fact, it examined a number of issues relating to private practice in general. It heard evidence on 12 occasions from representatives of the medical and nursing professions as well as from Health Authorities, BUPA and other organisations and individuals. The Committee reviewed the current state of knowledge about the extent of private practice and the specialties involved but was scathing about the lack of information on pay bed use and occupancy and the impact on the NHS and its staff of retaining private practice within the public sector. In hearing evidence the Committee focused primarily upon the alleged benefits of private medical care (both to the patients and the NHS) and the alleged costs and abuses. Although the views expressed in the Report are illustrative of some important arguments it is necessary to take account of the fact that these opinions were largely unsubstantiated by firm evidence.

The benefits of private medicine

Witnesses to the Committee identified a number of benefits of private practice. Many of them claimed that the ability to choose one's consultant and the time of admission and to have a pre-arranged date were the highest priorities. Others mentioned privacy, the ability to carry on one's business, the availability of a private telephone, unrestricted visiting and a choice of menu. Critics mentioned the 'snob value' of going private.

Witnesses claimed that the NHS benefited in four ways from the existence of private practice: every patient treated in the private sector was one less burden for the NHS; the doctors on part-time contracts gave good value to the NHS; Britain gained prestige from treating overseas patients; and the 'brain drain' of experienced doctors was averted.

The disadvantages of private medicine

The weight of opinion was firmly against private medicine ○
and a number of different arguments were raised. On pay beds
the critics maintained that monitoring procedures were slack
and beds were often left empty when they could have been
used by NHS patients. Conversely some consultants were
charging a fee to patients in beds which had not been designated 'pay beds'.

The Junior Hospital Doctors Association claimed that pri- ○
vate patients were jumping the queue and gaining admission
to hospital on a preferential basis. Private patients would be
entered onto surgical lists at short notice and were placed
early on the list when the consultant himself would be operating. NHS patients were seen later in the day when the risks
of error through fatigue were greater or they had their operations postponed altogether. The Medical Practitioners Union
described how, against all professional advice, private 'dirty'
cases would sometimes precede NHS 'clean' cases on operating lists. The Royal College of Nursing felt that queue-
jumping most commonly took place in 'cold' surgery where
private patients were seen much more quickly than NHS
patients. BUPA took the view that private patients were not,
in fact, queue-jumping but were 'moving out of one queue and
leaving a space in it' (p. 52).

A number of witnesses suggested that the existence of pri- ○
vate practice provided an incentive for consultants to maintain long waiting lists. The Junior Hospital Doctors Association remarked that 'there is a strong feeling that a minority of
consultants do nothing to reduce their waiting lists in the
certain knowledge that their private practices will benefit' (p.
58).

Another complaint was that private practice increased the ●
burdens on junior doctors and nursing staff in the NHS.
Junior doctors were sometimes required to assist the consultant staff in their private practices and bore the brunt of the
work in the NHS when they failed to turn up for clinics and
appointments. Few of them felt able to refuse this extra work:
'If a consultant says, "Will you come with me to the hospital

down the road and assist while I do a hysterectomy", you say yes. Even though it may be private and even though, strictly within the terms and conditions of your contract of service, you should not function there as a doctor, nevertheless you go' (p. 80). The financial rewards were minimal – a bottle of whisky, a book token or theatre tickets. The BMA recognised that it was 'difficult for the chaps working underneath' to complain to senior colleagues (p. 133) but suggested that it was simply an apprenticeship which all doctors served. One surgeon added: 'I would think the junior staff, just the same as when I was a lad, are only too pleased to go and assist their chief' (p. 145).

The nursing staff and junior doctors both complained that some doctors in private practice neglected their NHS duties. They 'failed to attend ward rounds, clinics, operating sessions' or put in a 'late or short appearance'. They neglected teaching and administration and their 'management and leadership functions' (p. 57), all of which led to inefficiency, lower standards and poor morale. Junior doctors felt that their career development was frequently blocked by consultants who opposed the creation of more senior posts in order to protect their private practice. Between 1949 and 1968 the number of consultant posts had increased by only 44.25 per cent while the number of Registrars had nearly doubled and the number of Senior House Officers almost quadrupled (p. 62).

Several witnesses gave evidence about the borrowing and theft of drugs and equipment by NHS staff engaged in private practice. Others complained that private patients were over-charged for the treatment they received.

Finally, the Committee set out to discover whether private and NHS patients received different standards of service and different standards of care. Opinions were mixed. Private patients were often treated in better physical surroundings and had a better meal service with more individual attention. They had shorter waiting times for appointments, tests and treatment. They received more visits from the consultant staff and saw them for longer periods of time than did the NHS patient. The Patients Association argued that people took the decision to 'go private' precisely because standards of care would be different and better: 'We think that extremely few people are private patients because they prefer to pay directly for treatment. They pay for standards which they would otherwise not get. It is therefore inherent in the system that the "free" service should in some ways be below the standards desired by many if not most people' (p. 192). But there were disadvantages. Some nurses pointed out that it was not always in the patients' best interests to be nursed in single rooms, especially when they were seriously ill and required constant supervision and specialist facilities. The Association of Hospital Matrons added that private wings were often staffed by agency nurses and maintaining continuity of care could be difficult.

The detailed report suggested that, on balance, the retention of private practice inside the NHS had damaging effects upon the public service and its patients. The Conservative majority on the Expenditure Committee, however, ensured that the status quo would be maintained and no action was taken on the Report.

Barbara Castle and the Pay Beds Dispute

The Report of the Expenditure Committee was followed by a White Paper, in April 1973 (DHSS, 1973). It accepted the Committee's conclusions reaffirming the view that people should have the opportunity to pay for medical care and that private practice operated to the overall benefit of the NHS. The White Paper claimed that pay beds in the NHS meant that overseas patients could receive treatment, thus enhancing Britain's reputation as a centre of medical excellence (and making profits for the service at the same time). It argued that it was beneficial to both public and private patients to have the consultant doing his private work in the one hospital, especially in emergencies, and also that 'private facilities in NHS hospitals can be subject to overall planning as an integrated part of total health care' (DHSS, 1973, p. 4). The White Paper was at pains to point out that the existence of

° private practice had only a marginal effect on the length of
waiting lists. It was able to show that the number of patients
treated in NHS beds and in pay beds had increased between
1963 and 1971 despite an overall decrease in both types of bed
(ibid., p. 5). The White Paper discussed the questions of abuse
but concluded only that specific incidents should be investigated and that there should be constant scrutiny of the situation. It referred problems about unauthorised admissions and
the 'borrowing' of NHS equipment for operations in the private sector to the hospital authorities. It rejected the notion
that large numbers of NHS consultants were neglecting their
duties. Bad time-keeping, it argued, was characteristic of some
consultant staff whether they were seeing private patients or
not! In conclusion, the White Paper commended the status
quo and felt, as the Report had done, that no radical changes
in practice were required.

The Labour Party in power

° This was not, however, the view of the Labour Government
when it returned to power in February 1974. The Party had
already committed itself two years earlier to the phasing out of
pay beds and to a reversal of the policy permitting part-time
consultant contracts in the NHS. These moves were a repudi-
ation of the cautious line taken by Bevan nearly thirty years
earlier. The new Secretary of State for Social Services was
known to have a personal commitment to the abolition of pay
beds and this had now become Party policy.

Klein described the attack on pay beds under the new
Government as 'essentially ideological: an attack on visible
symbols of privilege' (1983, p. 120) and contended that their
continued existence in the 1970s represented a 'flaw in the
pure crystal of the NHS's underlying conception' (ibid., p.
118). Certainly some members of the Labour Party now saw
the opportunity to finish off the tasks left undone (as they saw
it) by Bevan in the 1940s. Feelings ran high about lengthening
waiting lists and queue-jumping but – most of all – about the
breach of the principle that medical need and not money
should determine access to medical care.

Strike action in the NHS

Shortly after her appointment in March 1974 as Secretary of State for Social Services Barbara Castle set up a Working Party under David Owen (then Minister of Health) to examine the arrangements for private practice and to explore the possibility of a new consultant contract. However, before the Working Party had been able to reach any conclusions the pay beds issue was raised again as a result of industrial action in hospitals across the country. In May 1974 members of the National Union of Public Employees (NUPE) in the North-East started a ban on private patients which went on for many weeks and emptied almost all the 196 private beds in the Region. Another incident took place at the 'showplace' Charing Cross Hospital in London where, in June 1974, domestic staff decided to take strike action unless the private wing of the hospital was closed down or opened up to NHS patients. They were led by Esther Brookstone (whom the Press described as a 'battling granny') – a clerical worker and NUPE branch steward at the hospital. The situation was not resolved and in July the ancillary staff came out on strike (*Nursing Times*, vol. 72, no. 8, 2 Dec. 1976, p. 1866). Not only did this mark a turning point in the pay beds debate but it also signified a new phase in labour relations in the health service. Strike action was almost unheard of in the service and it was, as the *BMJ* explained, the first time that a group of workers within the NHS had 'set out to achieve a political change by industrial action' (*BMJ*, vol. 3, no. 5923, 13 July 1974, p. 71).

The dispute about pay beds took place in the context of increasingly militant action by health service unions over pay. The Halsbury enquiry had been set up to look at nurses' pay and the pay of radiographers and other groups 'supplementary to medicine'. COHSE and ASTMS members, having failed to win an interim pay award, began to take industrial action. Similarly, in June, consultants and other hospital doctors threatened mass resignations from the NHS unless their Pay Review Body recommended a large pay increase.

In June 1974 when industrial action was a threat rather than a reality, Dr Derek Stevenson, Secretary of the BMA,

wrote to Barbara Castle asking her to intervene in the Charing
Cross dispute. She regarded his letter as 'an insulting ulti-
matum' (1980, p. 130) and the relationship between the
doctors and the Government (and especially with the Secretary of State) deteriorated markedly. The doctors were well
aware that the Government would have liked to abolish
private practice completely. They were suspicious of the
Owen Working Party's discussions about consultants' contracts and of rumours that the part-time contract might be
abolished altogether. As a result, the BMA's Central Council
on Hospital and Medical Services threatened a work-to-rule
unless Barbara Castle personally put an end to the Charing
Cross dispute. When the Secretary of State did eventually
make a public announcement on the matter on July 6 she said
that she did not condone the strike action. A compromise had
been reached at the hospital to redistribute the pay beds, to
ensure that NHS patients could be treated on the 'private'
ward and that private patients would continue to be treated.
Mrs Castle also confirmed that there would be no arbitrary
reductions in the number of pay beds and that any substantive
changes would await the outcome of the Owen Working Party
Report. In response both the doctors and the unions called off
their industrial action.

Government proposals

When the Labour Government was returned to office in the
Autumn of 1974 after another General Election a number of
new recommendations were on the table (see Ryan, 1975;
Butcher and Randall, 1981; Klein, 1983). They included
proposals for a new consultant contract designed to make
full-time NHS work more attractive than a part-time NHS
contract with private practice. At the time there were around
11 500 consultants, 5000 of whom had full-time contracts.
Most of the remainder had maximum part-time contracts
which meant that, although they were contracted to do the
same number of sessions as the full-timers (11/11ths), they
were only paid 9/11ths of the salary – on the assumption that
they would more than make up the shortfall from their fee-
paying patients (Castle, 1980, p. 191). Proposals to introduce

'common waiting lists' for NHS and private patients (to eliminate queue-jumping) and to review pay bed utilisation were also discussed. When the consultants examined the package as a whole it became clear to them that their opportunities for taking on private patients while remaining NHS employees were to be dramatically curtailed and after unsuccessful negotiations they began a work-to-rule in protest in January 1975. This continued until the following April and, together with industrial action by NUPE directed against private patients, meant that considerable disruption was caused. The real inducement for consultants to resume normal working was not, however, a resolution of the pay beds issue, but a recommendation by their Pay Review Body that their salaries be increased by around 30 per cent.

On 5 May 1975 the Secretary of State announced firm proposals in the House of Commons. These included the intention to phase out pay beds as soon as possible and an extension of the regulatory and licensing powers over the private sector to limit its growth. Mrs Castle proposed an immediate reduction of 500 pay beds where occupancy levels were low, and the Government agreed to compensate health authorities for the revenue lost. Barbara Castle claims that the reaction was predictable. The Tories were 'furious', the TUC were 'delighted' and even the BMA was 'mild' in its response because it was to be consulted about the proposals (Castle, 1980, p. 384). Not all members of the medical profession shared the BMA's view and once more there was talk of strike action.

The consultative document on 'The Separation of Private Practice from NHS Hospitals'

In August 1975 the Government spelled out its intentions more fully in a consultative document entitled *The Separation of Private Practice from NHS Hospitals*. In this document it set out its plans to repeal the Health Services and the Public Health Act, 1968, which had authorised the provision of facilities for private practice. It was proposed that although private hospitals and clinics might continue to avail themselves of NHS services (such as radiotherapy) they would, henceforth, be expected to pay the full economic cost. Overseas patients were to be allowed treatment in NHS hospitals, on a fee-paying basis, with the income going to health authorities or university departments for research and development rather than to individual doctors. Private hospitals would be entitled to use donated blood free of charge but a fee would be levied for administrative costs.

The rest of the document was devoted to a series of proposals about the regulation of the private sector and the licensing of private homes and hospitals. The existing provisions were described as 'over-complicated' and 'inadequate'. The consolidation, which had taken place under the 1975 Nursing Homes Act, still left an unsatisfactory picture. It was argued that the deficiencies of the current system would become even greater where the private sector was increasingly involved in the kind of complex treatment which had, hitherto, only been carried out in the NHS. New legislation was proposed which would ensure that the total volume of private medical care in the future would not exceed that which existed (inside and outside the NHS) in 1974. A licensing system was to be instituted which would require the private sector to demonstrate the need for and suitability of new facilities and which aimed to ensure that any private sector developments would not be detrimental to NHS patients. Licences would be issued for 5 years and would normally be renewable.

Barbara Castle's original feeling that the reaction of the doctors and the private sector to the consultative document was 'muted' and 'pretty mild' (1980, p. 492) later proved a gross misjudgment and it became clear that the consultants were outraged by its contents. When she met representatives of the different interests in November she wrote that 'a united hostile chorus assailed me' and, after a very acrimonious meeting, concluded that 'an epoch of total non-co-operation lies ahead' (1980, p. 550). Nevertheless (and in spite of the 'cold feet' of some of her Parliamentary colleagues) the key proposals from the document, on licensing and pay beds, were included in the Queen's Speech less than a week later. As far as the BMA and the private sector were concerned this was the last straw and plans were now formulated for industrial action. The Central Committee for Hospital Medical Services announced that, from December 1, its members would work in emergencies only.

The Goodman compromise

It was at this stage that the Prime Minister, Harold Wilson, decided to intervene and Lord Goodman (a solicitor enobled by Wilson in 1965) was called upon as an intermediary.

Barbara Castle claims that she jumped at the opportunity to discuss the issue with Goodman and hoped that he would act as a go-between with the medical profession and the private sector. Her enthusiasm was short-lived. Goodman, by this time, had close links with the Independent Hospital Group (which had been set up by BUPA to oppose the pay beds proposal). Nevertheless, Harold Wilson had increasing faith in Goodman's ability to find a solution and decreasing confidence in his Secretary of State. A compromise was reached during the first two weeks of December which was that only 1000 of the 4444 pay beds in England, Scotland and Wales would be phased out or released to NHS service immediately. This was a much weaker proposal than the Labour Party Manifesto had envisaged and one which Barbara Castle herself found too modest. It was clear, however, by this time that the Secretary of State had been removed from the driving seat on the pay beds issue and the policy was now being propelled along by the Prime Minister and Lord Goodman, both of whom were eager to placate the doctors and the private hospitals.

It was agreed that an independent review body (the Health Services Board) would be set up to examine the demand for private medicine and the future of the remaining pay beds. Decisions about future closures would be made, not by the Secretary of State, but by the Board. The 'Goodman proposals' emphasised firmly that the Government was still 'committed to the maintenance of private medical practice' and that the real problem was how to preserve this 'right' at the same time as phasing out pay beds (Castle, 1980, p. 760). A key factor in determining whether and which of the remaining pay beds would be closed down would be the existence of alternative facilities locally where doctors would carry out private work. The proposals were agreed by the BMA, the Royal Colleges and other representatives of the medical profession and were duly announced on 15 December 1975. However, they refused to call off their industrial action immediately and insisted on balloting their members about the proposals. The results of the ballot, announced on 12 February 1976, showed a majority of two to one were in favour of accepting the Goodman proposals.

The trade unions were unhappy with the compromise as were some members of the Parliamentary Labour Party and the National Executive Committee of the Labour Party who felt that the proposals had moved too far from the commitment in the Queen's Speech to eliminate private practice from the NHS. However, many of them recognised that the compromise was probably the best agreement which could be reached in the circumstances and gave their support to the Health Services Bill when it was given its Second Reading on 27 April 1976. Barbara Castle described some of her Cabinet colleagues as 'craven' and 'cowardly' for their willingness to capitulate to the medical profession on all the key issues. The final stages of drafting the Bill were complicated by Harold Wilson's resignation as Leader of the Labour Party, and when James Callaghan took his place the task of shepherding the legislation through the House fell to David Ennals, whom he had appointed to replace Barbara Castle. It received the Royal Assent in November 1976 with few modifications.

The Health Services Board

Once the Health Services Act 1976 had become law, 1000 pay beds were abolished and the Health Services Board, under the chairmanship initially of Mr Ralph Gibson QC and then Lord Wigoder, was established to consider the phasing out of the remainder. Similar Committees were set up for Wales and Scotland. One of the first initiatives taken by the Board was the preparation of a document on common waiting lists for NHS and private patients (DHSS, 1977). This recommended that all private patients (apart from emergency ad-

missions) should be on the same list as NHS patients seeing
the same consultant. The criteria for moving patients up the
list or for admitting them for treatment should be the same in
both cases. It was recommended that NHS and private patients
should have parity of access to NHS diagnostic and other
services.

The other major activity of the Health Services Board was
the scrutiny of pay bed use and occupancy. The assumption was
that in hospitals where pay bed occupancy was normally less
than 50 per cent there was a *prima facie* case for withdrawing
authorisation for the beds. After local consultation it was
eventually agreed that 317 bed in England, 4 in Wales and
35 in Scotland should go (DHSS, 1978, para. 9). Similarly,
authorisations for private consulting rooms in outpatient departments were revoked when there was evidence of low (or
no) usage. In the second (and subsequent) set of revocation
proposals the Board decided to use 60 per cent occupancy as
its criterion for closure, rather than 50 per cent. It said that
the continuing existence of a large number of under-used pay
beds was attributable to a steady decline in preference for pay
bed treatment and a very marked decline in lengths of stay in
hospital. In fact, in England, the number of 'patient days' in
pay beds had decreased from 1010 in 1961 (with an average
length of stay of 12.2 days) to 624 in 1976 (with an average
stay of 6.7 days). A similar pattern was evident in Wales and
Scotland, although in Wales the length of stay had gone down
even further, from 11.9 in 1961 to 4.9 in 1976 (DHSS, 1978,
App. VI).

The other responsibility which fell to the Board was the
scrutiny of 'controlled' and 'notifiable' works. This meant that
anyone wishing to build or extend private sector facilities of a
certain size (100 beds in London, 75 beds elsewhere) had to
seek the permission of the Board. However, the Board was
obliged to grant an authorisation unless it could show that any
new development would adversely affect the NHS or its
patients to a significant extent.

The deliberations of the Board continued through 1978 and
1979, becoming ever more complex as the legislation was modified and as the Board was asked to look deeper into issues such
as non-resident private care in the NHS and the substitutability

of private and NHS facilities. In its Annual Reports the Board emphasised the difficulty of obtaining accurate information about facilities and bed occupancy, both from the NHS and the private sector. By the beginning of 1980 the numbers of pay beds had been steadily reduced to 2553 in Great Britain as a whole (from 3444 in mid-1977). Yorkshire, the West Midlands and the North Western Region had experienced the heaviest losses, with the four Thames Regions retaining most of their beds. The greatest concentration of beds was in the South of England, with Wales and Scotland left with only 36 and 95 beds respectively (DHSS, 1980, App. V).

The Impact of the 'Pay Beds' Dispute

The dispute over pay beds in the 1970s had a number of far-reaching consequences upon both the NHS and the private health care sector. Four issues in particular came to the fore. First, the private sector itself began to forge new alliances and, with the creation of the Independent Hospital Group, moved onto a different level of pressure group politics. Second, the proposal to separate off private practice from the NHS gave a boost to private developers to provide alternative facilities outside the NHS. Third, the debate about private practice and pay beds threw up a number of administrative difficulties in the relationship between the private sector and the NHS and, fourth, it heralded a new era in which health policy was to become increasingly politicised. Each of these issues will be discussed in turn.

The politics of the private sector

The election in 1974 of a Labour Government committed to the phasing out of private medicine galvanised the supporters of private practice in an unprecedented manner. Since the 1950s the private insurance companies and hospital companies such as Nuffield Nursing Homes Trust had steadily been extending their coverage. They had adopted a low-key approach and avoided confrontation over their activities. The incoming Labour Government, however, posed new and serious threats and led to significant liaisons between different interest groups in medicine. Robb and Brown claim that many of the meetings of these groups took place in a 'cloak and dagger atmosphere', often late at night (Robb and Brown, 1984, p. 24).

It was BUPA who took the lead in these negotiations. The association saw the removal of pay beds from NHS hospitals as a serious threat to its existence and was determined to resist the policy at all costs. It would restrict the freedom of choice of the insured population, BUPA argued, and the beds which currently existed outside the NHS were inadequately equipped to cope with the demands of modern medicine. They were no substitute (either in quantity or in quality) for NHS pay beds and access to important diagnostic facilities would be seriously curtailed. In August 1974 Derek Damerell, the newly appointed Chief Executive of BUPA, convened a meeting which included representatives of Nuffield, the Association of Independent Hospitals and two commercial hospital chains. This group (which became known as the 'Private Hospital Facilities Group') thereafter met regularly to discuss the Government's proposals on private medicine. By late 1974 this informal group had re-formed to become the Independent Hospital Group and, with financial backing from BUPA, started to circularise all private hospitals and nursing homes who might wish to join.

At this stage a significant split emerged in the private sector itself. Since 1949 the Association of Independent Hospitals had represented the interests of those private sector facilities which remained outside the NHS. The creation of the Independent Hospital Group clearly challenged AIH's role and threatened to draw away some of its membership. IHG claimed that AIH rejected all attempts to present a unified attack on Government and that it (IHG), therefore, had to 'take up the cudgels on behalf of the private sector on its own' (Robb and Brown, 1984, p. 27). IHG complained that AIH was unwilling to bite the hand that fed it (many of its members provided facilities for NHS patients on a contractual basis) and that it was not prepared to confront Government. AIH, on the other hand, maintained that it was essentially a non-political organisation, with charitable status, and that it would be inappropriate for it to be involved in the kind of action envisaged. Until 1987 (when they merged to form the Independent Hospitals' Association) AIH and the IHG remained divided, with the former representing the non-commercial providers of long-term care, and the IHG focusing upon non-profit and for-profit providers of acute medical and surgical facilities, though there was some overlap in membership.

The Independent Hospital Group campaigned vigorously throughout 1975, so that when the Consultative Document on 'The Separation of Private Practice from NHS Hospitals' was published in August their counter-arguments had been carefully rehearsed. Throughout their negotiations the IHG had received the support and guidance of Lord Goodman. The Group had also cultivated the support of senior members of the medical profession and in September it orchestrated a careful response to the Castle proposals. A memorandum was issued opposing the recommendations on pay beds, signed by representatives of all the Scottish and English Royal Colleges, the British Medical Association, the British Dental Association, the Hospital Consultants and Specialists Association and the Junior Hospital Doctors' Association. This displayed, as Robb and Brown remark, 'a degree of unanimity almost without precedent in the medical profession' (1984, p. 29).

Although the 'Goodman compromise' eventually won the rather unenthusiastic support of the doctors, the IHG continued to worry about its implications. It agreed, therefore, to launch a new publicity drive under the title of 'Campaign for Independence in Medicine' to encourage public opposition to the Government's proposals. The Campaign was financed largely by BUPA and issued a series of posters, leaflets, badges and car-stickers proclaiming 'Patients before Politics'. The Campaign achieved considerable coverage and may have had some effect on the eventual outcome of the dispute. The IHG viewed the successive changes of Secretary of State, after the dismissal of Barbara Castle, with increasing pleasure. When a Conservative Government was returned to office in 1979 and abolished the Health Services Board the Group regarded this as 'a happy ending to a gravely disturbing story' (Robb and Brown, op. cit., p. 35).

This brief but significant episode throws up a number of interesting issues. First of all, it reveals the power of a provident association 'tail' (BUPA) to wag the private sector dog. The key role which BUPA had forged for itself in 1947 was strengthened by its activities in the 1970s. Its ability to bring together the medical profession and leading opinion-formers around the pay beds issue was impressive and the organisation assumed a significance in the private sector which went well beyond its position as market leader in health insurance. It was able to attract the support not only of Lord Goodman, who went on to advise the Labour Government, but also secured the services of Lord Wigoder as BUPA Chairman when he ceased to chair the Health Services Board.

Second, it is clear that the Government (unintentionally but predictably) induced a strength and unity amongst its opponents which had hardly existed before. The medical profession which had been divided on most issues most of the time since the 1940s saw, in the pay beds debate, a threat to their independence and their incomes which produced a remarkable degree of unanimity. Similarly (and despite the differences between the AIH and the IHG) the heterogeneous and hitherto almost somnolent private homes and hospitals found a cause to arouse collective passions. The aggressive stance of Government provoked, in return, an aggressive response from private entrepreneurs who had been quietly developing their small corner of the market over many years. It politicised groups who had been off the political scene for some while and it did so in a way which probably damaged rather than enhanced the Government's cause.

A boost to the public sector

The second – and related – consequence of the pay beds dispute was that it gave precisely the boost to private sector developments which Bevan had been seeking to avoid in the 1940s. Lord Goodman, in a letter to *The Times*, noted that this would be the likely outcome of the Health Services Bill, 1976, which set up the Health Services Board. 'If this Bill is approved', he wrote, 'I believe it provides a secure base for private medicine and a springboard for its continuation and, I hope, enlargement' (*The Times*, 27 April 1976). It was even rumoured that BUPA were anxious about the prospect of a Conservative Government being returned to power lest it limited the gains which had been made under Labour! Barbara Castle had, of course, hoped to avoid strengthening the private sector by coupling the separation of private practice from the NHS with strict controls over private hospital building. In the event, only a weak package of regulations was agreed.

6   It is ironic that until private medicine became a live political issue in the mid-1970s the numbers of pay beds had been steadily declining and the number of doctors engaged in private practice (as far as one can judge) was decreasing. In 1956 there were 7188 pay beds in the UK, in 1965, 6239 and in 1976 4859. On the other hand, the number of patients treated in pay beds had increased annually since the 1950s to a peak of 120 274 (in England and Wales) in 1972, after which there was a slow decline. Between 1965 and 1976 pay beds accounted for a decreasing percentage of total beds in NHS hospitals and levels of occupancy were generally low. While it is not possible to establish with any degree of accuracy the extent of private practice at this time, it is clear that the number of consultants with part-time contracts (and therefore assumed to be doing private work) had gone down from 56.9 per cent as a proportion of all NHS consultants in 1965 to 42.8 per cent in 1976 (Royal Commission on the National Health Service, 1970, pp. 287–92). It is a moot point, therefore, whether it was really necessary to have the Health Services Board accelerate the closure of pay beds which were, in a sense, already phasing themselves out all around the country.

The *British Medical Journal*, in an editorial in 1975, argued that one of the outstanding achievements of the NHS had been that it had made private practice 'an expensive anachronism' outside London. Ten years earlier, it went on, private practice seemed to be 'on its way out' in Britain but a series of factors had reversed its decline. These included the underfunding of the NHS as well as the lowering of morale and decreasing job satisfaction, exacerbated by bitter disputes over pay and differentials. Consequently, consultant staff felt that there were more and more incentives to undertake private practice where they could not only enhance their incomes but have greater autonomy and more congenial surroundings in which to see patients. The low-key approach to private practice which had prevailed since the 1940s gave way to a much more highly-charged political atmosphere where confrontation between government and doctors replaced the 'gentleman's agreements' which had existed for 30 years (*BMJ*, 22 Mar. 1975, p. 648).

As many commentators had predicted, the outcome was growing divisiveness, with consultants increasingly being forced to opt for NHS work exclusively or for private practice. But some saw this as a healthy outcome. One general practitioner advised his colleagues that they should welcome the Government's proposals to phase out pay beds because it would bring 'richer rewards' to all members of the medical profession and would 'speed the growth of a new and more vigorous private practice' (Mayer, 1975, p. 3)

The first signs that the private sector was willing and eager to fill the gap left by pay beds were soon forthcoming. Nuffield Hospitals, which had expanded on a modest scale to 13 hospitals in 1968, had by 1978 acquired a total of 29 modernised or purpose-built acute hospitals. At the same time BUPA, which had been Nuffield's 'parent company' decided to move into hospital provision itself. In 1975 BUPA Hospitals Ltd was created and work began on the first hospitals which had been acquired for the company. Further properties were bought (or built) in rapid succession. Unlike Nuffield Hospitals (a charity), BUPA Hospitals was a for-profit organisation and gave preferential rates to subscribers. The other major entrant to the private (commercial) market at this stage was American Medical International (AMI) which first established itself in Britain in 1970 with the purchase of the Harley St Clinic and which, by 1977, had also acquired the Princess Grace Hospital. Another prestigious development was the opening in 1974 of the Wellington Hospital which had been built by a subsidiary of the British and Commonwealth Shipping Group, whose other main activities lay in luxury hotel and liner accommodation. Each of these companies (and others too) had, by the end of the 1970s, entered upon a period of rapid expansion which more than replaced the numbers of pay beds lost from the NHS – and often on a profit-making basis. The real watershed came in 1979, after which (as Chapter 3 illustrates) the private sector grew at an extraordinarily rapid pace.

Controlling the private sector

The policy debates of the 1970s threw up a series of administrative problems, especially at the boundaries between public and private medicine. One of the greatest controversies centred upon common waiting lists for NHS and private patients and how they should be drawn up and monitored.

Another key aspect of the debate centred around the issue of registration and licensing. This was important for a number of reasons. Most members of the 1970s Labour Governments argued that licensing was a crucial function of government because it would enable public authorities, after the separation of private practice from the NHS, to determine the size and scope of the private sector. However the proposed regulations stopped short of the more rigorous 'certificate of need' procedures adopted by other countries (e.g. the USA and France) where developers must demonstrate that they are satisfying unmet needs for medical care. The procedures which eventually emerged, in fact, were rather weak measures which did not deter private developers. The other function of such regulations is to enforce certain standards of care and to determine quality as well as quantity. As Barbara Castle's consultative document noted, the legislation which then existed for monitoring provision was both 'over-complicated' and 'inadequate'. The problems both of setting standards and then of monitoring them, which had been evident for many decades (and which are vividly described in Abel-Smith, 1964) did not, however, evaporate in the 1970s. Although the consultative document recognised the nettle which had to be grasped it did not, in fact, grasp it and the regulatory system at the end of the 1970s had all the deficiencies of earlier legislation.

Perhaps the most troublesome problem of all, however, lay in the gross deficiencies in information about private medicine both inside and outside the NHS. There was no means of measuring the true extent of private practice, because health authorities largely took the view that what the consultant did over and above his NHS duties was a matter between him and his tax man. Estimates about private practice were based upon the numbers of consultants holding part-time contracts and assumed to be doing other paid work or upon data on private patients from the General Household Survey. Although health authorities were also expected routinely to collect basic data on private facilities in their area this frequently proved incomplete and no clear picture emerged about the size and shape of the private sector. The Employment and Social Services Sub-Committee was constantly frustrated in its attempts to quantify the extent and nature of private practice in the NHS and problems of alleged abuse. Every witness was cross-examined closely about the validity of the evidence they were giving and most had to acknowledge that it was largely anecdotal. At best it was based on limited surveys with low response rates. Similarly, the Health Services Board, in its first Annual Report, complained that 'the most serious problem' it had faced and continued to face was 'a lack of information on the use made of NHS pay beds and facilities and on the availability and use of beds and facilities in the private sector' (HMSO, 1978, para. 7). It was a point reiterated in all subsequent Reports and also in the Report of the Royal Commission on the National Health Service. The Royal Commission observed that: 'Information is lacking that would enable us to reach precise conclusions about the relationship between the NHS and private practice' (Royal Commission on the National Health Service, 1979, p. 294) The consequence of this uncertainty was that policies relating to private facilities (inside and outside the NHS) which were developed in the 1970s were based largely on assumptions and 'best guesses'.

The politicisation of health policy

Finally, the dispute over pay beds in the 1970s led to a degree of militancy amongst health service staff which was unprecedented and provided a focus for the rapid politicisation of health policy issues. Perhaps the most critical factor which marked out the 1970s from other periods was the escalation of industrial disputes in the health service which involved not only nurses and ancillary workers but also medical staff. As the *BMJ* observed, it was the first time that NHS staff had sought to achieve political change through industrial action. Low-paid workers in the NHS who had traditionally taken the view that providing a service to patients was more important than their own pay and conditions became less reluctant to contemplate industrial action on their own behalf and a series of bitter disputes ensued. While it is not always possible to identify cause and effect in the pay beds dispute it seems reasonably clear that it became a convenient vehicle for trade union militancy. At the same time it provided a focus for existing resentment and ill-feeling not only about pay and status differences in the NHS but also about continuing in-equalities in a supposedly egalitarian service. NHS staff were angry that private facilities, built with NHS finance, were being reserved for a minority of patients who could pay for treatment. They were angry that pay beds often laid empty when NHS beds were sometimes under constant pressure and they were resentful that they were often expected to provide a superior service to paying patients (perhaps to the detriment of their NHS patients) for no extra pay. Many groups of staff complained that, while the consultants reaped the financial rewards of treating private patients, extra burdens fell upon them and with no monetary benefits.

It is also clear, as Butcher and Randall have pointed out, that the pay beds issue served several secondary purposes for some of the health service unions. Although they were con-cerned about the principle of unequal treatment, for its own sake, they also saw pay beds as a way of raising issues about pay and conditions and of winning new members. One NUPE official, for example, commented: 'Once we discovered the weapon we used it. We realised that we were likely to get a much quicker response if we attacked private patients. The consultants went berserk'. (Butcher and Randall, 1981, p. 290). Action over pay beds was also tied in to the rivalry between the Confederation of Health Service Employees (COHSE) and the National Union of Public Employees

(NUPE) and their competition for members. Traditionally COHSE had tended to attract the less skilled nursing staff and those working with mentally ill and mentally handicapped people; NUPE concentrated on the ancillary workers but there was an overlapping membership. By the 1970s, as Rudolf Klein put it, the NHS 'provided a tempting game reserve for recruitment' (1983, p. 111) and even though trade union membership in the health service increased from 40 per cent to 60 per cent between 1948 and 1974 the level of unionisation, compared with other branches of the public sector, was still low.

The threatened (and actual) strike action by doctors in the health service signified the end of a 30-year period of relatively peaceful relations between them and their employers. Many of the issues raised in the 1940s about clinical freedom, control and the 'right' to treat paying patients had been thoroughly examined and, if they had not actually been resolved, a series of 'gentlemen's agreements' and 'understandings' had grown up. The different political environment of the 1970s and the different political style of Barbara Castle meant that a different outcome was almost inevitable.

The broader impact of the pay beds dispute was that it raised questions about equity, fairness and social justice in fee-for-service medicine. It revealed injustices and inequalities in the relationship between consultants, their junior doctors and ancillary and nursing staff as well as between private and NHS patients. The striking aspect of the dispute was not perhaps that these divisions had now come to the fore but that they had lain dormant for so long.

The contrast between the 1940s and the 1970s was signifi-cant in several respects but especially in the changing relationships between public and private medicine which resulted from the conflicts. In the 1940s ideology had given way to pragmatism. Despite Bevan's passionately held views about the iniquities of fee-for-service medicine he was prepared to make concessions and tolerate private practice for the greater good of establishing a National Health Service. He recognised, in particular, that eradicating private practice from the NHS would lead to the growth of private nursing homes over which he would have little control. The compromise which emerged – while it can hardly have been palatable to Bevan because of its ideological 'impurity' – nevertheless secured gains which were felt to outweigh many disadvantages.

In the 1970s the opposite attitude prevailed and pragmatism, in this case, gave way to ideology. As the Butskellite consensus of the post-war years broke down, ideological disputes forced their way onto the public agenda. As far as the Labour Party in general was concerned, private medicine was a useful peg on which to hang a political debate. It was an impurity in the post-war settlement which was to be purged. For Barbara Castle it offered an opportunity to re-establish her left-wing credentials after her unhappy experiences with the trade unions and her Parliamentary colleagues over her White Paper, *In Place of Strife*, which had been designed to regulate industrial action. The eagerness to debate the ideological points led to a neglect of the pragmatic questions and also to a polarisation of attitudes which was probably unproductive. Bevan's discreet and subtle relationships with key doctors in the 1940s led to a rather different outcome than resulted from the confrontational approach of the 1970s. Although Bevan's political opponents were formidable (the voluntary hospitals, the insurance companies and provident associations and the doctors) their positions were more clearly defined than those of the interest groups Barbara Castle faced. In the 1970s there were many more conflicts and divisions between (and among) the doctors, trade unions, the private sector, insurance companies, hospital companies and public sector interests. Membership of a particular occupational group did not necessarily signify agreement with all its public pronouncements and the parameters of the debate were much more loosely defined than in the 1940s.

In broad terms, the stakes in the 1940s in the dispute over private medicine, were very much higher than those in the 1970s. There was much more to lose (e.g. the very existence of the NHS) but the eventual gains were substantial. In contrast, by the 1970s, the issue of pay beds and private practice – by most objective standards – had become rather marginal to the effective operation of the public service. Both were in steady decline and pay beds had decreased to less than 1 per cent of total bed numbers. They assumed a significance, however, which went far beyond their size and scale. The really interesting question is whether, if the Labour Government had ignored them, private practice in the NHS and pay beds would have withered away.

3. The Boom Years: The Private Market After 1979

By 1979 the private market in health care in Britain had begun to change in very significant ways. These changes particularly affected – and were influenced by – private insurance companies, hospital companies providing acute beds and nursing homes offering long-term care. The Conservative Government elected to office in May 1979 began to create conditions under which private practice would grow and flourish. Changes in government policy – modest in themselves – set in train a cumulative process which altered the traditional balance between public and private medicine and which, in the eyes of some critics, began the dismantling of the post-war NHS. This chapter is concerned with three main themes. First, it examines government policy towards the private sector and to private practice in the NHS. The changing ideological climate and apparent shifts in public opinion are also discussed. Second, it looks at the rapid developments which took place in private insurance, private hospital building and related initiatives from the late 1970s. Third, it makes some assessment of the impact of private sector expansion and looks at the contribution of private medicine to meeting health needs.

Changes in Government Policy

A number of changes in government policy, after the Conservative Party came to power in 1979, increased the potential for private sector developments in acute care and for private practice. Two months after the election the Report of the

Royal Commission on the National Health Service was published. After reviewing the scope of the private sector, its relationship with the NHS and alleged abuses it concluded that: 'it is clear that the private sector is too small to make a significant impact on the NHS, except locally and temporarily' (p. 244). The Conservative Party, in its election manifesto, was firmly committed to policies which would encourage the private sector and – although there is no evidence that politicians envisaged a strategy which would actively damage the NHS or reduce its role – there were firm directives designed to enhance both collaboration and competition.

The Health Services Act, 1980

The Health Services Act which became law in 1980 contained a number of provisions designed to reduce the restrictions on private medicine. In particular, it abolished the Health Services Board and restored to the Secretary of State the power to authorise the use of NHS accommodation for paying patients. As a result the number of pay beds in Britain increased very slowly from 1982 onwards by just 70 or 80 a year. However, the number of patients treated in pay beds and average daily bed occupation continued to decline (Grant, 1985, pp. 21–2). In 1980 the Secretary of State agreed with the medical and dental professions a voluntary code of conduct for private practice in NHS hospitals. Six principles were agreed:

the provision of accommodation and services for private patients should not significantly prejudice non-paying patients.

subject to clinical considerations, earlier private consultation should not lead to earlier NHS admission.

common waiting lists for seriously ill patients should be used and the same criteria should be used for categorising paying and non-paying patients.

after admission access to all facilities should be governed by clinical considerations.

standards of clinical care should be the same for all patients.

single rooms should not be kept vacant for private patients

longer than the usual time between NHS admissions
(HC (80) 10, DHSS 1980)

While the principles no doubt reflected honest intentions they
relied entirely on good will and co-operation for their implementation. The DHSS argued that it was unnecessary to
set up a formal system to monitor them and suggested that
authorities use peer pressure to ensure adherence: 'The authority should seek the help of the medical staff committee
which, being conscious that the use of authorised facilities by
individual consultants is an important privilege, can be expected to use its influence to maintain the proper operation of
the principles' (HC (80) 10, p. 12).

The Health Services Act also transferred some powers of
control over private hospital developments to the Secretary of
State. Any new or converted hospital of more than 120 beds
required his/her approval. In cases where other private developments would bring bed numbers in a District, as a whole,
above 120 the Authority could apply to become a 'designated
area' and have the developments restricted. However, the
Secretary of State would only withhold approval for private
sector initiatives where it could be demonstrated that they
would have an adverse effect on the NHS and its patients.

Changes in consultants' contracts

The most important single change in government policy,
especially in its long-term effects, was the decision to introduce revised consultants' contracts in January 1980. From
this date ʃall NHS consultants became entitled to do private
practiceʄ (where previously only 'part-timers' could do so).
The amount of private practice a consultant could undertake
depended upon which of three contracts he held. Consultants
with a *full-time* contract were permitted to earn up to 10
per cent of their gross NHS salary (including merit awards)
from private practice. *Maximum part-timers* were to forego
one-eleventh (previously two-elevenths) of their NHS salary
for a slight reduction in NHS commitments but could now
undertake any amount of private practice. *Other part-timers*
could also undertake unlimited private practice and receive an

NHS salary on a pro-rata basis according to their contractual commitments. The DHSS memorandum accompanying the announcement made it clear that authorities should take a low key approach to monitoring consultants' contractual obligations: 'Detailed accounts will not normally be required since such a system will work most satisfactorily on the basis of a large measure of trust and confidence between employing authorities and consultants' (DHSS, 1979). The system was to rely upon self-reporting. Whole-time consultants were expected to report annually on whether they had breached the 10 per cent limit. If they did so in two consecutive years they would be regarded as maximum part-timers unless they made a commitment to reduce their private practice.

The net effect of the changes was a rapid increase in the number of full-time and maximum part-time contracts. The number of consultants with such contracts went up from 5303 in 1979 (in England and Wales) to 6472 in 1984 – an increase of 22 per cent in just five years (Laing, 1985, p. 8). In total, 54.3 per cent of all consultants had full-time or maximum part-time contracts in 1984 as against 47.6 per cent in 1979. Similar trends were evident amongst hospital dental staff, though the numbers involved were much smaller.

The changes in contracts meant that consultants could undertake significantly more private practice without forfeiting their position and privileges in the NHS and – in the case of maximum part-timers – without losing so much of their NHS salary. These changes meant that in 1984 there were many more consultant staff available, willing and eager to do private practice than there had been in 1979. In a situation where there were so few wholly private practitioners and where the service was so firmly consultant-led the potential for the expansion of private practice was dramatically changed. Although the increase in private health insurance and the availability of new private sector facilities were important factors, their contribution to the changing scene would have been marginal were it not for the radical restructuring of consultants' contracts and the consultants' willingness to take on new work. Furthermore, there is some suggestion that this expansion took place at the expense of the NHS. Although the DHSS emphasised that consultants must give priority to their

NHS patients at all times the NHS Consultants' Association was able to conclude in 1983 that:

> There can be no doubt that, with at least the vast majority of consultants now being engaged in some degree of private practice, and in many cases keen to develop this, there has been a reduction in the level of commitment to the National Health Service amongst consultants generally. This trend has been noticed in most parts of the United Kingdom. (quoted in NHS Unlimited, 1983, p. 10)

The 1981 Budget

The 1981 Budget introduced further incentives to growth in private medicine, when it was announced that, as from April 1982, all workers earning less than £8500 per annum would be exempt from paying tax on the value of private health insurance premiums paid by their employer. At the same time the Government introduced the Business Start-Up Scheme and the Business Expansion Scheme which provided tax concessions against the expenses incurred in creating or expanding small businesses and which encouraged the growth of consultant-owned hospitals. The Government also allowed companies to set against corporation tax the health insurance premiums which they paid for their employees. It was estimated that this last item was worth £30 million per annum to the companies involved (*Hansard*, 28 Feb. 1984, p. 66).

Co-operation with the NHS

Finally, the Government actively set out to foster co-operation between the private and public sectors of medicine and to strengthen their interdependence. In 1981 it issued a circular HC (81) 1 entitled 'Contractual arrangements with Independent Hospitals and Nursing Homes and other forms of co-operation between the NHS and the Independent Medical Sector'. The circular suggested that the NHS might wish to use independent facilities on a temporary basis, for example to reduce waiting lists or when building work was being undertaken. Longer term arrangements were also envisaged where

the NHS would utilise spare capacity for specialised services
in the private sector, or vice versa. In a Press Release (23 Sept.
1982) the Secretary of State emphasised the importance of
'partnership in the service of the sick' and the need for
'co-operation and understanding' between public and private
providers. 'The Health Service', he maintained, 'should never
be made a battle ground between the different sectors and
interests concerned with health care.

Public attitudes to the private sector

Supporters of private medicine argued that changes in government policy were, in fact, simply setting the seal on a shift in
public opinion which was now clearly evident. One poll
commissioned by BUPA in 1982 claimed to show that two-
thirds of the respondents did not want an NHS monopoly of
health care in Britain and preferred a mix of State and private
medicine. A similar proportion felt that people should be
allowed to pay for private treatment if they wished to do so
(BUPA Press Release, 4 Oct. 1982). A further survey in 1983
purported to show that a very large proportion of the population wanted to see the NHS and private sector working
together more closely (BUPA Press Release, 1 June 83).
However, another survey taken around the same time by an
independent organisation showed much less overt enthusiasm
for private medicine than the BUPA polls might seem to have
implied. Although only 10 per cent of the sample felt that
private medical treatment in Britain should be abolished less
than a quarter felt that it should be encouraged to expand.
The majority favoured the status quo (Bosanquet, 1984, p. 88).

Meanwhile, a number of discussions were going on, both
inside and outside government, which embodied much more
radical ideas about the future of the NHS and private medicine. An unpublished report by the Central Policy Review
Staff in 1982 is said to have recommended that the NHS
become an insurance-funded service. This view apparently
had the support of the Prime Minister and the Treasury
Ministers but was strongly opposed by the so-called Cabinet
'wets'. The debate in Cabinet was allegedly so acrimonious
that no record of the discussion (held on 9 September 1982)

was made in the minutes (*Guardian* 21 Sept. 1982). Two years later the Adam Smith Institute, in a report entitled *Omega Health Policy*, went even further than the CPRS and recommended the introduction of charges for hospital accommodation and meals, family planning services, drugs, ambulances, visits to GPs and other items. Patients would be expected to insure themselves and those who could not afford to do so would be given 'medicards' entitling them to a certain level of basic treatment. Fees would be introduced for all services, to deter the 40 per cent of visits by people whom the Institute claimed were not ill and who were abusing the free service. Regional Health Authorities were to be abolished, District Health Authorities were to be managed by private firms and all other possible services were to be privatised.

Finally, in 1985, the Government examined the structure of Health Maintenance Organisations in the USA with a view to reorganising primary care along similar lines. The principle of HMOs is that patients pay an annual or monthly premium and, in return, are entitled to care from their GPs if and when they need it, without further payment. HMOs normally offer a wider range of services than is available under conventional insurance programmes, there is an emphasis on prevention and there are incentives to both doctor and patient to keep down costs. It has yet to be demonstrated convincingly, however, that they are more cost-effective than existing primary care services in Britain or that they provide better patient care. Government enthusiasm for HMOs appears to have cooled and, as yet, there have been no firm proposals to reorganise British services along these lines.

Private Insurance: Boom and Bust?

The numbers of subscribers to private health insurance schemes has shown a steady growth from the 1950s until 1974. In that year subscribers to the schemes operated by the 'big three' companies (BUPA, PPP and WPA) totalled 1 096 000 which meant coverage for 2 334 000 people. The following year, 1975, saw a decline in subscribers to 1 087 000 and the downward trend continued into 1976 and 1977 when the figure for both years was 1 057 000. The number of people insured also decreased accordingly but subscription income and expenditure on benefits rose steadily (Laing 1985, p. 20). A similar pattern was evident in the Hospital Contributory Schemes which began to lose contributors at the rate of 50 000 to 100 000 a year after 1974. Grant (1985) argues that this downturn can be attributed to a particularly high lapse rate and the Labour Government's decisions to tax health insurance subscriptions and to phase out pay beds. The future of private medicine under Labour grew increasingly uncertain and strong ideological arguments had been made against the whole notion of private medicine. Laing adds that broader economic problems of rapid inflation and a fall in real incomes were also contributory factors (Laing, 1985, p. 21). This temporary decline from 1974 to 1977 was followed by an equally temporary 'boom' for the provident associations between 1978 and 1981 when the number of subscribers increased by 745 000 and the number of insured by 1 675 000. In the peak year of 1980 the net growth in subscribers was 26 per cent. The good news for the insurance companies was that the value of benefits paid out, as a percentage of subscriptions, went down from a 'normal' figure of around 83–5 per cent to less than 75 per cent between 1976 and 1979, although it reverted to 83 per cent by 1980.

The 'mini-boom' can be explained in a number of ways – though each is slightly speculative. The election of a Conservative Government, dedicated to preserving private practice, was obviously an important factor though the Minister of Health, Gerard Vaughan's expectation that 25 per cent of the population would have private health insurance by 1990 looks wildly exaggerated. The changes in consultants' contracts were, in fact, a much more important spur to private sector expansion than exhortations to the general public to go out and insure themselves.

Problems in the NHS: image and reality

It is likely that problems in the NHS also contributed to the growth of private medicine. Public expenditure cuts in the 1970s led to the closure of a number of smaller hospitals and there were cash limits on capital and revenue allocations as well as freezes on manpower. At the same time, the RAWP formula (which had been devised in 1976 as a means of redistributing NHS resources to areas of greatest need) adversely affected those areas of London and the South where private medicine already had a foothold and where it had potential to expand and fill the gaps being left by the NHS.

Although the rationing devices – especially long waiting lists and charges – which had evolved since the 1940s had restricted access to the public service, the 1979 Conservative Government maintained that there was evidence of excessive use and abuse of the NHS. Secretary of State for Social Services, Patrick Jenkin, suggested that patients 'should pay for their own keep' in hospitals and claimed that 'what was wrong with the NHS was that people expected too much from it' (CIS, no date, p. 4). Patients and health authorities alike were encouraged to look beyond the public sector for health services. The Government advocated a greater use of volunteers and, in the Health Services Act, 1980, it legalised lotteries and permitted health authorities to engage in voluntary fund-raising. The following year it introduced tax relief on health insurance premiums for those earning less than £8500 p.a. and allowed premiums to be off-set against corporation tax. A further inducement for many patients to 'go private' was the strike action by health service workers early in 1979, which fuelled fears that people who needed treatment might be prevented from receiving it. The head of public relations at BUPA said that they had received many more requests for information and enquiries after the industrial action and the public relations manager of PPP painted a similar picture. 'You always get an increased interest', he commented, 'when people realise the NHS is in trouble' (*Observer*, 25 July 1982). It is evident, then, that the public image of the NHS – for a variety of reasons – had become rather tarnished and one outcome was a growth in private insurance. As Michael Lee remarked:

> The basic confidence that the NHS can provide for the needs of patients was eroded. The constraints on health service expenditure and recurring tales of cuts in services have further undermined confidence that the NHS will

meet needs as they arise. A growing number feel it necessary to cover themselves and their dependents for medical
care. Wholesale reliance on the NHS seems too great a risk.
(M. Lee, 1980, p. 19)

However, as William Laing has indicated, public percep-
tions of the NHS may have been influenced more by image
than reality. Although there was contraction in some areas of
the public service in the 1970s, overall expenditure on hospital
and community services continued to rise steadily. He concluded that: 'there is no evidence of any inverse relationship
between growth in NHS Hospital and Community Health
Services and expansion of insurance coverage during the mid
seventies and early eighties' (Laing, 1985, p. 22).

Similarly, he found that waiting times for elective surgery
did not change very markedly during this period and suggests
that alarmist accounts about the state of the NHS were fuelled
by 'frequently inaccurate media reports' (op. cit.) It is clear
that the sources of some of these reports lay on different sides
of the political divide. On the one hand, the political left were
anxious about what they saw as the 'dismantling' of the
post-war Welfare State and breaches of the principle of a free
and comprehensive health service. Their literature emphasised cuts in services and the steady erosion of a service faced
with growing demands and limited resources. On the other
hand, the private sector itself sought to strengthen its own
position by pointing to problems in the NHS – an overbur-
dened bureaucracy, production-line care and so on. Indeed
companies such as BUPA and PPP were a little over-zealous
in the denigration of the NHS in their literature and, according to Griffith *et al.*, the Advertising Standards Authority
'upheld a complaint against BUPA and looked hard at an
advertisement from PPP' (Griffith, Rayner and Mohan, 1985,
p. 21). Ironically, then – and for quite different reasons – the
NHS was being discredited by supporter and critic alike.

Marketing insurance

The insurance companies, of course, capitalised on this situation. They embarked upon a series of publicity campaigns
emphasising the peace of mind which private insurance

brought as well as the prompt medical attention and personal service and privacy. Nevertheless, as some observers have noted, the British insurance companies maintained a relatively genteel image, continuing to call themselves 'provident associations' (rather than insurance companies) 'for its comforting ring of Victorian middle-class prudence' (*Economist*, 18 Dec. 1982, p. 20).

Significant changes in the health insurance business (with the advent, in particular, of American for-profit companies) were only a little way off and the style of the provident associations seemed increasingly dated. Their critics, who were frustrated by their outlook argued that 'these niceties are signs of the preservation of a cosy world of charitable beneficence as out of tune with modern private medicine as Florence Nightingale would be with a brain scanner' (ibid., p. 90). Despite these criticisms, it is clear that the 'big three' British insurance companies did enjoy a considerable expansion in the number of subscribers and in subscription income from 1978 to 1981. It coincided with a steady growth (of around 9 per cent per annum) in the number of private acute beds outside the NHS – a growth which had been boosted by the phasing out of pay beds. As William Laing comments: 'It is likely that supply of new facilities and demand for medical insurance were mutually reinforcing in this period' (Laing, 1985, p. 21).

The growth of occupational schemes

The final and most important reason for the rapid expansion of private insurance in the late 1970s was the increasing success and popularity of occupational schemes. In 1977 almost half the subscribers to the 'big three' insurance companies were individuals, with the remainder in 'employee purchase' schemes (where trade unions or professional associations organised group discounts but the subscriber paid his/her own premium) or 'company purchase' schemes (where the employer paid the premium). By 1983 individual subscribers were only 32.3 per cent of the total (see Table 3.1).

This did not necessarily mean that subscribers were now a different group of the population. They were still predomi-

Table 3.1   *Breakdown of subscriber by purchase category (BUPA, PPP and WPA), 1977–83*

	% of total						
	1977	*1978*	*1979*	*1980*	*1981*	*1982*	*1983*
Individual purchase	44.0	40.8	39.1	36.3	34.5	34.0	32.3
Employee purchase	18.9	16.9	15.6	15.7	21.5	23.4	23.9
Company purchase	37.1	42.3	45.3	48.0	44.0	42.6	43.8

SOURCE: Grant, 1985, p. 79.

nantly male professional workers and many of those who had been individual subscribers simply switched to one of the other two types of scheme where subscriptions were lower or were paid by employers. By 1984, 69 per cent of managers were receiving free health insurance compared with only 44 per cent in 1978. It had become the fourth most prevalent 'fringe benefit' after life assurance, company cars and subsidised lunches (Grant, 1985, p. 85). Periodic wage freezes had underlined the value of 'perks' as a way of rewarding employees and their popularity had grown markedly. As Olivia Timbs observed, private health insurance became a way of 'slipping a few extra hundred pounds' to senior managers without infringing the terms of the government's incomes policy (Timbs, 1985, p. 18).

Although senior management were still the main beneficiaries of private health insurance, the movement towards group schemes of various kinds meant that benefits were also extended to lower income groups and sometimes to manual workers. Certain companies such as Rank Xerox, Allied Breweries, Black and Decker, IBM, Marks and Spencer, and certain financial sector firms and 'high-tech' industries already had a policy of offering insurance to all their staff. It was regarded both as a welfare measure and as a means of meeting the needs of business (White, 1983, p. 35). The decision to extend insurance cover to other 'blue collar' workers elsewhere had important consequences. First, it aroused considerable controversy among and between trade unions about the propriety of accepting private cover. Second, it had a profound impact upon the profits of the insurance companies and the relationship between subscription income and benefits paid out.

One of the most controversial deals struck between a trade union and an insurance company was that between the electricians union, the EETPU, and the Electrical Contractors Association and BUPA. The 1979 TUC Conference was fiercely critical of the union but failed to dissuade it from arranging private insurance for its members. Similar criticism was directed at the National Union of Seamen when it negotiated a scheme for 1000 North Sea oil riggers. Some branches of other TUC affiliated unions such as the Fire Brigades Union, NALGO and ASTMS also agreed to manage group schemes on behalf of their members. The national leadership of NALGO and ASTMS were firmly opposed to private medicine but recognised that some of their branches took a contrary view. BUPA argued that many of these unions were out of touch with their members. Of a sample interviewed for them by NOP 68 per cent claimed that they would be in favour of participation in a group scheme (BUPA, 1981). Of NALGO members 78 per cent interviewed felt that insurance companies should be able to distribute information to employees and 59 per cent strongly disapproved of union action to prevent the introduction of private schemes (BUPA, 1982). Certainly some of the growing demand for this new perk was employee-led. Almost all the organisations interviewed by Incomes Data Services in a survey of company schemes claimed that workers were enthusiastic about private medical insurance. One said it couldn't recall any other 'perk' which had 'resulted in a better reaction and certainly not one which cost comparatively so little', while other said the schemes were some of the most satisfactory deals they had ever negotiated (White, 1983, p. 37). One group of TGWU members at a fertiliser factory who had been denied private insurance by their employers took industrial action to obtain a company scheme (*Fightback*, no date, p. 38). Equally, there are cases where management proposals to introduce group schemes were opposed by the workforce. British Rail, for example, found that its deal with PPP was opposed by both the NUR and ASLEF while the plan to insure 652 000 civil servants (including those at the DHSS!) was strongly criticised by the

Civil Service Unions and the TUC. A number of large unions not affiliated to the TUC also provided opportunities for private health insurance. The Police Federation, for example, had an agreement with BUPA and the Royal College of Nursing with PPP.

By the early 1980s the private medical sector – led by private insurance companies and provident associations – had acquired a growing interest in the health of the British workforce. BUPA's Chief Executive, giving evidence to the Expenditure Committee in 1971, had described it as 'an embryonic business or occupational health service' (House of Commons, 1972, p. 32).

Ten years later this was to be an even more apt description, as private health insurance penetrated industries, groups of workers and social classes it had had no dealings with before. Although BUPA's claims to be covering large sections of the working classes were somewhat inflated, the General House-hold Survey in 1982 did show that the benefits of private health insurance were being felt, on a limited scale, by inter-mediate and junior non-manual workers, skilled and semi-skilled manual workers, non-manual workers and women (both as employees and dependents). A more detailed analysis of the subscriber population is discussed in Chapter 5.

However the immediate consequence of insuring these groups of the population was that claims shot up rapidly. The value of benefits paid, as a percentage of subscriptions, went up from 64 per cent and 69 per cent in 1978 and 1979 to 83 per cent in 1980 to a high of 95 per cent in 1981. The main reason for this was that the morbidity of the lower income groups and social classes (as the Black Report had amply demonstrated) was consistently higher than that of professional groups and the better off. Their use of the services was also higher (though still low in relation to their morbidity). This was most vividly illustrated in data from the General Household Survey (re-analysed in *Social Trends 1986*.) Although less than 1 per cent of out-patient attendances in Social Classes III, IV and V in Great Britain in 1982–3 were private, around 5 per cent of out-patient attendances in Social Classes I and II were pri-vate. However, the total number of private out-patient atten-dances by Classes III, IV and V was 9777 compared with only 1782 in I and II. Similarly, less than 2 per cent of all in-patient stays by Classes III, IV and V were private, compared with between 8 per cent and 20 per cent in I and II. The total number of in-patient stays, however, by III, IV and V was 2996 as against 1803 in I and II (*Social Trends 1986*, p. 127). While in each case the numbers are small the figures do show a greater use of the private sector by Classes III, IV and V, analogous to their use of the NHS. In general, women were more likely to 'go private' for out-patient care and men for in-patient care.

At the same time, some policies allowed subscribers who received treatment in NHS hospitals, rather than private hospitals, to claim a daily cash payment. Trade unionists who had found themselves in group schemes but who were uncomfortable about the fact were often happier to receive cash payments instead of treatment in a private hospital. Indeed the Electrical Contracting Industry JIB commented that its members felt 'socially out of place' in the private sector and 'felt more at home' in the NHS (White, 1983, p. 37). Nevertheless, subscribers were determined to get their money's worth and, according to one source, they were now 'insisting on seeing a consultant where before the GP would have done'! (*The Times*, 17 June 1982). The insurance companies complained that subscribers were submitting a large number of frivolous claims. One said that 'some people were expecting their toenails cut on their insurance' (Drummond, 1983) and another commented that there seemed to be an abnormally large number of policemen's wives who suddenly required D and Cs and hysterectomies! It was generally true that the number of claims increased most among dependents rather than subscribers themselves.

The end of the insurance boom?

By 1981, when benefits paid out almost equalled subscription income the insurance boom came to an end. The leading insurance companies increased their premiums substantially, by 31 per cent in 1981 and 39.8 per cent in 1982 and the growth rate in subscribers dropped from a high of 25.9 per cent in 1980 and 13.9 per cent in 1981 to 2.9 per cent in 1982 and 1.9 per cent in 1983. While the 1980 and 1981 figures were quite abnormally high, the later figures were very low, given a usual annual increase of around 5 per cent (Grant, 1985, p. 77). Medical costs (and hence premiums) went up for a number of reasons. Hospital charges, according to White, rose well ahead of inflation both as a result of substantial increases in pay bed rates and increases in the private sector where new beds were coming on stream at a rapid pace. Consultants' fees also rose rapidly – a factor, as White points out, over which the insurance companies had 'little control' (White, 1983, p. 40). The free-for-all in the insurance market with special offers, package deals, new benefits and loss leaders also contributed to the volatility of the situation.

The result, after an exhilarating couple of years, was that BUPA began to lose business to its two main non-commercial rivals, WPA and PPP, but also that the non-profit sector as a whole lost out to the small but aggressively competitive commercial sector which was just beginning to establish a foothold. Grant (1985, pp. 74–6) has shown that the number of BUPA subscribers declined by 2.7 per cent between 1981 and 1983, originally with the loss of individual subscribers and then through both individual and group schemes. In the same period PPP subscriber numbers increased by 24.8 per cent and WPA by 37.2 per cent with gains largely amongst individuals rather than groups. It should be noted, however, that they both were starting from much lower baselines than BUPA, that BUPA reasserted itself with new growth in 1984 and that BUPA still remains way ahead of any other single company in its dominance of the market, with more than 60 per cent of all subscribers.

The other development at this time, which may have a much longer term impact, was the growing importance of the commercial companies such as Mutual of Omaha, Crusader, Orion and Crown Life. In 1980 they covered only 2 per cent of all subscribers but by 1984 this had grown to 8.5 per cent (Grant, 1985, p. 73). As Grant observed, the activities of the commercial carriers 'seriously disturbed the cosiness of the providents' monopolistic control' and led to 'wars of words, frequently tetchy, occasionally vituperative, between the providents and the commercials and between the associations themselves' (op. cit., p. 68). Nevertheless, and despite considerable publicity, debate and aggressive marketing, at the end of 1984 only 4.4 million people in the UK were covered by private health insurance – less than 8 per cent of the population (*Social Trends 1986*, pp. 127–8). The benefits were spread unequally – both regionally and in terms of age, social class and gender. The beneficiaries were primarily middle-aged, male professional workers and senior managers, living in London and the South-East.

Hospitals and Beds

The expansion in private insurance went hand in hand with an increase in the number of private hospitals and nursing homes and private sector beds. The precise relationship between these two areas of expansion is difficult to assess but it has been argued both that the increase in subscribers led to a demand for more private beds (especially outside the NHS) and also that the growth of attractive, modern private hospitals made private insurance seem a worthwhile investment. Either way the number of private sector beds expanded as subscriber numbers rose.

Conflicts in the industry

It should not be assumed, however, that the relationship between insurers and providers was altogether harmonious. Conflicts of interest between the non-profit provident associations and the commercial hospital companies quickly came to the surface. The main differences (though they are usually denied) have been between BUPA and AMI (the largest American for-profit company operating in Britain). In 1982 a day conference organised by the *Financial Times* (and costing £400 per head) had to be cancelled because the 'big three' provident associations withdrew. They complained that the programme had become unbalanced in favour of commercial, profit-oriented companies and they were opposed to the interests they represented. The organisers complained that the provident associations were just 'trying to throw their weight about' (*The Health Services*, 12 Nov. 1982). Just one month later BUPA announced that, as from January 1983, its subscribers would no longer be covered in full for fees in some of the independent, for-profit hospitals (including those owned by AMI). BUPA insisted with (as *The Times*, 17 June 1982, put it) 'as straight a face as it can muster' that the initiative came from its subscribers but – the report went on – it did 'nothing to hide its delight at the decision'. The Managing Director of AMI explained that his first instinct had been to 'fire back' at BUPA but that he was not entering into a dialogue with them (Brown, 1983, p. 28). The problem was not resolved, however, and later, in 1985, the Chief Executive of BUPA was still complaining that AMI and other for-profit companies were 'killing the goose which lays the golden eggs'. AMI, in return, argued that BUPA was simply trying to 'blame the health care providers for the mismanagement of health insurance' and looking for scapegoats because their profit margins were tight (*The Times*, 12 Dec. 1985). The projected rise of 11 per cent in BUPA's subscription rates for 1986 could not, AMI argued, be attributed to escalating costs in private hospitals. PPP's plan to restrict subscription rates to only a 1.5 per cent increase but to introduce a whole range of exclusions provoked even greater bitterness and AMI claimed that they were simply 'taking the easy way out' (*Guardian*, 6 Dec. 1985).

The declining use of pay beds

Another key factor in the increase in private sector beds from the late 1970s was the decline in the numbers and occupancy of NHS pay beds (see Table 3.2).

The dwindling total between 1974 and 1977 is accounted for by the activities of the Labour Government and the Health Services Board in closing beds. The modest revival in 1979 was the result of three factors: the growth in the number of insured patients seeking treatment, the reinstatement of some beds by the Conservative Government and the willingness of health authorities to use pay beds as a source of income. Although the data on pay beds is surprisingly inadequate (see Grant, 1985; Laing, 1985) it is clear that levels of occupancy, length of stay and the numbers of patients treated declined

Table 3.2   *Authorised pay beds in NHS hospitals in England, Wales and Scotland, 1974–83*

	England	Wales	Scotland	Total
1974	4535	60	324	4919
1975	4136	60	234	4430
1976	4113	60	234	4407
1977	3213	47	184	3444
1978	3370	44	149	3563
1979	3171	39	114	3924
1980	3171	36	94	3301
1981	2677	48	94	2819
1982	2919	49	105	3073
1983	2987	49	108	3144

SOURCE: England, DHSS (SBH 211); Wales, Welsh Office; Scotland, Scottish Health Services.

steadily during the period. Average occupancy in England fell from 48.3 per cent in 1974 to less than 40 per cent in 1983 (Rayner, 1986, p. 16). In Wales it dropped from 29.95 per cent to 13.87 per cent and in Scotland from 30.2 per cent to 21.8 per cent (Grant, 1985, p. 144). The most marked change of all, however, in the period 1974–83 was the very striking increase in private out-patient attendances in NHS hospitals which went up from 78 811 in 1974 to 189 668 in 1983 in England (ibid., p. 22) and from 424 to 1980 in Wales (ibid., p. 144).

Private sector beds: numbers and ownership

If data on NHS pay beds is incomplete, information on private sector hospitals and beds is even more rudimentary and unreliable. However, the Association of Independent Hospitals has undertaken regular reviews and was able to provide authoritative and up-to-date statistics compiled both from DHSS data and from information supplied by the private sector itself. In a survey in July 1985, AIH showed that, between 1979 and 1985, there had been a net increase of 52 hospitals and 3577 beds in the UK as a whole. This represented a 35 per cent increase in the number of hospitals and a 54 per cent increase in the number of beds in a period of five and a half years. England had 185 private acute hospitals and 9416 beds, Wales 5 hospitals and 239 beds, Scotland 9 hospitals and 414 beds and Northern Ireland 2 hospitals and 86 beds, making a total of 201 acute hospitals in the UK and 10 155 beds (199 hospitals and 10 069 beds in Britain). Almost half of the private hospitals have been built within the last 10 years. In contrast, only one-tenth of NHS hospitals have been built since the Second World War and 70 per cent date from before the First (Davies, 1987, p. 412). New growth was concentrated in those areas with a tradition of private sector development, especially in the South and South-East. The most outstanding 'boom' area was Wessex with 8 new hospitals and 439 new beds but the North-West and North-East Thames Regions and the North-Western Region also saw significant new growth. Although the largest increase had been in England, Scotland experienced modest but interesting expansion with the opening of two new hospitals – Ross Hall in Glasgow (owned by AMI) and Murrayfield Independent Hospital (managed by BUPA) in Edinburgh. The most economically deprived areas of the country, especially in the North of England, Northern Ireland and Wales, saw only very small increases in bed numbers. By July 1985 the four Thames Regions had between 25 and 36 private sector beds per 100 000 population and Wessex 23 beds, while Wales had 9, Scotland had 8, Northern Ireland had 6 and the Northern Region of England had 5 per 100 000. (The average for England as a whole was 20 beds.) Although there was a large overall increase in the number of private hospitals from 1979 some also went out of business and 13 closures were noted between 1980 and 1985 (Association of Independent Hospitals, 1985a.).

Without doubt the most important change since 1979 was not, however, in the number or location of private acute beds but in the change in the pattern of ownership of private hospitals. Until 1979 the typical private hospital was small (30–40 beds) and owned either by a religious or charitable non-profit organisation or by an independent for-profit company; 95 per cent of all beds were in such hospitals. By 1985 only 68 per cent of beds were in this kind of institution and there had been a dramatic increase in the number of hospitals and beds owned by American for-profit corporations and British for-profit companies such as BUPA Hospitals, Community Hospitals and Grandmet. From having only 3 hospitals (366 beds) and 4 hospitals (156 beds) respectively the American and British for-profit companies acquired or built, in the space of 5 years, 24 hospitals (1924 beds) and 30 hospitals (1319 beds). The charitable, non-profit organisations which had owned 72 per cent of all private acute beds in 1979 now owned only 52 per cent and the for-profit groups which had owned only 28 per cent of all beds in 1979 now owned 48 per cent. By far the largest increase in the market share has been taken by American for-profit companies and there has been a trend towards the takeover of independent and charitable hospitals and small hospital chains. At the same time the average number of beds per hospital has gone up from 44 to 50 with some American owned hospitals having over 100 beds (ibid.). AIH's latest survey, published in December 1986, shows that although total bed numbers had gone down to 10 025 and the number of private hospitals to 198, the for-profit companies continue to strengthen their position in the market. In the charitable hospitals 473 beds were lost and, for the first time, the for-profit groups owned more than 50 per cent of all private beds (AIH, 1986).

The Disappearing Overseas Patients

A further important change in the private market which took place at this time was the decline in the treatment of overseas patients in Britain. For many years the overseas patient (especially from the Arab countries of the Middle East) had been the 'bread and butter' of private medicine, particularly in London. Although there are no entirely reliable figures to show what proportion of private patients come from overseas it has been estimated that they may account for 25–30 per cent of the total in London (Griffith et al., 1985, p. 50). However their numbers are 'falling fast'. In 1980, 1699 patients from Saudi Arabia had been treated in London but in 1983 the figure was only 398 (ibid.). Nicholl et al. estimate that 14 per cent of all surgery (excluding abortions) performed in the four Thames Regions involved patients not ordinarily resident in England and Wales. This compared with only 1 per cent of the private case-load in other Regions (Nicholl *et al.*, 1984, p. 92).

According to one report, in 1978, AMI were alleged to have recognised that any future expansion in the private sector would mean: 'providing hospitals in the regions for *British* patients and not for Arab ones, which at present make up 80 per cent of its patients' (Illman, 1978, p. 13). The United Arab Emirates were reported to be completing a 'massive hospital building programme' involving a five-fold increase in health care spending and AMI had concluded that there was 'no further scope in the Arab market' (ibid.). Illman claimed that the number of Arab patients seeking treatment had fallen by one third in 1978. He attributed this not only to the extensive hospital building taking place in Arab countries but also to the poor treatment they received in Britain.

The problem here is that British doctors now have a reputation among Arabs for over-charging. A spokesman for the United Arab Emirates told me:

> These people do not like the idea of being cheated. They may come to London and spend £10,000 gambling and go away feeling quite happy about it. They know what they are doing. But they resent paying £30 for a so called medical consultation which only lasts a minute or two.

What often happens, Illman said, is that the patient may have a simple question or two for their doctor which could easily be dealt with on the phone. However, the doctor will tell them to book an appointment at £30–£35 a time. 'They don't complain,' the spokesman added, 'they just don't bother coming back.' Illman concluded with the comment that: 'The new style native Briton patient will be treated differently, of course' (ibid.).

The leading British companies, Nuffield and BUPA, have always emphasised that they cater primarily for the British market and do not seek overseas patients. Their attitude was illustrated in some rather injudicious remarks made by BUPA's

Chief Executive to the Employment and Social Services Sub-Committee in 1971. The 'biggest trouble' in some of their London hospitals, he said, came from 'the Middle East contingent, who come in with their retinues' (House of Commons, 1972, para. 1311). Such patients were normally directed to the London Clinic (owned by AMI) a few streets away. 'I hope you will not tell the Charity Commissioners this,' he added, 'but we do our very best within the charity status to put the posts up in different directions away from our front doors' (ibid., para. 1315). Earlier the Chief Executive had said that he felt 'very militant' about overseas patients and the fact that, as charities, Nuffield Hospitals were expected not to discriminate between patients seeking treatment (para. 1209). Speaking 'quite parochially and narrowly', he went on, he thought that was wrong.

> I think we built these for this country, increasingly it is all too easy now for the Eastern Seabord of America – particularly in the New York area – to combine Stratford, Edinburgh and varicose veins in London plus an air fare at rather cheaper cost than having the whole thing done in New York. (ibid., para. 1214)

The indications are that a less than welcoming attitude to overseas patients in some hospitals in Britain and the increasing availability of high quality care elsewhere have reduced the demand upon British facilities. Not only have many Arab countries now built their own hospitals but it is often cheaper for foreign nationals to receive treatment in the USA or in Western Europe than in Britain. However, those patients who still come to Britain are said to come for "very complex treatment" (Griffith et al., 1985, p. 50) and the Opposition spokesman on Health, Frank Dobson, has established that a significant proportion of patients receiving heart transplants in Harefield Hospital are foreign nationals. Between 1979 and 1985 34 foreign nationals received a heart transplant there compared with 139 U.K. nationals. In the same period 6 U.K. nationals and 4 foreign nationals received heart-lung transplants. In Papworth hospital, by contrast, only one (out of 109 transplant patients) was from overseas (Hansard, 1 July 1985,

p. 58). The research conducted by the University of Sheffield on the work of private acute hospitals, shows that 1 in 8 private patients were non-U.K. residents and that the majority of these came from Eire and Europe; 84.5 per cent of them were in Britain for a termination of pregnancy. Apart from terminations, overseas patients (43847 in total) underwent 6.7 per cent of all other operations in 1981 (Williams *et al.*, 1984, p. 447).

The decline in the overseas market is also reflected in provident association statistics, which demonstrate that more and more private patients have insurance cover. The non-insured group (now growing smaller) have traditionally been overseas patients paying cash and elderly patients, ineligible for insurance, who pay for surgery such as hip replacements. In 1975, 40 per cent of hospital bills were paid by the patients themselves and 60 per cent by insurance companies. In 1984, only 25 per cent were paid direct by patients and 75 per cent by insurance companies (Grant, 1985 p. 65).

Although overseas patients are still in evidence in London, especially in hospitals which are foreign-owned, they represent a decreasing proportion of private patient numbers. The indications are that overseas custom in the 1980s comes less from individual consumers in rich Arab countries than from governments and embassies buying 'package deals' for their nationals. Griffith *et al.* describe deals with the Kuwaiti Embassy to treat 800–1000 patients each year (one-third of whom are government-sponsored), with the Qatar Embassy for 1500–2000 patients annually and with the Greek government to treat 450 Greek civil servants and their families (Griffith *et al.*, 1985, p. 50). Similarly, negotiations have been held with hospitals in London and elsewhere to treat nationals of several European countries on a contract basis.

In a number of ways the climate for overseas patients has become gradually less welcoming in recent years. In October 1982, for example, the Government implemented measures to charge fees to overseas visitors in NHS hospitals. There was considerable opposition to this move from both sides of the House of Commons on the grounds that it would be racially divisive and that it was unnecessary. There was very little evidence of any abuse of the NHS by overseas patients and many critics felt that the measures were a sledgehammer to crack a nut. Nevertheless, the Government persisted – in the expectation that charges would raise £6 million p.a. DHA returns suggest that the revenue has proved to be considerably less than this target and that in some areas the administrative costs of the scheme are higher than the income.

All in all, policies affecting overseas patients in Britain have been ambivalent. Some interest groups have set out to encourage greater use of private facilities by overseas patients as a means of maximising profits, while others – displaying fairly overt racism, especially against Arabs – have tried to restrict the trade from overseas. Government policies have reflected a similar tension between competing objectives. The net effect has been that overseas patients have gone elsewhere for their treatment, in increasing numbers, and seem unlikely to return.

Diversification of the Market

The radical changes which have taken place in private health care since 1979 have led to extensive diversification of the market. The rapid growth in the acute sector, for example, pales into insignificance when compared with the increase in private nursing home accommodation for the elderly and chronically ill. The 25 000 or so places available in England in 1979 increased to 29 807 in 1983 and 36 650 in 1985 – showing a 20 per cent increase in just two years. Wales experienced a 24 per cent increase in that period (from 1118 beds to 1382) and Scotland a very slight increase of 3.5 per cent (from 2377 beds to 2461) (Association of Independent Hospitals, 1985b).

Private primary care

Some of the other important changes, however, have been qualitative rather than quantitative in nature. First, we have seen new initiatives in private primary care, especially the much-publicised Harrow Health Care Centre which opened in November 1982. For an annual subscription of £85 (£52 for children) in 1985, patients received a range of GP services, together with the availability of screening, diagnostic tests and minor surgery. An additional annual fee of £32 was charged for drugs (or alternatively, patients could pay for each item). The Centre was set up by Dr Michael Goldsmith who had been an NHS GP for eight years but who resigned because he felt that patients wanted 'a more personal and caring service' (Levi, 1983). He raised £500 000 from Air Call Holdings Ltd and Electra Risk Capital and employed his staff on a salaried basis. By 1985 the Centre had enrolled 3200 patients and was just beginning to make profits. In July 1985 it was bought by AMI which, along with other private sector companies, is now planning to expand into primary care.

Apart from initiatives such as the Harrow Health Care Centre, however, private GP services have remained at a minimal level since the 1940s. Less than 1 per cent of all consultations are private and most of these take place in London and the South-East. A number of private GPs derive their business largely from embassies and hotels. Levi suggests that 'the reputable private GPs today' are: 'the traditional family GPs who wish to live and practise in an area which is closed to any more NHS practice and an unknown number of NHS GPs who are prepared to take some private patients' (ibid.). There are a number of disincentives to the growth of private GP care. Patients are not permitted to see their NHS GP privately and have to look elsewhere (or change their NHS GP) and they are not entitled to 'free' or subsidised NHS drugs from their private practitioner but must pay the price in full. One attempt by BUPA to set up insurance for private GP services in 1959 failed to attract sufficient subscribers and was abandoned. Similarly, a service launched by Medicover to provide private home visits by GPs for £60 p.a. survived only 20 months and went out of business in 1981.

Screening

Other developments in private primary care, especially screening have had much greater success. Many private hospitals and insurance companies now offer a screening service, both to individuals and to companies. In 1985 AIH listed 42 centres specifically providing such a service. BUPA, who are the market leaders in this fast growing area (and who describe themselves as 'the largest health screening operation in Europe' [BUPA, 1985, p. 8]), now screen around 50 000 people each year – 50 per cent of whom are not BUPA subscribers. Another 50 000 or so are screened by other organisations and pay £150–£200 for their consultation. One of BUPA's greatest successes has been its Women's Unit. Having established a London base in 1970 it then bought a mobile screening unit to tour the country. The Well Women Clinic at the BUPA medical centre in London now screens around 13 000 patients a year (10 per cent of them from overseas). A number of other imaginative initiatives in screening services are also evident. Dunbar Mobile Scanning, in 1982, was hiring out a body scanner and a radiographer at £750 per day. This service, run by the London Imaging Centre, was available to NHS and private hospitals alike (*The Health Services*, 26 Nov. 1982). Another 'first' went to the private Regent's Park Clinic for its successful bid to advertise its sexually transmitted diseases clinic on local radio (*Guardian*, 30 Jan. 1986).

Selling health care overseas

In 1977 BUPA announced a new service, which provoked rather more controversy than its well-established screening programmes. In conjunction with the British Tourist Authority (BTA) it issued a series of foreign-language leaflets on medical care in Britain to embassies in Greece, Turkey and the Middle East. It directed prospective patients to its headquarters in London and, for £20 it offered a basic consultation and preliminary examination. The aim of the service was to 'prevent a whole lot of shopping around' (Palmer, 1977, p. 3). Many overseas patients, it was said, came to Britain for treatment, but did not know how to find a doctor or to seek advice. A BTA survey showed that 17 per cent of all Arab and Iranian visitors in a six-month period were coming to Britain for medical care. The same was said to be true of many Greek and African visitors and a small percentage of Europeans. 'The first thing Italian businessmen do when they are ill', one writer claimed, 'is to telephone their travel agent' (ibid.). The service was given tacit approval by the Overseas Trade Board who hoped to increase 'invisible earnings', though the Department of Trade claimed that it did not wish to be too involved in the politically sensitive area of private medicine.

AMI, who were scathing about BUPA's initiative, and said that they had never needed to advertise their services, launched a package deal with British Airways in 1981. Clinic-Air, as it was called, offered what it described as its 'TTH package' – 'Travel, Treatment and Hotel' (*Family*, 1981, p. 3). For a pre-arranged fee, overseas patients were offered a deal which included their air fare, transfer from Heathrow Airport to an AMI hospital, all costs while in hospital (including accomodation and fees for treatment), convalescence in a top London hotel and a return flight from Heathrow. The package was designed for patients from Latin America, Africa, the Middle and Far East, Greece and Turkey, as well as British expatriates in Hong Kong, Malta and Cyprus. In 1984 BUPA opened its Gatwick Park Hospital which is conveniently located near the airport and which was jointly financed by BUPA, the Lovell Construction Group and the Caledonian Aviation Group.

'Chain-store medicine'

Other developments in primary care are many and varied including the growth of so-called 'chain store medicine' where GPs are setting up practices in department stores. In 1981 Debenhams in Oxford Street announced that it had rented space to a private GP practice, and walk-in opticians shops are now commonplace in large stores. This may be the beginning of what, in America, are now known as 'doc-in-the-box' centres.

Complementary medicine

At the same time, private allergy clinics have grown in number, as have many centres offering 'alternative' or 'complementary' medicine. Grant has estimated that there are now over 4000 professionally trained and organised therapists in the UK (excluding faith healers and creative therapists), in addition to 2 200 medically qualified complementary practitioners. Since 1978 their numbers have increased at a rate of 11.5 per cent a year. It was calculated that, in 1984, there were around 16.5 million consultations with such practitioners, involving a fee income of £160–£170 million (Grant, 1985, p. 62). By its very nature the field of complementary medicine is extremely diverse and these figures may well be an underestimate. In addition there are at least 3000 private chartered physiotherapists and 2000 osteopaths (*The Times*, 17 June 1982).

Dental and optical care

Ninety per cent of dentists undertake private work although only a small proportion are in full-time private practice. Insurance companies are now beginning to offer cover for dental care. Two major changes in government policy have also affected dentists and opticians. From 1 April 1985 dental charges increased substantially. Before that date patients were required to pay up to £14.50 for a routine course of treatment. After April 1, however, there was no upper limit for routine treatment, except the maximum charge of £115 for any NHS course of dental care. The patient pays the full cost of treatment up to £17 and 40 per cent of any costs after that. Dentists argued that not only would these charges deter those people who most needed treatment but also that they provided incentives to bad dentistry, where it became cheaper to remove a tooth than to preserve it. The rationale for the charges was that they would raise additional revenue and that they would cut down unnecessary treatment by dentists, because consumers would become more critical and cost conscious. In December 1984 opticians lost their monopoly on the sale of spectacles. From that date it became legal for any retailer to sell glasses to people over the age of 16 who were not registered blind or partially sighted. Anyone wishing to purchase them required a prescription from an opthalmic optician or a doctor which could be made up to suit their individual requirements.

Commercial deputising services

One further area of expansion in primary care has been in the
use of commercial deputising services for GPs. There are now
50 such services in operation (*The Health Services*, 17 June
1983), and in 1984, 45 per cent of all GPs had permission to
use such a service (*Hansard*, 6 Feb. 1984). In this case it is the
doctors, rather than the patients, who pay the fees to companies such as Air Call and Southern Relief Service to provide
out-of-hours (usually night-time) cover. In 1983 *The Sunday
Times* published an exposé of such services, alleging poor
standards of care, delay, inadequate controls and overwork by
deputising doctors. The allegations were investigated and in
May 1984 the Minister of Health announced new guidelines
on the control and use of deputising services.

Institutional care

Another main area of diversification has been in institutional
care for the mentally ill, for drug addiction, alcoholism and
eating disorders. These developments have taken two forms:
first, the adaptation of existing facilities to new markets and
second, the establishment of new facilities. One example of the
first line of development would be the changes which have
taken place at St Andrew's Hospital, Northampton. The
hospital was built by Freemasons and opened in 1838 as the
local asylum. It is a charitable organisation with a staff of
more than 400, including consultant psychiatrists, neuro-
psychiatrists and clinical psychologists, as well as a school of
nursing and school of occupational therapy. For many years,
after becoming a private hospital at the turn of the century, it
provided largely for the 'elderly rich' offering psychiatric
treatment and long-term care. In 1985 St Andrew's charged
£294 per week for long-stay non-geriatric care and £322 a
week for long-stay geriatric care. However, the 'boom' in
private nursing homes in the 1980s meant that more and
cheaper alternatives to hospital care suddenly became available.

As the traditional market fell away St Andrew's moved into

the provision of specialist treatment units dealing with alcoholism, eating disorders, brain damage, behaviour disorders, 'adolescent disorders' and behaviour modification. By 1983, 80 per cent of patients were under the age of 60. The hospital also provides secure facilities for the mentally ill on a contract basis with DHAs. The biggest expansion has been in the treatment of adolescent 'behaviour disorders' and in 1985, 7 wards were devoted to this purpose, charging £700 per week. Changes in the patient population have also meant changes in sources of income. Fewer patients now pay for themselves and, while some are covered by insurance policies, an increasing number are paid for by public authorities under contractual agreements. In 1983, out of a total of 680 admissions, 86 patients were paid for by Health Authorities and 25 by Local Authority Social Services Departments (i.e. 16.3 per cent of all admissions).

New provisions for the treatment of alcoholism and eating disorders reflect both a willingness to fill gaps left by statutory and voluntary organisations and an eagerness to move into very profitable areas. St Andrew's has also been associated with the unit, Spyways, in Dorset which is a 26-bed nursing home for adolescents with psychiatric problems. Dr Gavin Tennent was Medical Director of both institutions until leaving to join AMI. In 1983 St Andrew's acquired Bowden House Clinic in Harrow for use as a short-term psychiatric facility and a 'potential source of referral to St. Andrew's' (St Andrew's Hospital, Northampton, Annual Report 1984, p. 16) as well as premises in Harley Street for use as a psychiatric day clinic. Like many other private hospitals St Andrew's is now examining the potential of day and community services both as means of providing follow-up services to patients and as sources of recruitment to in-patient beds.

When AMI purchased the Harrow Health Care Centre in 1985, it was quite explicitly seen as establishing a primary care route into private hospital care. As Nicholas Timmins put it: 'AMI appears to see G.P. services as not so much potential profit-making centres, but as complementary, feeding patients into private hospitals, psychiatric facilities and alcohol rehabilitation centres' (Timmins, 1985).

In 1985 AMI also purchased Kneesworth House, a psychiatric hospital near Cambridge. It planned to operate at least part of the hospital as a closed unit offering secure surroundings for the severely mentally ill. According to *The Financial Times* (22 Jan. 1986), AMI's other plans for diversification included 'a network of Oakhurst alcohol treatment centres . . . other kinds of clinic and day care units'. Two specialist companies which have moved into the field of private psychiatric care and the treatment of addictions are Charter Medical of England and Community Psychiatric Centers, both of which are American-owned. Community Psychiatric Centers (European Division) owns Manor Clinics which specialise in the treatment of alcoholism. The British company, Nestor Medical Services Ltd, owns three hospitals and manages two others. The largest of them, Ticehurst House (90 beds) in Sussex, offers short-stay psychiatric care, psycho-geriatric assessment and alcohol treatment.

Abortion facilities and in-vitro fertilisation

The private sector has a long-standing interest in the provision of abortion facilities and is responsible for more than 50 per cent of all terminations carried out in the UK. The majority of abortion clinics were traditionally non-profit, voluntary organisations such as the British Pregnancy Advisory Service and the Pregnancy Advisory Service. However, since the 1967 Abortion Act commercial agencies have moved into the field and around two-thirds of all terminations in the private sector are now carried out by for-profit hospitals and clinics (Griffith *et al.*, 1985, p. 49). One third of these abortions in the for-profit sector are performed on overseas patients. Terminations, in fact, account for a large part of the work of private hospitals. Griffith *et al.* put the figure as high as 28 per cent in 1981 (ibid.) while Williams *et al.* (1984) estimate that the figure for England and Wales was 22.4 per cent (64 293 cases) with 28.1 per cent of this total being non-UK residents.

At the other end of the spectrum, as it were, we have seen the growth of a small but significant number of private infertility services. Since the birth of the first 'test tube baby' in 1978 a further 800 babies have been born, 550 of them at Bourn Hall, a private clinic near Cambridge set up by Mr

Patrick Steptoe and Dr Robert Edwards. A number of NHS hospitals in London, Bristol, Manchester and Glasgow offer in-vitro fertilisation on a fee-paying basis and two private hospitals in London – the Wellington Hospital and the Cromwell Hospital (both foreign-owned) – have infertility clinics offering in-vitro fertilisation (Marsh, 1986). A single course of treatment can cost anything from £1000 to £3000 but infertile couples may need several courses before conceiving a baby. The success rate of in-vitro fertilisation is generally put at 20 per cent and can be considerably lower than that in units with little experience of the technique. Both terminations of pregnancy and in-vitro fertilisaton have been procedures which the NHS has, in the past, been either unwilling or unable to undertake on a significant scale. The objections have been ethical and clinical as well as economic. The way has been left, therefore, for the voluntary sector (both non-profit and commercial) to plug the gaps and to develop the market.

Hospice care

Similar points can be made about care for the terminally ill where scanty NHS resources have gradually been supplemented by voluntary and charitable effort. In Britain today there are now around 100 hospices where 20 years ago there were none. All the hospices are run on a non-profit basis and they are supported by charitable effort, voluntary fund-raising and – increasingly – by health authorities who maintain patients on contractual agreements.

These private sector facilities, it should be noted, are only the visible side of the market and are organisations and institutions registered with District Health Authorities. They are subject to specific controls and are inspected regularly. Aside from these, there are a whole range of enterprises, including private pathology laboratories and clinics offering cosmetic surgery, which may not come to the attention of statutory authorities and where standards of care and treatment methods may be open to question. Indeed a number of disturbing incidents involving the use (and misuse) of laser therapy caused the Government to make specific mention in the Registered Homes Act 1984 of the need to register and monitor such facilities.

How is Private Medicine Doing?

The rapid changes in the private market in health care have led to a variety of provisions which was almost inconceivable only a decade ago. The question we must ask, however, is whether the boost given to private medicine by a series of social, economic and political decisions in the 1970s is of lasting significance. Is the private sector here to stay? Were the 'boom years' a brief honeymoon period in the otherwise strained (not to say 'forced') marriage between public and private medicine?

One important point should be made at the outset. Despite the attention given to the development and growth of the private sector in these pages and despite the considerable political controversy these changes have aroused, the size and scope of private medicine in Britain is still very limited. Pay beds in the NHS account for less than 2 per cent of all acute beds and levels of occupancy are low and falling. The 10 069 acute beds in the private sector represented less than 3 per cent of all hospital beds in Britain in 1985 and the 4.4 million people covered by private health insurance accounted for less than 8 per cent of the population.

Nevertheless, the private sector has begun to make a significant impact in Britain, particularly in its contribution to 'elective' non-urgent surgery. The most comprehensive figures on this subject came from national studies undertaken by the Department of Community Medicine at Sheffield University in 1981 and are now likely to be underestimates, given the growth in the market since then. However, even at that stage, they indicated that the private sector was bearing a significant burden of work in certain specific areas. One in eight patients (excluding non-UK residents) admitted for elective surgery (other than abortions) was treated privately either in a pay bed or in a private hospital bed. Of total hip replacements 26.2 per cent were carried out in this way as were 23.0 per cent of varicose vein surgery, 23.7 per cent of haemorrhoidectomies and 20.9 per cent of hysterectomies (Nicholl *et al.*, 1984, p. 91). Around three-quarters of all these operations took place in private hospitals and the remainder in NHS pay beds. Figures for other routine surgical procedures were smaller but, overall, 13.2 per cent of elective surgery was undertaken privately. Similar conclusions about the changing balance of work between the public and private sectors were drawn from a study of the gynaecology workload in the Winchester health district. Reductions in NHS bed occupancy accompanied an increase in the private work undertaken by the three gynaecologists (Noble, 1985, p. 124). The other major contribution of the private sector has been in abortions where more than 50 per cent of the total are carried out in the private sector.

It is now likely that the private sector is also undertaking a significant proportion of the treatment for alcoholism, drug dependency and infertility in Britain, though there are no firm statistics available in these areas. Its contribution to psychiatric care is growing, especially in the provision of secure facilities and treatment of 'behaviourally disordered' children, but the number of in-patient beds devoted to these purposes, as a percentage of all beds for the mentally ill, is still small. Some of the insurance companies and private hospitals, conscious of the criticism that they are living off the NHS, have sought to make contributions to total health care resources. A number of private schools of nursing, for example, are well-established and have good relationships with local NHS hospitals – often offering short courses to their nurses. BUPA has donated a £1 million lithotripter to St Thomas's Hospital and £250 000 to an acute ward at Stoke Mandeville Hospital as well as substantial sums for research and teaching. PPP has made similar contributions to medical research, to the funding of a teaching post and to transplant programmes and hospice projects.

By some criteria, the private sector is healthy and flourishing and identifying for itself a distinctive (and growing) corner of the health care market. However, by other standards, there are undeniable difficulties within the private sector. First of all there is the problem of over-bedding. The Association of Independent Hospitals (AIH) estimated that in 1984 average bed occupancy was less than 65 per cent, when most private hospitals needed 70 per cent to break even. In some hospitals occupancy fell well below this 65 per cent level and compared unfavourably with an average NHS occupancy level of 77 per cent (Grant, 1985, p. 32). John Randle, of AIH, claimed that the problem arose from a combination of: 'speculative building by commercial developers in areas where acute hospitals are not needed and the fact that much of the planning assumed that NHS pay beds would be phased out' (*The Financial Times*, 22 Jan. 1986). NHS pay beds were not, of course, phased out entirely and although small in number they still absorb a significant amount of work. The problem of over-bedding, which has been apparent in London for some time has now extended to the West Midlands and Wessex Regions where several private sector developments all came on stream at the same time.

Grant has suggested that factors other than the increase in bed numbers have contributed to under-occupancy. These include low pay-bed charges at levels where the private sector cannot compete, a substantial decrease in the growth rate of private insurance and fewer overseas patients. Shorter lengths of stay have necessitated increased throughput of patients to maintain profits – but these have not materialised. The tendency for some of the insured population to opt for treatment in the NHS and draw a cash payment has also contributed to low levels of occupancy in private hospitals (Grant, 1985, p. 32).

These changes in the market have affected the large companies as well as the small non-profit hospitals. In January 1986, Nuffield Hospitals announced that they were to close the 68-bed Nightingale BUPA Hospital in London. Oliver Rowell, General Manager of Nuffield Hospitals, explained that competition from the commercial 'for-profit' hospitals and the loss of patients to private hospitals outside London had caused particular difficulties. Since 1978, when Nuffield took over the hospital, 8 new private hospitals (with 800 beds) had been opened in central London and the competition had been too intense (*Financial Times*, 22 Jan. 1986). The hospital had been expensive to maintain and develop and its location deterred patients and staff.

Although the for-profit companies project a confident and

aggressive image they too have had difficulty in filling beds. The Chaucer Hospital in Canterbury, for example, owned by AMI, sacked nearly half of its full-time nursing staff and some ancillary workers within a year of opening in July, 1982. AMI admitted that it had over-estimated demand for acute in-patient surgery in the area and was hoping to move into day surgery and out-patient care. The 100-bed Chalybeate Hospital in Southampton, HCA's first purpose-built hospital in Britain which was opened in September, 1984, has had even more problems. Levels of occupancy have been very low – regularly at less than 25 per cent – and the hospital was, for some time, unsuccessful in attracting consultants from their usual locations in neighbouring private hospitals and pay beds. The Hospital Director and the Matron left the hospital at the end of its first year and it has gradually reduced its consulting room prices and room rates, so that from being the most expensive local hospital it now charges less than the local Nuffield and BUPA hospitals and less than NHS pay beds. Concern about over-bedding was also expressed by Bruce MacLeod, Executive Director of the Humana Hospital Wellington in London. 'It is tough going out there', he commented in 1984, 'I think we can expect to see a shakedown similar to that of the airline industry, with the Freddie Lakers falling by the wayside' (*The Observer*, 14 Oct. 1984).

John Randle of AIH complained that the NHS engaged in unfair competition by heavily subsidising pay beds and urged that, for the sake of the private sector, the remaining beds should go. Health authorities, he argued, should be 'made to use private hospitals' for non-emergency surgery as a way of reducing their waiting lists. If this did not occur, he warned, some private hospitals would 'certainly go to the wall' (ibid.).

Overall, the private sector has been plagued, in the last few years, with increasing costs but only modest profits. For some of the smaller non-profit hospitals the pressure proved too much and between 1980 and 1985 thirteen closed down altogether. A number of others have changed hands and been bought up by the larger chains. Several factors have been responsible for the escalation of costs in the private sector, though there is some disagreement about the weight which should be attached to them. The British non-profit organisations, such as BUPA and Nuffield, are of the firm opinion that it is the foreign-owned commercial companies who are pushing up costs in their expensive, 'luxury' hospitals. Robert Graham, Chief Executive of BUPA, has said that commercial providers have been operating with 'unrealistic profit levels' (*Financial Times*, 22 Jan. 1986). Not only are there more high-cost, for-profit beds than there were five years ago, but more and more patients are being treated in them, rather than in the charitable, non-profit sector. The new, commercial hospitals are increasingly involved with high-technology procedures which are also costly. The charges for all private beds, both in the NHS and outside it, have risen substantially in recent years – and at rates well above inflation. Where occupancy levels have been low, charges have been increased accordingly, to cover the cost of overheads.

The American for-profit companies, on the other hand, do not accept that they have spoiled the market, although they would agree that 'the glittery days of open-ended profits in the sector are over' (*Financial Times*, 22 Jan. 1986). Gene Burleson, Chief Executive of AMI, has commented that the industry has been experiencing a 'severe shakedown which will last another couple of years' (ibid.). He was critical of the British insurance companies, in particular, for restricting growth and for refusing cover for some psychiatric treatment and the treatment of drug and alcohol addiction. Indeed AMI had been exploring ways of moving into the insurance market in Britain. In short, Burleson concluded that it was 'totally asinine to say that the profit motive is killing the whole industry' (ibid.), and maintained that this was the essential ingredient keeping it going.

What of the plans to strengthen the private sector through collaboration and contractual agreements with the NHS? A number of studies have examined the extent and nature of collaborative arrangements (see Horne, 1983; RIPA, 1984; Rathwell *et al.*, 1985). David Horne has shown that the use of private contractual arrangements by the NHS between 1963 and 1981 declined steadily. The number of in-patient deaths and discharges under such arrangements actually fell from 37 376 in 1963 to 24 063 in 1981. During the same period the number of out-patient attendances decreased from 432 574 to

101 932. The decline continued even after Ministerial encouragement to make more use of private facilities. Indeed, the studies by the RIPA and Rathwell *et al.* show that the traffic was from the private sector to the NHS rather than vice versa. The most common form of contractual arrangement was the provision of NHS pathology services to private hospitals. The NHS made use of the private sector for convalescent care and terminal care in particular but contracted out only a small proportion of acute care (around 7 per cent). Laing comments that collaborative arrangements are very much 'second order issues' and are 'an avenue of last resort when efforts at achieving an in-house solution fail' (Laing, 1985, p. 50). Unless government policies change, therefore, and firmer directives to contract out patient care are issued to health authorities it does not seem likely that the NHS will be a major provider of business to the private sector (except in certain specialist areas). It is not impossible, however, that these changes will occur. In the longer term the NHS may increasingly be seen as a financier rather than a supplier of services. In this case the private sector may come to rely on a steady stream of work from the NHS on a contractual basis and the interdependence of the two sectors will be greatly strengthened. In a period of severe resource constraints it will, no doubt, seem attractive to central government to seek to fill empty private beds with patients from NHS waiting lists. Whether such an arrangement is necessarily cost-effective remains to be seen.

In 1987, and just a few years after the boom in private health care began, the prospects for private medicine are uncertain and the situation volatile. The trends indicate only modest growth in private insurance, with a search for new subscriber populations and attempts to consolidate past growth. Cost control is a serious and growing problem and is likely to be exacerbated by the entry into the market of commercial insurance companies – especially the larger groups such as Mutual of Omaha and AMI. In the hospital sector the weak will go to the wall or be bought out by for-profit organisations. The process of transformation from what Wood calls 'a cottage industry' into 'a sector of corporate activity' (Wood, 1986) is likely to speed up and to reflect more energetic activity by foreign-owned for-profit groups.

The private sector, in some form, seems here to stay, but it is
likely to be dominated by American commercial interests
rather than by the charitable non-profit organisations of the
past. The precise nature of that market will be determined
only tangentially by the NHS and will arise out of political
calculation, entrepreneurialism, clinical need, opportunity
and profit-oriented economics. The crucial role in all this of
American corporations is examined in detail in the next
chapter.

4. A Taste of American Medicine

The most striking change in the private health care market in Britain in the last decade has been the growth of for-profit medicine and the contribution to that growth of American-owned hospital corporations and insurance companies. In 1979 there were just 3 hospitals in Britain owned by American companies, with 366 beds. By 1986 there were 31 acute hospitals with 2239 beds and AMI was rivalling Nuffield Hospitals as the single biggest provider in the country. Although it had fewer hospitals, the ones it did own were relatively large and sophisticated and its total bed numbers were rapidly reaching comparability with Nuffield. Each of the American for-profit corporations in Britain is an organisation with extensive commercial interests in many parts of the world. They have both the power and resources to mould the British market in ways to suit their needs. The outcome is likely to be a major shift from the 'cottage industry' gently nurtured by Nuffield and BUPA since 1948, towards a much more aggressive, competitive, profit-oriented enterprise. This chapter examines the recent growth of American-owned for-profit facilities in Britain. It looks at the context from which they have emerged and at the possible consequences of growing commercialism in health care. It examines the thesis that these developments are aspects of a medical/industrial complex with far-reaching significance in western capitalism.

American For-Profit Corporations: Who They Are and What They Do

In 1986 there were eight American for-profit corporations operating in Britain, with the possibility that others would follow. Three of them had opened London offices in the 1970s but the rest had moved in later when the prospects for expansion looked encouraging.

American Medical International Healthcare Ltd

The biggest and most expansionist American corporation in Britain, American Medical International Healthcare Ltd, the UK subsidiary of American Medical International (AMI), came to Britain in 1970 and purchased the Harley Street Clinic. In 1977 it went on to buy the Princess Grace Hospital and between 1980 and 1985 added ten more hospitals as well as one other (Ross Hall in Glasgow), which it managed rather than owned. By the end of 1984, AMI overtook Nuffield Hospitals to become the largest single provider of acute beds in Britain – although in 1985 Nuffield reasserted itself as the front runner (*Financial Times*, 13 Feb. 1985). Even so, the speed and determination with which AMI has moved into the market is very striking.

AMI is the fourth largest hospital company in the USA after Hospital Corporation of America, National Medical Enterprises and Humana. In 1985 its sales were $2000 million and its net profits $137.1 million, and it employed 40 000 staff (*Financial Times*, 22 Jan. 1986). At that time it owned more than 150 hospitals worldwide, with around 100 of them in the USA and the remainder being in Switzerland, Austria, Spain and Singapore as well as in Britain. As well as acquiring new hospital chains (such as the 25 hospitals owned by Lifemark Corporation in the 'Sun Belt' states of the USA) and individual hospitals at home and abroad AMI has sought to diversify its activities on a wide range of fronts.

In 1984 it became the first investor-owned company to buy up a teaching hospital in the USA (St Joseph's Hospital in Omaha) and was appointed to equip, staff and operate all the medical facilities for the Los Angeles Olympic Games. It claims to have given away $2.5 million worth of equipment and services to athletes and trainers during the course of the Games. It has also started a Health Maintenance Organisation at the George Washington University and has acquired the Fidelity Life Insurance Company.

In its attempt to take a lead in the US private health care market AMI has been paying particular attention to staff development and to the visual image created in its hospitals. In 1984 it embarked on a joint venture with a fashion designer and a cosmetic company to set up a 'personalized image workshop' for all its American employees (*Federation of American Hospitals Review*, Nov./Dec. 1984, p. 62). The AMI Image Apparel Care Team was established to visit all AMI hospitals and give advice to staff on uniforms, fitness, skincare and make-up. The rationale, AMI claimed, was that : 'a properly packaged hospital employee who looks good and feels good can deliver a better quality of patient care' (ibid.).

In recent years AMI has moved into the provision of out-patient facilities ('ambulatory care centres') which are equipped for day surgery as well as more routine work. Another part of the company (AMI Diagnostic Services Inc.) provides diagnostic imaging services to 120 hospitals and has a fleet of mobile CT scanners. In 1984 it moved into psychiatric care for the first time in the USA and now offers psychiatric in-patient treatment and alcohol and drug rehabilitation programmes in special clinics. It has made available a new range of domiciliary health services and occupational health services and is now moving into the provision of information systems for health care facilities (*Federation of American Hospitals Review*, Nov./Dec., 1984, pp. 24–6).

In Britain AMI is aiming for similar variety and has moved in a number of different directions, promoting several kinds of service – some of them successful and others less so. In addition to its 13 acute hospitals (with 1203 beds) AMI has now established a number of clinics specialising in alcohol and drug addiction, in association with the charity ACCEPT. These are clearly areas of the market which are likely to expand and where American for-profit companies are playing a leading role. Not only is the treatment of addiction an area where public provision is very limited but alcoholism and drug dependency are serious and growing problems. If AMI is correct in its estimates that 'alcohol-related illness will be the world's third major health hazard by the year 2000' (*Independent Medical Care*, September 1985, p. 3) the field is wide open for entrepreneurial activity.

AMI is clearly alert to the danger of putting all its eggs into the hospital basket and, as in the USA, has begun to move into the field of primary care, with its acquisition in 1985 of the Harrow Health Care Centre. The Centre's founder, Dr Michael Goldsmith, became Executive Director of AMI's UK branch of the Family Health Programme Inc. The company has plans to move further into primary care, with a second health centre in Manchester, a £5 million health centre programme in London in 1987 and a feasibility study of Health Maintenance Organisations in a British context. The health centre is important in providing a route into in-patient care. As AMI's Chief Executive commented, the primary health care centres give the company 'access to a large segment of the population' and 'more to market to large industrial customers' (Cooke, 1985, p. 14).

Alongside this development AMI has established a range of occupational health services and screening services in Britain. In October 1985 AMI launched a new health and screening programme called Physiometrics, which specialises in cardiovascular monitoring. Some of its hospitals run sports injury clinics and pain clinics, and at the Park Hospital in Nottingham in-vitro fertilisation is available.

One of AMI's more controversial ventures has been the London International Transplant Centre based at the Clementine Churchill Hospital. The Centre collates information on kidneys available for transplant and supplies organs to surgeons working in London hospitals. Most of the kidneys come from the USA and most of the patients are from overseas. The Centre claims never to use British organs for non-nationals and does not aim to make a profit on the sale of kidneys. In fact Britain is a signatory to a Council of Europe resolution which prohibits the sale of organs and when AMI's activities came to public notice in September 1984 the Department of Health was pressed to launch an investigation. AMI had allegedly issued advertisements to all West German patients undergoing dialysis offering them 'cadaver kidneys' at £14 300 (1983 prices) and the prospect of surgery in Britain within just 4 weeks. Professor Peter Morris, head of the transplant unit at the John Radcliffe Hospital, Oxford, addressing the Transplantation Society's world congress in

1984, said that he deplored this practice of trading in kidneys and said it was an example of 'insidious commercialism' (*Guardian*, 1 Sept. 1984). AMI responded by denying any impropriety and denied all knowledge of the West German advertisement even though the *Guardian* claimed it possessed a copy (*Guardian*, 6 Sept. 1984).

Two other recent ventures by AMI have also provoked controversy. The first was the purchase of Kneesworth House in Cambridgeshire, which began operating in Autumn 1985 as a secure unit for the severely mentally disturbed. The hospital faced early teething problems because it admitted its first patients without having the approval of the full Cambridge Health Authority and it also ran into opposition from the Community Health Council and pressure groups for the mentally ill. In October 1985 the hospital was charging £690 a week and was expecting to attract interest from health authorities who might use its facilities on a contractual basis. The second controversy centred around AMI's proposal to buy the 252-bed Royal Masonic Hospital in Hammersmith in 1984, which is discussed later in this chapter.

In February 1986 AMI announced a new and unusual service for the victims of serious road accidents. It opened a head injury rehabilitation centre at Grafton Regis in Northamptonshire and offered assistance to patients who wished to sue for damages. After a period of 4 to 6 weeks' assessment, detailed medical reports were supplied to lawyers representing the crash victims. According to the *Guardian*, AMI anticipates that patients may then wish to spend some of the damages awarded to them by the courts on rehabilitation at the centre. The two-year programme offered at Grafton Regis cost £75 000 per patient at 1986 prices (*Guardian*, 4 Feb. 1986).

One of AMI's better known interests has been in the management of NHS facilities. In May 1985, when it was disclosed in the House of Commons that the Government had discussed the possibility of an American corporation running an NHS hospital, the District General Manager of Portsmouth and South-East Hampshire Health Authority, Chris West, revealed that he had discussed with AMI a proposal that they might manage the District's 673-bed General Hospital. Although the idea was put on a back burner until new

NHS management changes had been completed, another proposal that AMI open a private wing in the hospital was still under active discussion (*Guardian*, 22 May 1985). Later in the year the Lewisham and North Southwark Health Authority supported a motion to institute talks with AMI about managing the 65 pay beds in the private wing of Guy's Hospital. The hospital anticipated that AMI could help it double its £500 000 annual income from the beds (*The Times*, 30 Oct. 1985). Each of these developments has received the enthusiastic support of central government, which, since 1983, had been urging private management of NHS beds, where this seemed appropriate.

Conscious of the need to ensure that patients can actually pay for the treatment they receive, in 1984 AMI introduced a credit card known as the AMI Card. It operates on a credit rating basis similar to Access and Barclaycard and has an upper spending limit. Patients receiving treatment then repay their bills at a fixed monthly rate. In early 1986 AMI announced that, because of disagreements with British insurance companies, it was thinking of setting up its own insurance schemes, along the lines of the AMI Care programme in the USA.

Finally, AMI has been involved in a number of projects designed to enhance the image of the organisation. One such was the sponsorship of a series of master classes and concerts by the Royal Academy of Music at the Princess Grace Hospital in 1983 (*The Health Services*, 3 June 1983). It is also rumoured that the company was holding discussions in 1986 with the University of Cambridge about the possibility of funding the Chair in Clinical Criminology vacated by Professor Donald West.

In September 1985 AMI announced that it was planning to launch the first fully comprehensive private health care service in 1988. This was described as a service 'to rival the NHS'. Part of the package would be an insurance scheme which would cover individuals 'from the embryo to the grave' (*Guardian*, 30 Aug. 1985). In addition there would be private casualty units (the first was planned for Windsor) to complement the health centres, hospital and out-patient facilities already acquired. Gene Burleson, Chief Executive of AMI, said he was 'very bullish about the market' and was confident that it would 'continue to grow for those who can make a profit' (*Financial Times*, 22 Jan. 1986). He was aiming for a substantial increase in insurance cover to 'dwarf' that offered by BUPA, PPP and WPA and envisaged further diversification of his company's activities. 'There have to be additional markets out there, and', he added, 'we should be going after them' (ibid.). Just the previous year he had declared that 'The market isn't the $4\frac{1}{2}$ million people covered by health insurance. It is the remaining 50 million people and giving them access to the private sector' (*Financial Times*, 13 Feb. 1985). He was keen to explore new markets – naming geriatric care and occupational health schemes as obvious areas ripe for development – but, as a long-term strategy, he wanted to see the main expansion in private primary care. Developments here would provide a jumping-off point for other new types of facility. Burleson's other long-term goal is to have a network of facilities where services can all be incorporated under one roof with, for example, hospitals containing primary health care centres. 'More and more', he explained, 'we are trying to move towards a one stop shop. That is where the future lies' (Cooke, 1985, p. 14).

A recent article aptly describes AMI as a 'hustling, profit-motivated enterprise in a realm where the sacred cows of public service take up so much of the space' (Foster, 1985, p. 25). It is clear that AMI intends to maintain its position as the leading American for-profit company in Britain.

HCA United Kingdom Ltd

The second American entrant into the British health care market in recent years has been HCA United Kingdom Ltd, a subsidiary of Hospital Corporation of America – the world's largest for-profit hospital company. In 1981 it had revenues which, at $2064 million, were almost twice as great as those of its nearest rival Humana (*The Financial Times*, 12 Jan. 1983). Only two or three years later HCA had revenues 'in excess of $4000 million' and in 1984 was trying to arrange a merger with the largest American medical supplies company (American Hospital Supply Corporation) when revenues were expected to rise to $7600 million (Grant, 1985, p. 46). In the event the deal fell through and AHS was bought out by Baxter Travenol, a medical products manufacturer. HCA owns or manages 390 hospitals in the USA and another 30 in other parts of the world including Australia, Brazil, Saudi Arabia and the Virgin Islands. HCA's rapid growth has been all the more remarkable since it was only formed in 1968 when it started with one 200-bed hospital in Nashville, Tennessee. The company is registered in the Cayman Islands and 51 per cent is owned by physicians (Ashton, 1983, p. 26). Some of its hospitals in the USA are reserved solely for the treatment of doctors and their families. One of the founders of HCA, Jack Massey, previously Chairman of Kentucky Fried Chicken, was highly optimistic about the possibilities of expansion in private health care: 'The growth potential in hospitals is unlimited. It's even better than Kentucky Fried Chicken' (quoted in Widgery, 1979, p. 104).

The company first opened a London office in 1974 but this was largely as a recruitment base for its operations in the Middle East. Its major task was to staff the King Faisal Specialist Hospital in Riyadh. Its first important project in Britain was initiated in 1981 when HCA began negotiating with Southampton City Council to purchase a piece of land adjacent to Southampton General Hospital, on which it planned to build a 94-bed hospital to be known as Chalybeate. Despite strong local opposition, the scheme went ahead and the hospital was opened in September 1984. In the meantime HCA had acquired a chain of 6 small hospitals in 1982, owed by Seltahart Holdings Ltd and YJ Lovell Holdings. Seltahart itself was owned by Peter Townsend, a builder, and Ken Turnbull who, after their £15 million deal with HCA, went on to set up Nationwide Hospitals, which is now building a number of small 'cottage hospitals'. By the end of 1986 HCA owned 9 hospitals and partly owned one other, giving a total of 452 beds.

On the whole HCA has been keeping a very low profile in Britain, perhaps because of its difficulties with Chalybeate Hospital. The failure to win planning permission for a 76-bed hospital in Edinburgh in 1982 was also a setback and one which brought the company further into conflict with local interest groups. In 1985 it was rumoured that HCA had found a site for a new hospital in Croydon and was planning to move into psychiatric care (Grant, 1985, p. 47) but there was no sign that the company would adopt the aggressive style of AMI in Britain. Plans to diversify were modest and HCA was taking a very cautious line.

Nevertheless, the Managing Director of HCA United Kingdom Ltd, Art Ouelette, claimed in 1983 that the company's goal was 'definitely to be "number one" in the United Kingdom'. Their aim, he said, was to provide quality rather than quantity and although they would not necessarily be the largest they would be 'most assuredly the best' (Brown, 1983a, p. 16). HCA has an almost Messianic view of its worldwide operations and, indeed, its public statements set out what it describes as its 'Mission'. This refers to meeting the needs of local communities with a humanitarian approach but it is clearly combined with very hard-nosed commercial calculations. In fact HCA has been rather over-zealous in its expansion in recent years in the USA, and has been involved in legal action in several states where it is alleged to have contravened legislation regarding the over-provision of hospital beds and monopoly of the market.

Both AMI and HCA emphasise their sensitivity to local needs and the importance of responding to community demands, though their record on relationships with their host communities in Britain is, to say the least, mixed. In fact, both are concerned principally with satisfying the needs of consultant staff rather than any other particular interest group. HCA's approach in planning the Chalybeate was fairly typical. First, it examined the demographic picture and the size of the insured population in the area, then it went on to look at existing private facilities. Art Ouelette explained that two factors were crucial. They were looking for areas where there were not enough private beds to satisfy demand or where the quality of existing beds was 'sub-standard' (Brown, 1983a, p. 16). The next stage was a survey of local consultants to determine their interest, followed up by personal contact and – in the case of Chalybeate Hospital – a reception at a local hotel. The first administrator of the hospital, John Rabjohns, emphasised the prime importance of wooing local consultants and claimed that the hospital had been sited within yards of

Southampton General Hospital largely to suit their convenience. Local industrialists, neighbours and allotment holders (who had lost some of their land during the building of the hospital) were all invited to look round the building on pre-opening tours.

The concern with community support and interest was also a feature of HCA's planning at its Fylde Coast Hospital in Blackpool. As the hospital administrator put it: 'We want very much to project the idea that we are a hospital for the community. . . . And we want the community to feel responsible for the hospital in much the same way as they feel responsible for the local NHS hospital' (quoted in Brown, 1983a, p. 17). This very localised interest is reflected in the management style of HCA, where hospital administrators have considerable autonomy. As Art Ouelette put it:

One thing I learned very quickly when I came to this country is that you can drive 25 miles between two points and move virtually from one world to another. . . . If there was ever a case for de-centralised management, it exists in this country, because what is important in making a hospital a success in Blackpool is not necessarily identical to what is important in making a hospital a success in Southend-on-Sea. (quoted in Brown, 1983a, p. 17)

The future of HCA's involvement in the private sector in Britain remains open to question. It will, no doubt, involve a process of consolidation (especially where levels of occupancy are low) and may involve cautious expansion into psychiatric and out-patient care. However, in 1987 there were no indications that the company would replicate in Britain the kind of feverish activity which had characterised HCA in the United States.

Humana Inc.

The third American group in Britain is Humana Inc. which, although a leading hospital company in the USA, has only one hospital in Britain. This is the 265-bed Humana Hospital Wellington in London. The hospital was opened in 1974 and was bought by Humana in 1976. It has a wide range of

facilities and sophisticated equipment, including its own CT
scanner. It is equipped for a variety of surgical procedures
from day surgery to open heart surgery and has a 13-bed
intensive care unit. Resident medical officers provide 24-hour
cover. The Wellington is the largest private non-psychiatric
hospital in Britain.

On the whole Humana was developed very slowly in Britain. In 1979 the company had only one hospital with 101
beds and by 1986 this same hospital had just 265 beds. This is
remarkably modest progress for an organisation which had a
turnover of $2600 million in 1984 and operated 91 hospitals
worldwide (Grant, 1985, p. 47).

In recent years Humana has assumed a high profile in the
USA not least because of spectacular experiments with arti-
ficial hearts in transplant surgery. The much-publicised plas-
tic heart (Jarvik) was first used at the Humana Hospital in
Louisville, Kentucky, amidst extensive media attention and
personal messages of support from the US President. Although Humana won an international advertising award in
1985 for its promotion of health services, the company was
eager to emphasise that it was 'not simply a money machine
but a chain with a serious interest in medical excellence'
(*Guardian*, 3 Dec. 1984).

In the early 1980s Humana Inc. began to diversify its
activities in the USA with a programme of 'ambulatory care
centres' known as Humana Medfirst, and then an insurance
package called the Humana Care Plus programme. The
Senior Vice-President of the company explained that they
were aiming to create an 'integrated health care system which
blends together a pre-paid health plan with a hospital delivery
system' (*Federation of American Hospitals Review*, Nov./Dec.
1984, p. 34). The strategy was both to increase the utilisation
of Humana hospitals and to drive down costs and reduce the
employer-paid premiums. It would result, he said, in a 'win-
win situation' for Humana and for employers.

National Medical Enterprises Inc.

National Medical Enterprises Inc. of Los Angeles became one
of the newest entrants to the British market when, in 1984 and

1985, it bought two small hospitals – the Alexandra Hospital in Chatham (44 beds) and the Elland Independent Hospital in Yorkshire (47 beds). Both have out-patient consulting rooms, facilities for certain surgical specialities and 24-hour resident medical care. In 1985 NME strengthened its foothold in the British market by purchasing most of the assets of a government-backed British company, United Medical Enterprises. UME had originally been set up under a Labour Government in 1978, by the National Enterprise Board, with public investment of £6.2 million. It started with ambitious plans to finance hospital projects both in Britain and overseas but made relatively slow progress. It took over the management of a number of hospitals but encountered a good deal of local opposition over its UK operations, especially when it planned to take over the London Jewish Hospital – a disused hospital in Tower Hamlets – to turn it into a 90-bed private acute unit. Similar complaints were lodged in 1982 when UME proposed to build a luxury private hospital on the site of Battersea General Hospital, which had been set aside for residential provision for the homeless and the mentally ill. The NME buy-out in 1985 left UME free to concentrate on its overseas market and to withdraw from what had proved to be a problematic British scene.

Meanwhile, in the USA, National Medical Enterprises has edged Humana out of its number two position amongst the leaders in the health care industry. Only HCA now outstrips NME in terms of revenues (which were $2100 million in 1984) and employees (69 100 in 1984). This growth has been the result of what NME's Senior Vice-President describes as 'extremely aggressive, market-orientated advertising campaigns' (*Federation of American Hospitals Review*, Nov./Dec. 1984, p. 29). NME has sought to establish what it terms 'patient feeder mechanisms for our acute care hospitals' through the provision of primary care facilities in a so-called 'multi-delivery system'. NME's most ambitious project to date in the USA has been a 40-acre complex in Delray Beach, Florida (said to provide 'the ultimate opportunity for controlling patient distribution') which includes a whole range of treatment and rehabilitation facilities for both the physically and the mentally ill as well as 'retirement housing' and administrative services. It is clear that NME has both the potential and the resources to take a larger market share in Britain if it should choose to do so. Mr Judd Osten, Vice-President of NME's international group, has said that NME intends to 'use its acquisitions as a base for expansion into Britain and Europe' (*The Financial Times*, 13 Feb. 1985): 'We feel the UK market offers very good long-term growth opportunities we realise there are some areas that are over-supplied, but the private care system has not expanded uniformly in this country and we will be looking at areas which still offer opportunities for acute care services' (ibid.).

NME's operations in the USA have met with some criticism. Wohl argues that the company philosophy is to practise the best medicine for the least amount of money and that it aims to meet all the requirements of the accreditation agencies but not to go beyond them: 'A good doctor by NME standards is one who fills beds and overutilizes X-ray and laboratory facilities. Glorious as its reputation is on Wall Street it is often criticized in the medical community' (Wohl, 1984, p. 110).

Charter Medical of England and Community Psychiatric Centers

Two other American companies, Charter Medical of England and Community Psychiatric Centers, both had a small share of the private market in Britain in 1986 with 78 beds (in 2 clinics) and 241 beds (in 4 hospitals) respectively. They specialise in the treatment of mental illness and in certain addictions, especially dependence upon drugs and alcohol. Although Charter Medical, a hospital and insurance multinational based in Macon, Georgia, has only a small number of in-patient beds, its ambitions and desire for legitimacy in the British market are reflected in the deals it has been trying to strike with the Institute of Psychiatry and the Maudsley and Bethlem hospitals. The Dean of the Institute, for example, explained that Charter was 'anxious to see their new London base established as a prestigious academic centre' (*Guardian*, 12 Nov. 1985). It planned to fund a Chair in Addiction Behaviour as well as scholarships and training courses. The proposals met with some opposition, however, and one of the trade unions involved accused Charter of 'paying peanuts for our good name and reputation' (ibid.).

Charter Medical has had a more successful run in the USA. It is second only to HCA in its market share of psychiatric care with 2776 beds and 30 hospitals in 1984 (i.e. 19.9 per cent of all investor-owned beds). The previous year it had provided 481 034 days of care and had total revenues of $422 million. Sherlock comments that 'because of the relative size and inherent profitability of the psychiatric hospital business, Charter Medical's margins are among the highest in the hospital industry' (Sherlock, 1984, p. 13). This is despite the fact that occupancy levels in Charter Medical's hospitals in the 1980s only stood around 58 per cent.

Community Psychiatric Centers (CPC) was established in 1962 and is a multi-national organisation which owned 28 hospitals in 1986 including the Manor Clinics in England which deal primarily with alcoholism and drink-related problems. The CPC Group, which is based in Santa Ana, California, also owns Community Dialysis Services of Roehampton, which in 1985 won an NHS contract to supply kidney dialysis units to the East Dyfed and West Glamorgan Health Authorities. In the United States CPC is the second largest provider of dialysis services as well as being the fourth largest supplier of psychiatric hospital beds. In 1984 it had 1835 beds in the USA and a 13.1 per cent share of the investor-owned market. The other leading company there in the psychiatric field (in third place) was NME. CPC derives two-thirds of its profits from psychiatric services (again with around 58 per cent occupancy of its beds), though dialysis is also proving profitable. In Britain the other American company in the dialysis business is Travenol Laboratories, a subsidiary of Baxter Travenol of Chicago, which won an NHS contract to provide a small dialysis unit in Bangor.

Nu-Med Medical Inc.

One of America's fastest growing hospital companies, Nu-Med Medical Inc. made its first purchase in Britain in 1985 when it acquired Holly House Hospital in Essex. Nu-Med's fortunes improved dramatically in the USA in the early 1980s when its total assets went up from $1.9 million in 1982 to $173.8 million in 1984 and its profits increased accordingly. During this time the company bought up five hospitals from Humana and two from AMI as well as acquiring a management services organisation, a consulting firm and the Valley Park Medical Centre in California. In purchasing two further companies Nu-Med bought itself a number of acute hospitals, a chain of psychiatric hospitals and counselling centres, three home health-care agencies and an ambulance service. The main interest and expertise of Nu-Med in the USA has been largely in the field of health service management, rather than direct provision, where it owns only 15 hospitals and 1600 beds.

On his arrival in Britain the company's Executive Vice-President commented that: 'We look upon the UK as a market with considerable potential. We would be interested to hear from anyone wishing to dispose of their private hospital facilities' (quoted in Davies, 1985, p. 983). Despite Nu-Med's air of optimism, however, the company was obviously moving into the British market as much out of necessity as of choice. They had been hit, like all hospital companies, by restrictions upon public financing of hospital care through Medicare, and in 1984 had an occupancy level in all their hospitals of only 36.2 per cent (ibid). Davies remarks that Nu-Med 'reacted to increasing competition for patients in the US with aggressive expansionism, buying up existing health care companies for instant expertise and increased profits' (ibid.). He was sceptical, however, of the kind of reception they would receive in Britain with their evident wealth, their 'eagerness to take over ready-made facilities' and what he described as 'a rash desire to muscle in on NHS management'!

Universal Health Services Inc.

Finally, Universal Health Services Inc. of King of Prussia, Pennsylvania, began to build a 90-bed hospital in 1985 on the London Jewish Hospital site which had originally been developed by UME. By the end of 1986 it owned 3 hospitals with 131 beds. These were its first hospitals in Europe, though it owned 42 in the USA. According to the Managing Director, the aim of UHS is to 'build a community hospital, for the community, and for British patients' (*Financial Times*, 7 June 1985). In the United States UHS owns a range of services from Health Maintenance Organisations, to diagnostic centres, some 'health agencies', day surgery clinics and a health insurance programme.

Although the private market in health care in Britain only began to expand to any significant degree in 1979, the American for-profit companies have wasted no time in procuring a share of that market. The 'big three' companies (AMI, HCA and Humana) who already had London offices had a head start, but other companies have moved rapidly to fill the gaps. Typically they have bought out existing or almost completed hospitals and clinics, thus establishing their presence with the minimum of delay. Each of the companies already settled in Britain has sufficient resources to expand further if the opportunities arise, and other US companies not yet a part of the British scene are already poised to enter the market.

American Medicine in America

It will be clear from Chapter 3 that part of the attraction to the American for-profit corporations in entering Britain was the *pull* of political and economic developments in British health policy from the 1970s. Equally important, however, was the *push* to develop new markets because of changes in American health care. A number of these assumed particular importance in the late 1970s and early 1980s.

Changes in health care financing

The history of the current problems in the American health care system goes back many years and reflects increasingly uncontrollable pressures and costs. The traditional *laissez-faire*, free market approach with its combination of public and private hospitals and fee-for-service was modified in the 1960s with the introduction of the federal programmes, Medicare and Medicaid, which paid some of the medical costs of the elderly and the poor. Although the market began to organise itself around these new sources of federal finance after 1965, the situation remained volatile and was exacerbated by rapid inflation in medical charges and costs, especially in the hospital sector. Between 1970 and 1982 expenditure on health care went up from $74.7 billion to $322.4 billion and increased its share of the GNP from 7.5 per cent to 10.5 per cent. Some observers speculate that, by 1990, this figure will be 12.0 per cent (Halpern, 1986, p. 215). The post-1979 recession and the election of an administration opposed to extensive public expenditure led to pressure to reduce costs and a number of changes have occurred. For the purpose of the present discussion two have been of particular significance. First, there has been the growth of Health Maintenance Organisations (HMOs) and, second, the reorganisation of federal financing around Diagnostic Related Groups (DRGs). Both of these innovations began to take shape in 1983 and have had a significant impact upon health care provision.

HMOs are a means of providing health care on a fixed premium basis. Individuals or employers pay a prescribed annual or monthly sum and patients then receive treatment without further payment. There is an emphasis upon early diagnosis, preventive care and out-patient treatment, and there is little incentive to the salaried doctors and patients to run up large bills. HMOs have been widely acclaimed in the USA as an effective means of controlling costs and in 1985 (only two years after the first HMO was established) 16 million Americans paid for health care through HMOs – as against 150 million who were covered by conventional insurance programmes (*Financial Times*, 13 Feb. 1985). It is estimated that, by 1990, 70 per cent of the population may be covered by HMOs (Halpern, 1986, p. 216).

The second innovation was the change in the Medicare rules and the introduction of fixed prices for a wide range of treatments according to Diagnostic Related Groups; 486 Groups were identified and each attracts a specific payment per patient, regardless of the actual costs of treatment. This change imposed strict limits on reimbursement rates and drew limits to the hitherto open-ended scramble for profits in the federally-financed sector of health care. While many observers welcomed the order which HMOs and DRGs had brought into the chaos of health care finance in the USA, these measures did restrict certain kinds of growth and limit profit-making in several areas of medicine. One consequence was that the weaker health care providers went to the wall while the stronger groups sought to diversify their activities both at home and abroad. The non-profit hospitals, teaching hospitals and public hospitals have been the hardest hit, while the for-profit, commercial organisations have risen to the new challenge with spectacular inventiveness and energy.

However, a report in the *Financial Times* (22 Jan. 1986) indicated that, in 1985, the for-profit operators were also beset by the same problems as the smaller non-profit groups and began to see a downturn in their fortunes. In just one day on Wall Street, in October 1985, the report claims, 'the industry lost its glitter which had attracted investors to give it star rating after its 20-year rise from obscurity. As share prices plummeted so did the image of invulnerability in which the companies had basked during a period of staggeringly rapid expansion.'

Three particular difficulties were evident. First, it became clear that the for-profit companies had enjoyed their considerable financial success not only because they were marginally more efficient but because they charged higher prices. The ceiling imposed by HMOs and DRGs affected their profitability in the same way as it affected that of other groups. Second, employers (who are the largest subscribers to health insurance schemes) looked more critically at the deals being offered to their employees and at the cost to the company of providing cover. As a result, some of them have negotiated packages which have limited their liability and placed ceilings on the services to which employees are entitled. One report claimed that employers' costs had been rising so rapidly that a company like Chrysler was now spending more on health insurance for its employees than on steel or rubber and that, in 1983, employee health premiums added $600 to the price of every new Chrysler car! (*Guardian*, 13 Nov. 1985). The same source claimed that many companies were now insisting that employees acquire three medical opinions before agreeing that hospitalisation was really necessary and were requiring employees to meet as much as 20 per cent of the costs of their treatment. Third, there has been a dramatic decrease in hospital admissions and levels of occupancy of hospital beds. One estimate suggests that admissions fell by 8 per cent in 1984 and 1985 with occupancy levels declining from 75 per cent in 1980 to 65 per cent in 1985 and an expectation that they could fall to 60 per cent in 1990 (*Financial Times*, 22 Jan. 1986). Indeed, Griffith *et al.* have shown that some of the American companies operating in Britain already have levels of occupancy below that figure. In 1983 Humana was operating at a rate of 58.5 per cent in the USA and AMI at 55.9 per cent (Griffith *et al.*, 1985, p. 38). These figures alone provided sufficient incentive for profit-orientated companies to reassess their performance and to look elsewhere for business.

The reactions to financial pressures

The pressures on American health care providers (and especially the for-profit groups) have caused them to respond in three different ways. First of all, they have begun to talk in terms of developing 'health care systems' rather than simply hospital services (which were the traditional bread and butter of the industry). As the Chairman of the Board of HCA put it, the hospitals which were once regarded as 'medical meccas' were 'no longer the quintessential solution to patient care' (*Federation of American Hospitals Review*, Nov./Dec. 1984, p. 26). As a result HCA has been moving into the provision of out-patient and day surgery facilities and into drug and equipment research. It has established a company known as TransMed to provide home health services, such as convalescent care and rehabilitation, and another, PriMed, which is a preferred provider organisation. As one HCA spokesman put it: 'rather than mourn the passing of the status quo, investor-owned companies like HCA are taking a leadership position with solutions that enhance the whole system of health care delivery' (ibid., p. 28). Most of the major hospital companies are developing along similar lines, often adding their own insurance schemes and HMOs to existing programmes. The growth area in American medicine in 1987 was no longer the hospital but the 'alternative health care delivery system'.

The second response has been the growing 'corporatisation' ◦ of American medicine. It was estimated in 1984 that for-profit chains owned 15 per cent of all non-government acute beds and more than 50 per cent of psychiatric beds – almost twice the proportion they had owned in 1979. As the not-for-profit and government sectors contracted rapidly, it was expected that, by 1990, the for-profit chains would own more than 30 per cent of all acute beds. Added to this there are increasing numbers of hospitals which are managed by the big for-profit companies (Salmon, 1985, p. 144). At the same time, there has been a growing concentration of resources in fewer companies and the incorporation of smaller organisations which had been unable to weather the financial storm. This grouping of hospital companies applies both to the for-profit and not-for-profit sectors. Geof Rayner has shown, for example, that the number of voluntary hospitals in groups went up from virtually none to 35 per cent in just 10 years. They have been drawn in by the promise of economies of scale, by bulk purchasing and the availability of specialist skills as well as by their decreasing viability as independent organisations. It has been suggested that, by the end of the decade, just 20 multi-hospital corporations will dominate the market (Rayner, 1984, p. 503).

Third, the companies have moved into and developed new ◦ specialities either because health needs themselves have changed or because the insurance companies have made provision for new needs (or both). Two of the major growth areas have been in adolescent psychiatry ('ad psych') and chemical dependency ('CD'). They have filled the gap left by the apparent decline in cardiac surgery, intensive care and obstetrics. As hospital admission rates for many specialities have fallen rapidly, those for adolescent psychiatry have shot up. One hospital chief executive who had moved into ad psych explained his position: 'To remain viable you have to produce a bottom line. We can make money around behavioural medicine, but we don't make money on open-heart or cardiac specialities. So we go for the lines of business that we can provide at a profit' (*The Times*, 17 Oct. 1984).

The parallels with the growth of behaviour disorder units and alcohol and drug clinics in Britain are clear and reflect a similar response to similar pressures, but British experiences differ in a number of important respects. American entrepreneurs have so far had two significant advantages over their counterparts in Britain. First of all, health insurance for psychiatric disorders and chemical dependency is widely available in the USA – indeed it is mandatory in some states. Insurance cover for psychiatric care went up from 53 per cent of the privately insured population in 1959 to 90 per cent in 1977 (Sherlock, 1984, p. 7). This is not the case in Britain where insurance companies, such as PPP, have tried to restrict this type of cover in recent years rather than extend it. The nature of psychiatric illness is such that payment for treatment has to be more flexible and open-ended than with other illnesses. Hospital companies have benefited from this. There has been growing evidence of 'third-party-payment-driven diagnosis' (Rutherford, 1986, p. 155) in which treatment patterns reflect DRGs and insurance companies' reimbursement categories and rates. As Sherlock put it:

> Because mental diagnoses are so difficult and the treatment protocols are so varied, reported diagnoses may reflect predominant financial incentives. According to New Jersey officials, admissions for psychoses increased from 58 per cent to 80 per cent of all psychiatric admissions between 1978 and 1982; during this time, the state had implemented a DRG payment system that paid substantially more for psychoses than for other psychiatric diagnoses. (Sherlock, 1984, p. 3)

The second advantage which the American developers have had in ad psych, chemical dependency and alcohol treatment has been in marketing. Television advertising has been widespread and health company officials are explicit in their targeting. Rutherford quotes one spokesman as saying that the market they are aiming to reach is 'white, middle-class America' and that their advertisements on programmes such as 'The Rockford Files' reflect this. Marketing also extends into the schools and classrooms where teachers are seen as important sources of referral. The outcome has been that increasing proportions of children admitted to psychiatric hospitals are diagnosed as having 'conduct disorders', 'adolescent adjustment reactions' or 'attention deficit disorders' (Rutherford, 1986, pp. 153–5). Sherlock has argued that marketing these specialised programmes is considerably easier than marketing psychiatric care in general and can generate demand in a way which was never possible for routine medical or surgical care (Sherlock, 1984, p. 10).

The private market in psychiatry in the USA has expanded significantly and is dominated by the for-profit companies. In advising investors to buy shares in this market Sherlock advises that it is 'an attractive subsegment of the hospital industry'.

Inpatient psychiatric care is widely insured, occurs with predictable and increasing incidence and is complex enough to render cost control efforts difficult. In addition, psychiatric hospitals enjoy a number of advantages over general hospitals: these include the widespread acceptance of two classes of psychiatric care (high quality care in private psychiatric hospitals or in the psychiatric units of general hospitals versus lower-quality care in government-owned mental health centres) the ability of the industry's services to be marketed and certain cost advantages. (ibid., p. 1)

In particular, he argued, revenues and profits are spread more evenly throughout the length of stay in psychiatric than in acute hospitals and, because the average length of stay is greater, fewer admissions are required in order to make profits. All in all, Sherlock maintained that between 1984 and 1990 the private market in psychiatry could grow by 60 per cent.

With the exception of developments in psychiatric care, then, changes in the American market – cost containment, low occupancy, restrictions on reimbursement, declining hospitalisation – have all provided strong incentives for American for-profit operators (especially those which can afford short-term risks) to develop alternative markets overseas. England became an obvious target, particularly for the groups which already had British interests. As Salmon put it: 'In anticipation of a growing "market" American multinational management companies have staked out England for their greatest foreign investment' (Salmon, 1985, p. 174). However, Griffith *et al.* (1985, p. 36) have argued that the foreign operations of American companies are 'strictly subsidiary to their American assets'. Their interest, in the short term, is not so much financial gain (which is in any case distinctly limited) but the prestige of a British base which 'renders them a slight marketing advantage at home'. But how has Britain reacted and how receptive have the new markets been to what one critic has described as 'the American invasion' (Mohan, 1984, p. 16)?

Over-ambitious, Over-bedded and Over Here: Opposition to American Corporations in Britain

Opposition to the presence of American health care corporations in Britain has been of four main types, usually reflecting different vested interests. First of all, there has been opposition to new development proposals and building plans for new hospitals from a range of different groups. Second, there has been opposition to the acquisition of existing institutions or facilities. Third, there has been criticism of the aims and methods of American companies and, fourth, opposition from other parts of the private sector to American entry into the market. Each of these will be discussed in turn.

Objections to local developments

Although many of the American companies lay great stress upon meeting community needs and upon blending into their environment, it is clear that their presence in many areas, especially outside London, has provoked considerable controversy and sometimes hostility. The interest group giving most encouragement to these companies has been consultant staff seeking to undertake their private practice outside the NHS and keen to avail themselves of the good facilities which the American hospitals invariably provide. Many of the other interest groups involved – health authorities, community health councils, insurance and hospital companies, local residents, health service unions and non-consultant hospital staff

– have been much less welcoming and, in some cases, have actively opposed such developments.

The best documented case of opposition – and one which raises issues common to other situations – has been that of HCA's Chalybeate Hospital in Southampton. HCA made its first move late in 1980, when consultants at Southampton General Hospital received a questionnaire asking whether they would be interested in working in a new private hospital. The results of these enquiries were, as one critic put it, 'represented by the company as a measure of the "need" for further hospital facilities in Southampton and as an invitation to HCI [sic] from the people of Southampton to come and set up shop' (Ashton, 1983, p. 25).

However the general public did not become aware of HCA's plans until they had reached the stage of formal proposals to the City Council nearly one year later. Shortly afterwards a group known as SCOTCH (Southampton Citizens Opposed to Chalybeate Hospital) came together to oppose the development. It included doctors, trade unionists, local residents, allotment holders, environmentalists and local politicians. One of the stronger groups in the lobby were the environmentalists who claimed that the hospital site would extend into an important natural habitat and adversely affect both the trees and the birds to be found there. The allotment holders had a particular interest because they were to lose their land. HCA responded by providing a woodland walk along the edge of the site and new allotment facilities with piped water and toilets.

One particular criticism of HCA's proposals was that the hospital was to be built on a site separated only by a road from Southampton General Hospital. HCA regarded it as particularly suitable because of its convenience for local medical staff. It was the proposed location of the hospital, amongst other factors, which aroused the opposition of the Wessex RHA, the Hampshire AHA, the shadow Southampton and South-West Hampshire DHA and the CHC. When each of these organisations came to voice their concern, however, it became clear that they could only object to the development on planning grounds, i.e. with regard to its siting, traffic access, car parking facilities and so on. This was despite the recommendation of the DHSS Health Circular HC(80)10 which argued that health authorities had the right to oppose private sector developments where they would 'have a significant effect on the provision of NHS facilities' (p. 19). In practice it was the Department of the Environment Circular (2/81) which prevailed. This maintained that it 'would not be appropriate for them to express a view or offer guidance to planning authorities on the need for additional private nursing homes or hospitals in the area'. Furthermore, the Circular went on, it was for planning authorities and not health authorities to determine the desirability of any proposed development: 'their decisions in respect of each application will continue to be based solely on planning considerations, regardless of whether, in their view, the proposal to develop a private nursing home or hospital would be prejudicial to the interests of the National Health Service.' One city councillor said that this amounted to saying that 'a well designed, unobtrusive gas chamber for exterminating the Jews would receive planning permission provided it didn't contravene the Clean Air Act' (quoted in Ashton, 1983, p. 27).

In fact, the problems highlighted in the Chalybeate dispute were of long standing and, indeed *The Times* commented that HCA 'may feel justifiably unfortunate to find itself at the centre of controversy given that doubts about the adequacy of development control have been growing for some time' (*The Times*, 17 June 1982). Nevertheless, it was sympathetic to the view expressed by *The Lancet* (30 Jan. 1981) when it called, in an editorial, for a public enquiry into the siting of Chalybeate. At the same time the Royal College of Nursing, some health authorities and part of the private sector itself were calling for tighter control over developments in private health care and a more orderly approach to hospital building.

While the dispute about development control went on, the two main parties to the debate mustered their forces. HCA continued to insist that their hospital was a response to local demand: 'It is not a question of saying we are going to wack one up anywhere', a spokesman insisted, 'We want to be part of the community in which we decide to go ahead and to serve it' (*The Times*, 17 June 1982). They retained a public relations consultant to present their case locally and studiously avoided the controversy which continued to rage. Even so, the words of Robert Crosby, HCA's Vice-President, rang rather hollow: 'We try to maintain a low profile when we enter a country because we don't want it to appear that there is a big American company coming to take over the medical care system'! (quoted in Rayner, 1982, p. 1467).

SCOTCH, meanwhile, mounted a publicity campaign in the local media and printed leaflets and information sheets, posters and lapel badges. They were eventually successful in staging a public debate with HCA, chaired by the editor of the local newspaper, where there was overwhelming opposition to Chalybeate. No doubt as a result of their efforts also the local authority planning committee was 'besieged with letters opposing the proposal, with few in its favour' (Ashton, 1983, p. 27). This provoked the Chairman of the Private Practice Committee locally into writing to all consultants asking that they notify the Planning Officer of their support for the proposal.

In the event, the Conservative majority on the Planning Committee and on the full City Council (where the issue was debated early in 1982) ensured that HCA's planning application was approved. Building work progressed speedily and the new hospital opened in September 1984. Although the opponents of the hospital had been defeated by planning regulations – and in particular by DOE Circular 2/81 – HCA's traditional line that they were in Southampton to serve the local community and at their request sounded less than convincing. Subsequently the company got quietly on with business and the official opening in September 1984 was a rather muted affair. The first administrator of the hospital, John Rabjohns, said that they did not wish to attract publicity, because of local antagonism to the project. They concentrated their efforts on local consultant staff, courting their custom, providing receptions and circulating newsletters about developments in the hospital. Some two years after Chalybeate opened, occupancy levels at the hospital remained very low, although local opposition appeared to have subsided.

Concerted opposition to private sector developments has also occurred in Scotland where the number of private beds and private hospitals has traditionally been very small. In

1979 Scotland had just 7 private hospitals with 265 beds (Association of Independent Hospitals, 1985). In the early 1980s a group of health service workers, calling themselves the Committee to Defend the NHS, came together to oppose the growth of further private sector provision. There was opposition, in particular, to the opening in 1983 of Ross Hall Hospital in Glasgow, which is managed by AMI, and to Murrayfield Independent Hospital in Edinburgh in 1984 (managed by BUPA Hospitals Ltd). Clare Donnelly notes that although Glasgow District Council twice refused planning permission for Ross Hall this was subsequently granted by the Secretary of State and the hospital was 'born into a world which was already hostile to its arrival' (Donnelly, 1985, p. 18). The main reaction against Ross Hall came from the health service unions who refused to handle blood supplies to the hospital. Their argument was that blood products which were freely donated should not become the subject of charges in a profit-making institution. The outcry which subsequently ensued led to the imposition by the DHSS of standard blood handling charges to private hospitals. This, in turn, provoked an angry response from the private sector and continues to be the subject of considerable debate between the DHSS and private hospital companies.

Problems over development control and the establishment of new facilities in a hostile environment has meant that American companies have looked increasingly towards the purchase of existing institutions where they face none of the problems of planning permission or initial registration. This kind of tactic, however, has opened up a second area of controversy.

Buying British hospitals

Most of the American hospital companies have been attracted to the takeover and merger strategy as a way of establishing a foothold in the British market very quickly. One well-publicised proposal was the plan in 1984 to sell off the Royal Masonic Hospital in Hammersmith to AMI. After a ballot of Masons it was decided not to sell but the issue raised its head again the following year and, on this occasion, six organisations, including two American companies made bids for the hospital. The reluctance of the Governors to relinquish control of the hospital at all was coupled with a growing suspicion that the financial position of the hospital had been deliberately portrayed in a bad light in order to persuade them to sell. In January 1986 the Grand Vice Patron of the Royal Masonic Hospital took its managers to the High Court alleging that they had concealed the true financial status of the hospital. He argued that the accounts had been presented in a manner which suggested the hospital was making a loss when it was, in fact, in profit. More than £1 million was outstanding in unpaid fees and had been allowed to go uncollected. There is no suggestion that the American companies wishing to buy the hospital had colluded in deception but the majority of the Masons associated with the hospital were, nevertheless, suspicious of their interest and hostile to any kind of takeover. Some of the leading members of their body commented that not only were the bids of £20 million less than half the insured value of the hospital but that they were also opposed to what they described as 'the increasing American domination of the private care sector of British medical care' (*Health and Social Service Journal*, 21 Nov. 1985).

AMI was involved in another controversial deal in October 1985 when it opened Kneesworth House, formerly an approved school, as a secure unit for psychiatric patients. Some of these patients were legally detained on orders from the court. This led the *Health and Social Service Journal* to remark, in an editorial that:

> it is a moot point whether private organisations should carry out functions which are generally identified as belonging to the state. It is one thing for the state to divest itself of carrying out functions such as the provision of utilities it is quite another when it begins to divest itself of functions such as those connected with justice or law and order. (*Health and Social Service Journal*, 17 Oct. 1985)

The *Journal* was concerned both that the NHS had a responsibility itself to make provision for such patients but also that there was potential for abuse where private (and profit-orientated) interests were involved. The CHC objected to the development because of the way it had been rushed through without adequate consultation and discussion, while a former director of MIND complained that 'this could be the start of the privatisation of mental hospitals and prisons following the American example' (*Guardian*, 9 Oct. 1985).

A third example of the controversy concerning the changing ownership and functions of institutions in which American companies have an interest was that of Charter Medical's involvement with the Institute of Psychiatry. Here there was considerable anxiety amongst the staff because Charter's interest did not stop at funding for educational and training purposes and it planned to purchase land at the Bethlem Royal Hospital on which to build a private clinic.

In each of these examples the view of the American company was that it was making a positive contribution by stepping in to assist ailing institutions or that it was plugging gaps left by the public sector. Their opponents argued that they were taking parts of the health service down the road of privatisation, along American lines, and in a way which was both distasteful and inappropriate. In these cases the main opposition came from staff and trade unionists, but there was broader concern too about selling out to American interests.

Treatment methods

The third area of concern centres on what the Americans have been doing and how they were doing it, especially in relation to clinical practice. There has, as yet, been little evidence to suggest that American-owned hospitals in Britain have replicated the pattern in the USA where fee-for-service medicine appears to lead to excessive surgery. However, there has been some concern about other areas of treatment, especially adolescent psychiatry, where American as well as British companies have been criticised for a heavy reliance upon behaviour modification.

When AMI, in 1985, bought Spyways, the private mental nursing home in Dorset, one commentator remarked that the company had 'bought itself controversy' (Alleway, 1985, p. 1006). It did not change the treatment methods in the home (now renamed Langton House) but was criticised not only for robbing the residents of basic rights but also of doing so at public expense. Of the young people in the home 80 per cent were paid for by health authorities or social services departments on a contract basis. Criticisms of the methods used both at Langton House and at Kneesworth House have come from the Health Advisory Service, the Mental Health Act Commission, the Association of Community Health Councils, MIND and the Children's Legal Centre. However, the enquiries conducted at Langton House and similar institutions have not produced evidence of any actual abuse, though lengths of stay do seem to be longer in private adolescent units than in the public sector and may be influenced by the profit motive.

Opposition from competitors

The fourth main source of opposition to the American presence in Britain has come, not surprisingly, from within the private sector itself. The Americans have provided a very real challenge to the 'cottage industry' in private medicine which had for so long been dominated by BUPA and the Nuffield Hospitals. British competitors in the private market have accused the Americans of contributing to over-bedding, especially in London, and of setting off an explosion in the costs of private treatment. As a spokesman for BUPA put it: 'We haven't welcomed the profit-making hospitals, they have been attracted by exaggerated and glowing reports. . . . The accusation of making money out of the sick is grist to the mill for the left wing, it gives us all a bad image' (quoted in Rayner, 1982, p. 1468).

The conflict between British and American companies came to a head in 1982 when BUPA and some employers declared a number of for-profit hospitals (most of them American-owned) 'out of bounds' to subscribers. BUPA argued that patients would have to choose between 'good private care and extravagant private care' and accused the Americans of doubling bed rates and introducing large mark-ups on drugs (*Guardian*, 13 May 1982). One of the companies involved, Charter Medical, replied that 'we may not all be lily white' but denied overcharging (ibid.). This particular dispute has grown worse since 1982 and there is considerable conflict within the private sector itself. BUPA has argued that the Americans have misunderstood the British market and have exaggerated expectations of the kind of expansion which may be possible. In its view, there is a natural limit beyond which private sector growth is unlikely to occur and they fear that the aggressive marketing style of the Americans may queer the pitch of all private sector organisations by putting the costs of treatment beyond the average patient. Robert Graham, BUPA's Chief Executive, describes his organisation as 'traditionally a middle class movement and not a wealthy man's club', concentrating on low-cost, routine medicine (*Financial Times*, 22 Jan. 1986). On more than one occasion BUPA has accused the Americans of killing the goose that lays the golden egg. It has taken the opportunity to restyle its own advertising to emphasise that it is offering reasonably priced, 'no frills' British medicine.

The Americans, however, do not appear to agree that the market may already be saturated. Their view is that the weaker elements will disappear (or be bought out) and that the private sector will acquire a slick, new professional image. They are critical of the British insurance companies for withholding or withdrawing cover for certain treatments and argue that they are applying an unnecessary brake to progress.

It cannot be said, then, that the Americans in Britain have had an easy ride. Quite apart from any party political opposition around the principle of fee-for-service medicine there has been a general scepticism about their aims and methods – not to say outright hostility. This hostility has had a number of sources – ranging from blatant anti-Americanism, through competitive aggression to fear about the longer term impact upon British medicine and health policy. Although there is little evidence that any interest group, other than consultant staff, has actively sought the American presence, this has not deterred their entrepreneurial activity to any significant degree and they might best be said to have 'toughed it out'. Toughing it out, of course, becomes considerably easier when – as in the case of American hospital corporations – there is powerful financial backing and where companies have a long term time perspective.

The medical-industrial complex

It is important to examine these changes in the private market in Britain not only in terms of their implications for domestic health policy but also as a feature of what Relman has called the 'new medical-industrial complex'. This he defined as: 'A large and growing network of private corporations engaged in the business of supplying health care services to patients for a profit – services heretofore provided by non-profit institutions or individual practitioners' (Relman, 1980, p. 963). It was different in character and scale from the 'old' medical-industrial complex, involving the private provision of drugs, medical supplies and equipment, which were part of a different and (in his view) less controversial market. Relman argued that the growth of for-profit health care corporations was 'an unprecedented phenomenon with broad and potentially troubling implications' (ibid.) but one which had attracted very little analytical discussion, expect on Wall Street. It was his view, however, that it was 'the most important recent development in American health care' and was 'in urgent need of study' (ibid.).

It is clear that, if we are to understand these changes in American medicine and their impact upon the British market, we need to develop a new conceptual framework. The language of public policy analysis and an understanding of public sector organisations are largely irrelevant in looking at the 'new medical-industrial complex'. Here the goals and strategies are essentially those of the business world and the aims of health care corporations are often antithetical to those prevalent in 'welfare' organisations.

First, the hospital corporations are concerned with the maximisation of profit and securing returns to investors rather than with the enhancement of health and welfare. Medical care is a product to be bought and sold in the marketplace like any other goods. As Stanley Wohl puts it: 'Corporations, by their nature, are bottom-line creatures whose sole organizational purpose is the creation of profits for their shareholders' (Wohl, 1984, p. 96).

Second, and a related point, the business ethic leads to a distribution of the product strictly upon the basis of ability to pay and not on the basis of need. Morone has commented recently that: 'When a hospital defines itself as a business, it defines medical services as a commodity rather than a right. Business logic leads away from allocating services on the basis of need' (Morone, 1985, p. 29). At the same time the nature of the discourse and the terms in which it is couched could change too: 'Phrases such as "patient mix", "cost reimbursement", "header sheets" and "profits per square foot" have become the language of the new healers". (Wohl, 1984, p. 79).

Third, the hospital corporations will move to those areas where prospects for growth seem brightest. Because they seek out the wealthiest consumers and the least-regulated markets these are unlikely to be the areas of greatest medical and social need. Relman remarked that in the USA:

> Most are located in the Sunbelt states . . . in relatively prosperous and growing small and medium-sized cities and in suburbs of the booming big cities of those areas. Virtually none are to be found in the big old cities of the North or in the states with strong rate-setting commissioners or effective certificate-of-need policies. (Relman, 1980, p. 964)

Fourth, although hospital corporations are very cost-conscious they have no strong incentive to restrict the inflationary spiral in medicine. Their responsibility is to sell their products at the highest possible price and not, as they see it, to contribute to moderation in prices and costs. Morone summarises their priorities as follows. They are to 'provide more expensive care in more expensive facilities set as far as possible from poor people . . . or government regulators. . . . There is no obvious return on controlling hospital inflation, much less getting better care to those who cannot afford it' (Morone, 1985, p. 29).

Consistent with these other aims there is also what Relman describes as 'cream-skimming'. In other words, the hospital corporations concentrate on providing 'the most profitable services to the best-paying patients' leaving other suppliers to deal with unprofitable services to patients who are less able to pay or who cannot pay at all. The second element of 'cream-skimming' is that the for-profit sector makes little contribution to educational and teaching programmes. Other hospitals must therefore provide services 'that are not economically viable, simply to provide an adequate range of training experience' (Relman, 1980, p. 968).

Each of these implications of medicine as a for-profit industry is familiar in and relevant to the situation in Britain. A further point made both by Relman and Morone may, however, have an even deeper and lasting significance. In Morone's view, corporate medicine has flourished in America for two particular reasons: first, because of the commitment to the free market and second, because the desire to protect its autonomy led the medical profession to oppose all state intervention and control. However, as Morone points out: 'For-profit chains scramble the traditional discourse over American health policy by pitting the principle of free enterprise against physician autonomy' (Morone, 1985, p. 29). After five decades of resisting state control, physicians are now finding that controls in the marketplace can be just as strong: 'free enterprise means large corporations whose profit-seeking nature and business hierarchy provide both ends and means to threaten that autonomy' (ibid., pp. 28–9). The assault on medical autonomy takes a variety of forms but the overall aim of the hospital as a business is to ensure that clinical practice is carried out in a way which will ensure profitability. Although there is a dialogue between manager and physician, Morone argues that it is increasingly the businessman who shapes the 'style' of modern medicine. The for-profit corporations have the power to make their decisions stick, even in the face of opposition from the medical profession. As Stanley Wohl put it, 'The companies that sign the cheques call the shots' (Wohl, 1985, pp. 80–1). It is clear that the real power in the medical-industrial complex is beginning to shift away from the professions and towards the corporate managers. The hospital corporations are, according to Wohl, 'raiding' Government and the insurance companies for their managers because these people have perfected their adversarial relationship with the doctors and know how to dominate them. The net effect is that, in the control over the nation's health, 'the gray flannel suit is replacing the white coat' (ibid., p. 178).

The movement from not-for-profit to for-profit hospitals and from a small private sector with modest ambitions to multi-national corporate activity, which began in Britain in the late 1970s, is much more advanced in America. There the process began in the late 1960s and accelerated quickly during the 1970s. It meant a concentration of power in fewer and fewer hands in the private sector with many of the leaders of the industry having seats on the boards of associated companies. This corporate network became complex and powerful and it meant, in Wohl's view, that the independent private hospital was following the family farm and the corner shop into extinction (ibid., p. 179). He argues that the dominance of the for-profit corporations and their methods is now so great that 'the transition of the practice of medicine from a science and art dedicated to the preservation of life to a boardroom activity in pursuit of shareholder profits is virtually complete' (ibid., pp. 1–2).

What is more, the hospital corporations have become an increasingly important interest group on the national political scene in America and, to a lesser degree, in Britain. Relman observes that pressure groups have long been a feature of decision-making in America and one more would not be a cause for concern if it were not the largest, richest and most powerful of them all (Relman, 1980, p. 30). Quoting Eisenhower, who first developed the notion of a 'military industrial complex', Relman argues that it is crucial to guard against the acquisition of unwarranted influence. There is a good deal of evidence from Relman, Morone, Wohl and others to indicate that the new hospital corporations operate strictly on business principles which are, in almost very case, the exact opposite of the 'welfare principles' which have otherwise informed health policy. Furthermore, as has been shown above, it is increasingly true that it is the needs of business which are shaping the provision and focus of medical services, rather than the people's needs for health care.

It is not only hospital corporations which form part of the medical-industrial complex. Other participants include insurance companies, commercial banks and pension funds and companies such as ARA Services which is one of America's largest food service companies. It began by supplying vending machines in hospital waiting rooms but now supplies food and linen to hospitals. Moreover, it actually contracts to supply physicians to hospitals, prisons and nursing homes as well. It is the second-largest operator of skilled nursing homes in America, the largest garment and textile retail firm (supplying uniforms to the US Army) and the largest national school bus operator. A number of other listed corporations such as IBM, Hewlett-Packard, Apple, EMI and General Electric have a large investment in the medical market, supplying high technology equipment to hospitals and clinics. Yet others, including Du Pont, Dow Chemical and Monsanto, have recently established subsidiaries in the health care field (Wohl, 1984). McKinlay has shown that 'incursions into the house of medicine', as he puts it, have also been made by aerospace companies selling medical information systems (Lockheed) and life-support systems (United Aircraft), tobacco companies manufacturing surgical supplies (Philip Morris) and even the Greyhound bus company moving into the manufacture of drugs (McKinlay, 1985, pp. 5–6).

McKinlay has argued that the growth of the medical-industrial complex must be seen in terms of the 'logic of capitalist expansion' which is governed by 'the inexorable requirement of profitability'. 'Predatory' corporations, he claims, have now penetrated (in a 'rapinous' manner) a whole range of health care activities around the world. They are responsible for: 'invading, exploiting and ultimately despoiling a field of endeavour – with no necessary humane commitment to it – in order to seize and carry away an acceptable level of profit' (ibid., pp. 2–3). McKinlay maintains that they have a number of factors in their favour which have encouraged expansion in the market:

a large and captive group of consumers
demand for medicine is often given primacy over other needs
control of vital technology
the state acts as a guarantor of profits in many cases
(ibid., p. 5)

The overwhelming emphasis on profitability, it is argued, sets in train a series of developments including competition and accumulation, culminating in the search for new markets at home and abroad. In all this, McKinlay concludes, 'there is only a coincidental relationship between the production of goods and services in accordance with the logic of capitalism and any resulting improvements in the health and general welfare of mankind' (ibid., p. 7).

In summary, then, the growth of the medical-industrial complex has heralded three particular trends in health policy and medical care which have their origins in America but whose significance goes much wider. First, there has been the application of business principles in health care delivery, as illustrated above.

Second, there has been the growing 'corporatisation' of health provision with large, investor-owned for-profit corporations swallowing up an increasing share of the market. This has been accompanied by the concentration of resources amongst a few dominant hospital chains, which have bought up the smaller and weaker institutions lying in their path. As Salmon put it, these smaller hospitals have been 'targeted for acquisition' (1985, p. 160). Public hospitals and hospitals run by religious orders have been particularly vulnerable and many Catholic hospitals especially have been bought out by the chains. HCA, AMI, Humana and NME have all been front-runners in mergers and buy-outs and in 1984 the 10 top chains operated over 70 per cent of all 'proprietary' (i.e. private, for-profit) hospitals in the USA (ibid., p. 161). These takeovers have occurred with great rapidity and have involved very little discussion with key figures in the hospitals themselves. As Wohl remarked:

> History shows that the corporations simply marched in because there was a profit to be made. Doctors, government, insurance companies and so-called leaders in health care exercised about as much influence as a feather in the wind. All they could do was study the phenomenon after the fox had raided the chicken coop. (1984, p. 25)

The only real check on the voracious acquisitions policy of the biggest corporations has come from outside the health care industry. In 1982, for example, the Federal Trade Commission filed a complaint against HCA alleging that its

purchase of Hospital Affiliates International reduced free
competition in hospital care in some parts of the country. A
number of other cases, along similar lines, have also been
brought alleging infringements of certificate-of-need procedures and monopolistic control. These challenges, however,
have made only a marginal impact upon the overall growth.

The third trend has been towards multi-nationalism in the
health care enterprise. Some of the British private sector firms
such as United Medical Enterprises and Grand Metropolitan
have overseas interests but these are on a small scale when
compared with the growth of American overseas interests.
Britain was targeted for special attention, according to the
Federation of American Hospitals, because of its 'ailing national
health program' (quoted in Salmon, 1985, p. 165). The
Americans have begun to deal with early problems of culture
conflict by softening their marketing style and recruiting
British personnel to fill senior management posts.

It is increasingly apparent in the multi-national enterprise
that private sector hospital companies have begun to compare
themselves with hotel chains as much as with medical suppliers. Indeed some of their charging practices (e.g. extra
payments where rooms are not vacated early on the day of
departure) are exactly the same. The American multinationals now make a virtue of standardising hospitals so that
they are almost indistinguishable from one country to
another. Indeed, as Wohl points out:

> The same question that McDonalds asked a few years ago
> concerning the eating habits of America is now being asked
> by Humana concerning the health habits of the country.
> Are we, as a nation, ready for quick, medium-quality,
> medium-cost medical care? Are we ready for 'fast-food'
> medicine? Humana is betting we are. (1984, p. 113)

Humana's Chief Officer himself has been quoted as saying
that it is his aim to 'provide a product as uniform as Mc-
Donalds' hamburger' (Griffiths *et al*, 1985, p. 37). This comparison with the fast-food industry is no coincidence and
comes up time and again. The corporate executives maintain
that if you can achieve the same homogenisation in health

care as has occurred in the fast-food industry the marketing possibilities are endless.

This chapter has shown the extent of the penetration of the British health care market by American companies and the reasons for that expansion. It has argued that these changes must be analysed in terms of business policy rather than as developments in welfare thinking and practice. The scale of American involvement in Britain is small but significant. It is important not just because it extends the plurality of provision in health care but also because it is the first time there has been substantial overseas investment in the direct provision of health and welfare services in Britain. The activities of American hospital corporations are likely to have a crucial influence upon the shape of the private market in health in the future.

5. Winners and Losers

Some of the most important questions in assessing the impact of private medicine in Britain relate to distributional issues. Who 'goes private' and why? If some groups benefit from the growth of the private sector do others lose out? Does private medicine contribute to an overall increase in health care resources or does it lead simply to a redistribution of existing resources and a readjustment of priorities by default? Many of these questions are impossible to answer conclusively because of large gaps in current knowledge about the private market and about its impact on the NHS. The balance sheet of gains and losses can only be drawn in a rudimentary fashion. This chapter focuses upon the winners and losers in the battle for health care – both in an individual and an institutional sense.

Who are the Private Patients?

In looking at the users of the private sector two separate questions must be addressed. First of all, who subscribes to private health insurance and who is covered by it and, second, who actually receives private treatment both inside and outside the NHS? For the first time, in 1982, the General Household Survey asked questions about private health insurance, about ill health and insurance and about private in-patient stays and outpatient attendances. The questions were repeated in the 1983 Survey and, even though the figures were two years out of date by the time they were published, they provide the most complete set of information yet available on private patients in Britain (OPCS, 1985, pp. 174–9).

Insurance cover

1. Marital status The 1983 General Household Survey (GHS)

with a sample of 26 155 individuals showed that 3 per cent of the population were policy holders and 7 per cent of the population were covered by private medical insurance in Great Britain. Considerably more men than women were policy holders but roughly equal proportions of men and women were actually covered by the policies. The proportion insured was highest among people of working age (between 16 and 64) and relatively few men and women over retirement age were insured for private treatment.

Questions on marital status revealed that 9 per cent of married men were policy holders compared with only 1 per cent of married women but that married men and married women were equally likely to have insurance cover because wives were included as dependents on most policies. Individuals who were widowed, divorced or separated were less likely to have the benefit of insurance than others but perhaps the most striking finding was that single women were much more likely to be policy holders and to be covered by private insurance than single men. This was especially true for those in their middle years or over the age of retirement. Twice as many women as men aged between 45 and 64 had policies and were covered (8 per cent as against 4 per cent) while 5 per cent of single women over 65 years had policies and cover compared with none of the single men of the same age.

Not surprisingly, the working population were much more likely to be policy holders than the unemployed or the economically inactive, though a certain proportion of women in these two groups were covered by their husband's policy. The breakdown according to socio-economic group was also quite predictable with 23 per cent of professional workers and 22 per cent of employers and managers having insurance cover compared with only 1 per cent of manual workers. Relatively few women in the higher socio-economic groups were insured in their own right but a significant proportion benefited from their husband's scheme.

There were large regional differences in insurance cover with 14 per cent of the population of the Outer Metropolitan area of London being insured compared with only 3 per cent in Scotland and the North of England. The South-East, South-West and Greater London all exceeded the national average while every other region was at or below it. The North-South divide was very clear, with Wales joining the least covered regions (with a figure of 5 per cent).

2. Age and type of scheme The 1983 GHS figures confirmed information from other sources about the proportions of the insured population participating in different types of scheme, according to age, employment status and socio-economic group. However, the GHS data is arranged according to who organised the scheme rather than who paid the premium, which leads to a slightly different presentation of the results from previous analyses (see, for example, Griffith *et al.*, 1985, p. 16). Of the GHS sample 24 per cent were in individual schemes, 34 per cent in group schemes (which had been organised by their trade union, professional association or employer) and 38 per cent were in company schemes where the employer paid the subscriptions either wholly or in part; 4 per cent of the sample could not say which kind of scheme they were in. More than half (55 per cent) of the over-65s were in individual schemes where they had enrolled themselves. Another 41 per cent of this age group were in group schemes and just 3 per cent in company schemes. The majority of subscribers of working age were in group or company schemes where the employer paid the total premium with the largest group of 45–64 year olds in group schemes not run by their employer.

3. Employment status When employment status was considered, the figures highlighted the very different positions of those in work and those not working. Not surprisingly, very few of those who were out of work (8 per cent) were in company schemes and most were in individual schemes (47 per cent) or group schemes (42 per cent). Policy holders who were in work, on the other hand, were more likely to be in company schemes (44 per cent) or group schemes (32 per cent) than they were to be individual subscribers (19 per cent).

4. Socio-economic group The figures on the socio-economic group of the policy holders produced some interesting differences, with manual workers and other groups at the lower end of the scale being slightly more likely to be in individual schemes than professionals or managers (28 per cent and 25 per cent as against 24 per cent and 22 per cent). The majority of professionals and intermediate and junior non-manual workers (42 per cent and 38 per cent) were in group schemes while the majority of employers and managers and manual workers (44 per cent and 37 per cent) were in company schemes. Around one quarter of all subscribers had their premiums paid in full by their employers while another one in seven enjoyed part payment of their premium. The exception was the group of professional workers, where only a small proportion (15 per cent) had their subscriptions paid in full.

In short, the distribution of insurance cover across the population of Great Britain according to age, sex, employment status, socio-economic group and place of residence occurs along quite predictable lines. The typical subscriber is a middle-aged man, in a white-collar occupation, living in the South of England.

Private insurance and ill health

The actual use of private health insurance to finance private medical services (and the relationship of insurance to ill health) also provides few surprises. Generally speaking the insured population appear to be significantly healthier than the non-insured population: 20 per cent of the non-insured reported long-standing illness which limited their activities compared with only 12 per cent of the insured. The greatest differences lay between the older age groups of insured and non-insured, especially amongst the over-65 year olds. Of the insured in this age group 49 per cent said they suffered from longstanding illness compared with 65 per cent of the non-insured. Almost half (47 per cent) of the non-insured elderly said that their ill health restricted their daily activities while only 32 per cent of the insured elderly complained of any restriction. As the 1982 GHS points out, the relative healthiness of the insured can be explained in several ways. First, the insured population are drawn predominantly from those socio-economic groups (professionals, employers and managers) which have lower rates of chronic sickness than manual

workers, who are rarely insured. Second, the Provident Associations require subscribers to declare any pre-existing
medical conditions and can screen out the unhealthy and,
third, this requirement may deter potential subscribers with
longstanding illnesses from seeking medical insurance in the
first place (OPCS, 1984, p. 157).

Questions about restricted activity through ill health during
the 14 days preceding the survey also showed up differences
between the insured and the non-insured, though these were
not so great as in the case of chronic sickness. Similarly the
figures on in-patient stays during a 12-month period and
out-patient attendances during a 3-month period revealed
consistent but relatively small differences between the insured
and the non-insured, with the former having fewer dealings
with the medical services than the latter. Once again, the
greatest distinction was between the insured and non-insured
over-65 year olds. Of non-insured elderly men 13 per cent had
been in-patients in the last 12-month period compared with only
8 per cent of insured men. However, the biggest differences were
in out-patient attendances which involved 17 per cent of the
non-insured elderly (both men and women) and only 9 per cent
of the insured. These figures reflect the fact that Provident
Associations will only take on, or retain, the healthy over-65
year old but also that inequalities in health status according to
socio-economic group may be especially likely to show up in
old age.

Finally, the 1982 GHS revealed that, overall, only 5 per cent
of in-patient stays and 2 per cent of out-patient attendances were
private. Women in-patients aged 45–64 were more likely to
have had private treatment than men and women in other age
groups. Children were less likely to have had private treatment than other age groups and the 1982 survey recorded no
private in-patient stays amongst unskilled manual workers
(OPCS, 1984, p. 160). At that time around one third of
private in-patient stays and out-patient attendances were in
NHS hospitals. The 1983 GHS showed that 58 per cent of all
in-patient stays amongst the insured population had been
private – that is, a charge had been made for medical care or
accommodation or both. This compared with only 2 per cent
of in-patient stays for the uninsured (and was 14 per cent

higher than in the previous year). The corresponding figures for private out-patient attendances for the insured and non-insured were 23 per cent and 1 per cent respectively.

Private patient surveys

Two other surveys give a fuller picture of the use of private medicine, both inside and outside the NHS and contribute to our knowledge about private patients. The first was under-taken by David Horne (1984) and was a study of patients in two private hospitals – one in Cambridge and one in Bristol. Horne found that 60 per cent of his combined sample were aged between 25 and 54. Only 9.5 per cent were younger than 24 but 17.7 per cent were over 65. There were no significant differences in usage between men and women and the majority of patients in these two hospitals were drawn from the immediate locality of the surrounding area. More than three-quarters of all the patients were seeking treatment in four specialities – general surgery (28 per cent), gynaecology (16.9 per cent), orthopaedics (16.6 per cent) and ENT (16.9 per cent) – and a similar proportion (72 per cent) were paying for their treatment through private health insurance. According to Horne his results closely correspond with unpublished information about private patients and with data supplied by Nuffield Hospitals and BUPA. The only significant difference between Horne's findings and those of the GHS related to the type of scheme under which the private patients were covered. Horne found that only 3 per cent of the insured patients were in company schemes, 14 per cent were covered as individuals and 83 per cent were in 'family groups'. However, his results may reflect the way in which the question was asked. As the 1982 GHS points out, respondents are often confused about the exact nature of their cover and may give misleading replies initially (OPCS, 1984, pp. 154–5).

The second survey, by the Medical Care Research Unit at the University of Sheffield, provided a considerable amount of detailed information about short-stay clinical activity in the private sector and included data about private patients themselves. It was based on a study of in-patients and day patients in 148 of the 153 independent acute hospitals which existed in

England and Wales in 1981 (Williams *et al.*, 1985). The study showed that, at that time, 76 per cent of all private patients (excluding those seeking maternity care or abortions) were young or middle aged adults (15–64 years). Children and the elderly were under-represented and were less likely to be patients in the private sector than they were in the NHS: 8 per cent of all persons seeking treatment in the private sector were under 14 (compared with 13 per cent in the NHS) and 16 per cent were over 65 (compared with 23 per cent in the NHS). Women between the ages of 15 and 44 were greater users of the private sector than men in their middle years (even when maternity and abortion cases were excluded) and they were more likely to be in-patients than women of the same age in NHS hospitals. Over 45 and under 14, males were in the majority in independent hospitals (William *et al.*, 1985, pp. 20–21). In total 120 206 women (56.8 per cent of all private patients) used independent hospitals in 1981 compared with only 91 132 men. In practice, the use by women of the private sector is much higher than these figures might suggest because they exclude maternity care and abortions. Of all operations in private hospitals in England and Wales in 1981, 22.4 per cent were for termination of pregnancy and 10.9 per cent were for other gynaecological procedures. These operations involved 95 470 women. Overall, then, women in 1981 were much greater users of the private sector than were men and benefited more from health insurance (as dependents) than did male contributors to insurance schemes.

Overseas patients accounted for 13.6 per cent of all private patients in the Sheffield study. Their age and sex composition varied considerably according to their country of origin. A very large proportion of private patients who were resident outside England and Wales used the private sector for termination of pregnancy: 85–90 per cent of other UK and Eire patients, for example, were seeking abortions, while 84 per cent of West European patients came to England (usually London) for the same purpose. The private patients who came from outside Europe originated primarily from Arab countries in Asia and Africa and were predominantly male. They included a significant proportion of male children but very few elderly people (ibid., pp. 32–3). Generally speaking, private patients from these overseas countries were undergoing more serious operations than their British counterparts. Of the small number of private patients having major heart surgery in 1981, three-quarters came from overseas (ibid., p. 35).

Although the 'typical' private patient is a somewhat elusive personage, we can draw some conclusions from these three surveys about the individuals covered by medical insurance and about patients using the private sector. The most significant finding is, perhaps, that women are greater users of private medicine than men. Although this broadly replicates the pattern in the NHS, because of the large number of abortions carried out in the private sector (64 293 in 1981; Williams *et al.*, 1985, p. 22), the proportion of private patients who are aged 16–44 and female seems strikingly high. Even when the abortion figures are omitted from the calculations, women appear to be deriving greater benefits from the private sector than do men, despite the fact that men are more likely to be paying the insurance premiums. All these studies confirm that the young and the old make relatively little use of the private sector as do the poor, the sick and the unemployed and residents of areas outside London and South.

Why Do Patients 'Go Private'?

Given the commercial interests involved in encouraging the growth of the private sector there is surprisingly little information on why patients 'go private'. However, it may be that the data which do exist on patient preferences remain closely guarded within the research departments of insurance companies and hospital corporations. That which does emerge in the publicity literature simply confirms popular assumptions about avoiding NHS waiting lists, the desire for privacy, freedom of choice and so on. Apart from this, the little evidence which is available underlines the essential heterogeneity of 'the private sector' and those who use it. It suggests quite firmly that different people go to different parts of the private sector for different reasons.

One of the earliest investigations into patient preferences took place during the course of the inquiry into *National Health*

Service Facilities for Private Patients (DHSS, 1972) which was discussed in Chapter 2. The inquiry team asked most of the witnesses appearing before it why patients would wish to pay for their medical care when they were entitled to receive it free-of-charge under the NHS. Many of the witnesses gave similar answers. They agreed that 'going private' gave patients the opportunity to choose their time of admission to hospital and enabled them to gain admission more quickly than they would have done on the NHS waiting list. The team commented that although private patients also acquired the right to choose their own consultant they only exercised this right indirectly because access was still via the GP in most cases. A number of the witnesses agreed that desire for privacy in a single room was also a factor but some claimed that demand for pay beds was often inflated, because patients were unaware that they could have an 'amenity bed' without incurring such heavy charges. Other witnesses mentioned the availability of private telephones, flexible visiting hours, choice of food and 'a feeling that better service can be demanded if necessary' (DHSS, 1972, p. xiii).

The Chief Executive of BUPA, in evidence to the Committee, maintained that the company's own research indicated that two factors were particularly significant in relation to private practice. One was the patients' freedom to choose their doctor and the other was the ability to fix their in-patient stay for a pre-arranged date. Private patients, he argued, were less concerned about jumping queues than they were about having good notice of their admission date and arranging the time to suit themselves. In his view privacy came 'fairly low' in the list of priorities and having a private room 'a very poor third'. The other incentives to go private such as unrestricted visiting were, he argued, 'insignificant' because of recent improvements in these areas within the NHS (ibid, p. 49).

Witnesses from Birmingham Regional Hospital Board agreed with previous submissions about the reasons for going private but one of them, a consultant physician, also added that some patients did not think they were getting good treatment unless they paid for it: 'They take the view that you get what you pay for and if they are paying for nothing they do not think it is the best.' This was simply human nature, he added, and was 'just a general innate feeling of a certain section of the British population' (ibid., p. 177).

The Expenditure Committee did not attempt to survey private patients themselves – indeed few pieces of research on patient attitudes to 'going private' have done so! However, they did take evidence from the Patients' Association.

In fact the Association did not differ substantially from other groups in its evidence, although it did focus upon the disadvantages to patients in the NHS of the existence of private practice. It believed that the private sector was attractive to patients largely because of the inadequacies of the NHS which, in its view, had been caused or exacerbated by consultants undertaking private work. It maintained that all patients should have the right to privacy if they wanted it, to choice of doctor within the constraints of supply and demand, to choice of admission time and to all the other 'so-called amenities for which private patients pay' including 'more of the doctor's time and more consideration generally'. It concluded that if the NHS ceased to be 'sub-standard' the private sector would wither away (ibid., p. 192).

The Royal College of Nursing did not consult private patients either but it did ask its membership in a questionnaire: 'What, in your opinion, are the factors which make a patient choose to have private medical treatment?' The majority of responses referred to the physical facilities, choice and visiting times mentioned by other witnesses but members also mentioned the benefits of consulting a doctor unaccompanied by a retinue of medical students, being made to feel a 'person' rather than a 'case' and they also noted reasons such as fear of seeing 'gruesome sights' in a public ward and 'not so many people asking unnecessary impertinent questions'. One or two added that private patients took pride in paying for themselves and said they had an 'honest desire' to pay for what they received (ibid., pp. 442–3).

Many of the witnesses echoed these comments and there was extensive speculation about the motivation of private patients. However, the modest survey undertaken by Horne (1984) does confirm that most of these assumptions were correct. In his sample of 307 private patients the most frequently given reason for seeking private treatment was avoid-

ance of the NHS waiting list. Nearly 60 per cent of the Bristol
patients and 42 per cent of the Cambridge patients cited this
as their primary motivation. Other factors such as the choice
of consultant, pre-arranged admission, better nursing care
and additional services were mentioned much less frequently.
It was interesting that only a minority of the respondents had
previous experience of the private sector or had received
treatment in the previous 10 years in the NHS. At the same
time, only 37 per cent of the sample chose private treatment
after taking advice from their GP or consultant. This suggests
that a majority of private patients made their decision to 'go
private' on the basis of untested assumptions about the length
of NHS waiting lists and waiting times. Indeed, Horne refers
to an earlier study which suggested that the majority of
patients made their decision to 'go private' before they were
aware of their expected NHS appointment date. Most of
Horne's sample were reacting against an NHS with which
they were not familiar and were also opting for a private sector
of which they had no experience. Nevertheless, the majority of
them emerged satisfied and appreciated 'being treated like an
individual' (p. 71). 52 per cent of the sample said they would
still continue to use the NHS for treatment for which they
could not afford to pay and 12 per cent said they would use it
for any care. A further 36 per cent indicated that they would
only use the NHS in an emergency. The few words of criticism
which were voiced against the private sector related to feelings
of isolation in single rooms and the comparative lack of
medical resources in private hospitals.

A number of witnesses, in evidence to the Expenditure
Committee in 1972, had emphasised that some patients
sought private treatment for conditions which were not accorded a priority in the NHS and favoured private facilities
only because NHS facilities were unavailable in their area or
non-existent. This factor became even more important in the
1980s when the private sector began, quite deliberately, to fill
gaps which had been left by the NHS in, for example, the
treatment of infertility, drug and alcohol abuse and certain areas
of psychiatry. However, the biggest and most obvious gap in
NHS care which had been filled by the private sector for many
years was the termination of pregnancies. Since the 1967

Abortion Act a significant number of abortions had been carried out in the private sector either in charitable or in commercial institutions and after 1978 the number of abortions carried out privately on UK residents began, consistently, to exceed those undertaken in the NHS. A recent study of the use of the private sector and the NHS for termination of pregnancy in the London Borough of Camden provided some useful insights into patient preferences in this rather special area of treatment, which accounted for nearly one quarter of all private patient admissions.

The study was based upon a census of all Camden women residents having abortions in the NHS and the private sector in a three month period in 1981, and 180 of them were subsequently interviewed. Of the sample 42 per cent were aged between 20 and 24 (compared with 26 per cent for England and Wales as a whole) and fewer of them were teenagers or older women. A much higher proportion of them (80 per cent) were single or cohabiting than in the total population (54 per cent) and only a small proportion (14 per cent) were married, although three-quarters were in a steady relationship of some sort; 78 per cent had had no previous live births and for 76 per cent this was their first abortion; 51 per cent had their abortions in NHS hospitals, which was a little higher than the national average at that time of 46 per cent and the remainder went to charitable or commercial centres (Clarke *et al.*, 1983, pp. 6–13).

The aim of the research was to establish why some women opted for private abortions and whether they actively chose the private sector rather than being forced to use it because of lack of suitable NHS alternatives. A number of conclusions emerged. One significant finding was that the type of doctor the women saw in the first instance was a clear determinant of where she had her operation. All of the women who consulted a doctor in a commercial clinic had their abortions in the private sector as did almost all the women seeking help from a charitable agency. In contrast, most of those (69 per cent) who first saw an NHS doctor had their operations in NHS hospitals. The women who originally consulted a doctor in the private sector did so either because they did not wish their GP to know about their pregnancy or because they assumed he would be unsympathetic or because they expected that NHS abortions would be difficult to obtain. Only 16 per cent of this group felt that it was fairly or very easy to get an NHS termination in Camden. One woman commented: 'my doctor put me off straight away' while another felt it was 'nigh impossible' to get an NHS appointment quickly enough. Others remarked that the NHS was 'only for extreme cases' and 'not for people like me' (i.e. single and healthy). Several women had heard that they needed strong medical reasons to get into the NHS. One commented that: 'My girlfriend said she didn't have enough reasons for a termination and one of her friends in a similar situation was refused', while another said that 'some consultants want evidence of a nervous break-down before they'll do it'. In fact, the researchers concluded that Camden was relatively well endowed with NHS abortion facilities and, unlike other areas of the country, there were no real difficulties (other than delay) in obtaining NHS abortions for most of those who wanted them. Not only were the relatives and friends of the women often misinformed but doctors also played a part in discouraging women from seeking NHS treatment.

When the women who had private sector abortions were asked about their reasons for going private – other than their assumptions about the problems of obtaining an NHS abortion – 47 per cent of them mentioned either the speed of treatment in the private sector or delays in the NHS, 20 per cent had expected to get either better personal or better medical treatment and a further 14 per cent mentioned their desire for anonymity. Some of them had been afraid that NHS staff would be unsympathetic or punitive in their attitudes and one or two even feared that sterilisation would be forced upon them. They were also concerned about being in public wards where other women were either having babies or wanting them. Only 16 per cent of the women who had their abortions in the private sector said they would have preferred to go into an NHS hospital and 64 per cent expressed a preference for private clinics. On the other hand 78 per cent of the women who had NHS abortions said that, given a choice, they would still have preferred an NHS hospital and only 1 per cent would have gone private. The other women in the sample were either uncertain or had no strong feelings either way. Almost half of the women preferring the NHS did so for financial reasons (i.e. they could not afford the expense of a private abortion) while others mentioned their antipathy to private medicine, high standards of treatment in the NHS and favourable past experiences (ibid., pp. 38–43).

However, the majority of women in this study, like the private patients surveyed by Horne, do not appear to have based their choice of private care on actual knowledge or recent experience of either the National Health Service or the private sector. Only 10 per cent of women nationally have had more than one abortion and the 23 per cent in the Camden sample was particularly high. Seven of this group went into the private sector after a previous NHS abortion but only two of them did so because of dissatisfaction with the NHS. Many of the women took advice on where to have their abortion from friends and family as well as from the medical profession and were also influenced by 'word of mouth' and advertising. Only 18 per cent of the women in Camden had found that a doctor gave them the most helpful advice about their abortion although another 19 per cent did mention the help of a counsellor. The majority (36 per cent) referred to the support of husbands, friends and their mother while 12 per cent had found no one helpful (ibid., p. 59).

In Horne's survey 20 per cent of the sample had taken the advice of family and friends in seeking private treatment and another 28 per cent claimed that they had made their decision without consulting anyone. Both studies cast doubt upon the image of the well-informed consumer making rational and considered judgements on the basis of professional advice. Indeed, three-quarters of the women in the Camden survey had made up their minds about the treatment they wanted *before* consulting a doctor. Their attitudes to the medical profession were similar to those in an earlier study where doctors were regarded as 'intrusive' and 'hurdles to be overcome in the race to get an abortion' (Clarke, 1983, p. 60). It may be that the rather adversarial relationship between doctor and patient is peculiar to this medical speciality but there is no evidence from other studies that the doctor–patient relationship is necessarily a real partnership in the pursuit of private care.

A number of other studies of patient expectations and preferences suggest that, while they may seek treatment in the private sector, they are not always 'anti-NHS'. One very small survey of 56 patients at the Centre for the Study of Alternative Therapies in Southampton drew out a number of reasons why people sought 'alternative' medicine in a private clinic. All but two stated that they were there because conventional medicine had failed them. The majority (30 patients) were suffering back pain or other pain while 10 patients had allergies. On average they had experienced their symptoms for 9 years. Despite this most of the respondents claimed that they had a good relationship with their GP and felt that the NHS treatment they had received had been satisfactory. Many of them appeared to be philosophical about what the NHS could and could not do for them and most said they would return to conventional medicine for future problems (Moore *et al.*, 1985, pp. 28–9). The Director of the Centre, Dr George Lewith, has argued that his patients are also motivated by the fear of technology in orthodox medicine and their dislike of drugs as well as by the accessibility of the Centre, its informal atmosphere and the prospect of self-referral. His view that patients were wanting to spend more time with their doctor was probably accurate, though the 19 patients who had claimed to be rushed by their GP were joined by another 18 who felt they had also been rushed by the doctor at the Centre! Nevertheless, almost all the patients (53) said that the latter had a good appreciation of their problems and was more understanding than their GP. The Centre provided a range of services which were either unavailable or not widely available in the NHS.

Although it would be wrong to generalise from these findings they are consistent with other views about the attractions, to the patient, of private medicine. Different accounts, which are largely anecdotal in nature, refer to other attitudes towards private treatment which seem to be widely shared even if they are not major reasons for going private. Dr Stanley Balfour Lynn (1982), for example, who worked for AMI but who had also been a private patient, complained about the lack of respect for patients in the NHS: 'How often did I hear during my 10 years of working in National Health hospitals, the men in the wards, who have reached pensionable age, referred to by the nurses as "Dad".' Balfour Lynn argues that this does not occur in the private sector and should not occur in the NHS either. Other writers refer, along similar lines, to the greater degree of personal attention and dignity accorded to private patients. Alina Reagle, for example, explained: 'I was not a number or a statistic. I was another human being with whom they (the nursing staff) could chat as well as give me reassurance'. (1983) Along with several others, she mentioned the 'peace of mind' which going private brought and the belief that she was being treated by 'the best brains in the country'.

Some patients have rather special reasons for going private. A report by Central Birmingham CHC in 1979, for example, suggested that because of a reluctance to go to male GPs, a number of Asian women in the city preferred to consult female doctors privately and to pay for a home visit. Another group who have rather particular reasons for taking out private health insurance and seeking treatment in the private sector are NHS staff. Some of them argue that, despite their commitment to the public service, they are embarrassed to be cared for by their colleagues or by staff they have trained. Some feel that it is rather undignified to have their junior colleagues see them in intimate positions of dependence or discomfort. Female nursing staff sometimes give this as a reason for having gynaecological treatment privately. Similarly, medical staff may be inhibited about being admitted to hospitals in their own or neighbouring districts and there are particular sensitivities where the treatment sought is for psychiatric disorders, say, or alcoholism. Some of the private psychiatric hospitals, such as St Andrews in Northampton, claim that they attract pop stars and royalty as well as doctors precisely because they are scrupulous about preserving privacy and confidentiality and because they offer patients the opportunity of treatment well away from home.

Finally, a proportion of patients appear to go private in order to 'get their money's worth'. This comment has been particularly applied to those new entrants to the health insurance market who were drawn in during the period of expansion in the late 1970s and early 1980s. Grant, for example, has remarked that:

Having sampled private medical treatment, and apparently approving of it, insureds have tended to increase their usage, often for trivial ailments, of both inpatient and outpatient facilities. Not only are they exhibiting a greater claims consciousness but they are also proving more adept at using their insurance, with a growing number of claims coming from wives and dependents insured through the breadwinner's policy. (Grant, 1985, p. 83)

In many cases it was not so much a case of these patients getting their own money's worth as of enjoying the premiums paid by their employers. Either way, certain groups of the population who might not have done so before were induced to go private.

The discussion in this section will have underlined the fact that we are unable to answer categorically the question of why patients go private. Some of the reasons for doing so appear to involve negative feelings about the NHS while others reflect very positive attitudes towards the private sector. Most observers think they know why patients go private but most research on private patients is conducted through third parties and asks them to speculate about motives. The fact is that there is very little information from patients themselves about their expectations of the private sector and whether these expectations have been satisfied.

Who Benefits from the Private Sector?

If the previous section was concerned essentially with patients' assumptions about private medicine this one looks at the advantages they *actually* appear to purchase by going private. Once again the data is so sparse that any conclusions on this point are largely speculative. Even so, there is perhaps a little more information about what patients get from the private sector than there is about the benefits to NHS consultants of doing private practice, the advantages to nursing and other staff of working in the private sector and the gains and losses experienced by hospital corporations and insurance companies. Only small portions of the distributional map can be pieced together on the basis of current knowledge about the operations of the private market.

The benefits to private patients

One of the most recent surveys of private medicine in practice was conducted by the Consumers' Association late in 1985. It received completed questionnaires from a randomly selected group of *Which?* readers, 1032 of whom provided information on the NHS and private treatment they had received in the previous five years. One third of the sample had gone private and two-thirds had been NHS patients. The results showed that, on average, the patients who went private waited for two weeks less to see a consultant than did the NHS patients: 55 per cent of the private patients had a consultant appointment within one week (compared with 32 per cent of the NHS patients) and 26 per cent were seen within a further week. Only 12 per cent of them waited for more than 2 weeks, compared with 44 per cent of the NHS patients. When it came to hospital admissions, however, the NHS patients had a considerable edge over the rest: 53 per cent of them were admitted within a week of knowing that treatment was necessary, as against only 38 per cent of the private patients. However, this probably reflects the fact that the NHS was treating more urgent admissions and considerably more accident and emergency cases than the private sector. Most private patients were admitted for 'cold' elective surgery. It also underlines the comment made by BUPA that what private patients wanted and got was not earlier admission but a pre-arranged admission. At the other end of the scale 29 per cent of NHS patients waited for more than one month for admission to hospital compared with only 15 per cent of the private patients.

The Consumers' Association survey also confirms that the private patients did, indeed, find the mechanics of consultation and admission much more convenient and satisfactory than did the NHS patients: 96 per cent of them were given exact appointments by the consultant (NHS patients, 81 per cent), 89 per cent had their appointments at times convenient to themselves (NHS patients, 64 per cent), 95 per cent of them were seen on time by the consultant (NHS patients, 63 per cent), 80 per cent were given a choice of hospital admission dates (NHS patients, 31 per cent) and 98 per cent were admitted on the day planned (compared with 92 per cent of the NHS patients). The advantages of going private, which are much vaunted by the hospitals and insurance companies, do in these respects appear to be very real to the private patient. The private sector, on the basis of this survey, certainly appears to give the patient what he/she wants in terms of speedy consultations, convenience and courtesy.

Patients seeking privacy and a single room also do considerably better out of the private sector than the NHS, though the distinctions may not be so great as is often assumed. It is true that 85 per cent of the private patients and only 14 per cent of the NHS patients were in single rooms but, at the same time, few of the latter were in the large public wards so disliked by some potential private patients. In fact 49 per cent of the NHS patients were in wards shared with five or fewer patients and only 5 per cent were in a ward containing 21 or more beds. Only 13 per cent of the NHS patients in the survey complained that they were sharing with too many people.

It is hardly surprising that the private patients having, for the most part, got what they paid for expressed high levels of satisfaction: 72 per cent pronounced themselves very satisfied, compared with only 50 per cent of the NHS patients. However, nearly one third of the NHS patients described themselves as 'fairly satisfied' and when the totals for the two categories are taken together levels of satisfaction were high amongst both groups: 89 per cent of the private patients were 'fairly' or 'very satisfied' compared with 81 per cent of the NHS patients (Consumers' Association, 1986, pp. 322–3).

Women in the Camden abortion study also tended to purchase greater speed and convenience in the private sector, in a situation where prompt attention was of paramount concern, and they were generally satisfied with their treatment. Although women who had abortions privately did not have the first appointment with a doctor as quickly as NHS patients, they received the results of their pregnancy tests much earlier: 82 per cent had their results on the same day, compared with only 57 per cent of the NHS patients. This was because many of the tests were either self-administered or carried out at a Pregnancy Advisory Bureau, rather than being sent away for analysis. Private patients had fewer consultations with doctors (and therefore fewer delays) before the pregnancy was terminated: 42 per cent made only one visit to the doctor compared with 3 per cent of the NHS patients, most of whom made at least three visits. Finally, the private patients had their abortions at earlier stages of gestation, despite paying later initial visits to the doctor: 63 per cent of these patients and only 49 per cent of the NHS patients had their abortions at less than 10 weeks (Clarke *et al.*, 1983, pp. 15–27).

All these factors combined to make the process of having an abortion less stressful for the private patients and the women generally expressed high levels of satisfaction. The distribution of satisfaction and complaint was much the same as that in the Consumers' Association survey. The only real difference was that women attending commercial clinics were much less likely to agree that they had been treated 'very well' than women receiving treatment either in the NHS or at charitable clinics. These women in the commercial sector complained not only about the food (or lack of it) but also about the impersonal treatment, the feeling of being in a 'cattle market' and the preoccupation with collecting fees (ibid., pp. 52–4).

Is private treatment better treatment?

Although these surveys provide only sketchy evidence about the benefits which patients perceive in going private they do suggest that, on the whole, the private patient is purchasing real advantages and is satisfied with the treatment he/she receives. However, there is also the separate question of whether patients in the private sector are receiving 'better' care. The measurement of quality in medical and nursing care is still only at a rudimentary level in Britain so there are few acceptable criteria which can be used to answer this question. Nevertheless, it can be said that – since the private sector employs few consultant staff of its own – most private patients are being treated by the same consultants who would have dealt with them in the NHS. They may feel it advantageous to deal with the consultant rather than his junior colleague and they may purchase more of his personal time but it is rather unlikely that the medical care they receive from him will be qualitatively different from that which they would have received in the NHS. A similar point can be made about other grades of staff, most of whom come directly or indirectly from NHS hospitals.

The benefits of intimacy, personal attention and so on, which may be available in a small hospital (whether public or private), are also accompanied by serious disadvantages. Such hospitals do not have the range of support services, facilities and qualified staff available in a large hospital. In particular, it has been estimated that 74 per cent of private hospitals do not have a resident doctor (National Health Service Consultants' Association, 1984) and, in an emergency, they have to rely on the services of local GPs or an urgent call to the responsible consultant. However, there is some controversy about this figure and in 1987 the private sector was maintaining that 60 per cent of private hospitals did, at that time, have medical cover. Those hospitals which do have a resident doctor often employ overseas doctors who have been unable to find work in the NHS and, because most private hospitals have not been accredited for training purposes, they cannot attract the high calibre staff they would wish to employ. A number of hospital managers have expressed disquiet about the quality of staff they employ as resident doctors and at their high turnover. Some hospitals will also take on junior NHS doctors (who already work long hours in their normal jobs) to provide part-time medical cover.

As the Consumers' Association survey suggests, the private patient may also find that going private does not necessarily mean a shorter wait for treatment. The National Health Service Consultants' Association (op. cit.) quote the BMA who warn that 'waiting lists in the private sector can be as long, if not longer, than in the National Health Service'.

There are many other issues concerning the treatment of private patients where popular assumptions abound but where hard data is almost non-existent. One such area is the nature of the relationship between doctor and patient in the private sector. A number of writers have argued that the patient who pays a fee is transformed from supplicant to client and may acquire not just an equal status with the doctor but a superior one. Sir Thomas Holmes Sellors, in his evidence to the Pilkington Commission on doctors' pay in 1958, for example, commented that: 'To put it rather unofficially . . . to put it rather crudely, in an [NHS] out-patients session the patient listens to the doctor, whereas in a private practice, the consultant listens to the patient' (quoted in Open University, 1985, p. 67). Other similarly plausible, but equally impressionistic, accounts are legion but it may well be that the private patient is buying status vis-à-vis the doctor as well as his/her time and expertise.

The benefits to consultant staff

The benefits to consultant staff of working in the private sector, not least the financial benefits, are assumed to be well known but are, in fact, badly documented. Most of the health authorities who hold consultants' contracts take the view that what a doctor earns from his private practice is between him and his taxman, and figures about consultants' earnings tend to be based on informed guesswork and are derived from insurance company statistics. Since 'whole-time' NHS consultants are only permitted to earn up to 10 per cent of their NHS salary from private practice their employing authorities are, in fact, responsible for monitoring their earnings. However, the Labour health spokesman, Frank Dobson, found, in a survey of the DHAs in the four Thames Regions and all the RHAs in England, that only a minority were doing so. Even those authorities which claimed to be monitoring contracts did so on the basis of verbal reassurances from consultants and few employed more stringent measures. Nevertheless, Dobson was able to demonstrate that the financial benefits to consultants doing private practice had increased significantly during the four years after the liberalisation of their contracts in 1980. In five regions alone the total number of whole-time consultants who earned more than 10 per cent of their NHS salary from private practice trebled during this period (Dobson, no date).

In 1984 it was estimated that 85 per cent of all NHS consultants (i.e. around 12 000) did some private practice – the highest proportion since the NHS came into being (see Griffith *et al.*, 1985, p. 57). Many of the hospital and insurance companies reject the comments made by the BMA, in 1980, that the average consultant was earning only £5000 a year from private practice and that this was unlikely to increase, though they have difficulty in producing exact figures themselves. They are nevertheless anxious about, and critical of, the way in which consultants' fees have risen well beyond the level of inflation and Oliver Rowell complains that too many consultants possess what he calls 'wallet motivation' (ibid.). From statistics provided by the Provident Associations, Laing (1985) has argued that: 'private medical fees from all sources probably exceeded £200 million in the UK in 1984'. (p. 8), though only a proportion of these fees went direct to the consultants themselves. Since the late 1970s consultants' fees have risen significantly both in absolute terms and as a proportion of benefits paid out by the Associations. As Grant comments: 'the medical profession, making the most of its monopoly and improved opportunities for private work, has tended to maximise its prices' (1985, p. 83).

Consultant staff, of course, make money not only from the fees charged to patients but also from their ownership, wholly or in part, of private hospitals. Those who have invested resources under the Business Expansion Scheme are eligible for substantial tax relief and are typical of what Oliver Rowell has described as: 'a new breed of consultant who would like to see a financial return for the contribution to the hospital and who is interested in getting a true commercial dividend for the investment involved' (quoted in Griffith *et al.*, 1985, p. 56).

As Griffith *et al.* point out, this type of financial investment has brought some consultants to the boundary of professional ethics and, in some cases, has driven them beyond it. Both the BMA and the General Medical Council have been forced to issue warnings to doctors about the dangers of having financial interests in hospitals to which they refer their patients and the conflicts which may ensue (ibid., p. 56).

Many consultants undertaking private practice would argue that, aside from the financial benefits, there are inherent satisfactions in the work. These include a degree of selectivity in admitting patients, as well as a more leisurely pace and the freedom to spend more time talking to patients. The cynic would argue, however, that these reasons come a poor second to the 'wallet motivation' referred to earlier. The benefits to consultant staff of a growing private sector, therefore, appear to be direct but – as yet – unmeasured.

Benefits to other hospital staff

Other staff groups derive much smaller financial benefits from working in the private sector but do enjoy certain advantages. Pay is usually based on the same Whitley Council rates which determine the salaries of NHS staff but salaries are often supplemented by benefits in kind such as free meals, clothing allowances and health insurance. Conditions of work in the more modern and well-equipped hospitals are often more attractive than those in the NHS and the lower levels of occupancy can mean a less frenzied working day. Some of the nursing staff feel that only in the private sector do they have the time and resources to practise their skills in the ways in which they were taught (and wish) to do. Many of them appreciate the less hierarchical structure of nursing in private hospitals and enjoy a greater sense of responsibility. Some have the opportunity to try their hand at a range of tasks in ways which would be less possible in the NHS.

However, there are also drawbacks to working in the private sector. Some of the older and smaller hospitals, for example, have relatively few amenities and struggle for funds. Staff may feel isolated and bored with the lack of variety and intellectually undemanding nature of some of the work. The contractual position of many staff is often less secure than that of their counterparts in the NHS. A high proportion of them may be on short-term and part-time contracts and some are required to bring in 'custom' in order to retain their jobs. Furthermore, the prospects for promotion within the private sector are distinctly limited, by its very size, and the ability of staff to get back into the NHS may also be limited, sometimes through prejudice. It is clear, then, that the benefits which accrue to patients and staff in the private sector, though real in many areas, are not without their negative features.

Benefits to the NHS

Finally, it should be said that the NHS does itself, to a certain degree, benefit from assistance by the private sector. A number of hospital companies and insurance companies have donated pieces of equipment to NHS hospitals, to be used both by NHS and private patients and some private sector organisations have made contributions to teaching and research. BUPA would go so far as to argue that 'The private sector makes available an additional £500 million a year to health care from the pockets of ordinary people who, through taxation, have already made their contributions to the NHS' (BUPA, 1985, p. 10), though it is not clear where these extra resources come from nor how they are distributed. The claim should be treated with caution.

Calculating the Losses

If these are some of the positive features of private sector growth (if only for a minority of the population) where, then, are the losses? Much has been made of the argument that the gains made in the private sector have taken place at the expense of the NHS and its patients. There is now evidence to substantiate this argument and the losses can be shown to have occurred for a whole variety of reasons from administrative inertia to outright abuse and occasionally to criminal activity. This section deals with those developments which have been a consequence of private sector growth in Britain.

Loss of NHS staff to the private sector

The most frequently cited impact on the NHS of the growth of the private sector has been through the loss of nursing, medical and other specialist staff, trained at public expense. Oliver Rowell has consistently maintained that this charge is unfair, at least when applied to Nuffield Hospitals. He argues that the majority of his nursing staff are not 'poached' direct from the NHS. They are either people returning from abroad, or women coming back into the labour market on a part-time basis after having children, or nurses drawn from the dole queue. 'Certain colleagues have, with me, examined our critics' accusation of poaching staff,' he argues, 'and we have found no evidence that the independent sector deprives the NHS of nurses' (quoted in Griffith *et al.*, 1985, p. 54). On the contrary, he would maintain, private hospitals were often creating employment for nurses who were unable to find jobs in the NHS.

Furthermore, the private sector points out that it does make a contribution to staff training through its own schools of nursing around the country and through centres such as the School of Occupational Therapy at St Andrew's Hospital (though most of the students there are on DHSS bursaries). Private hospitals also maintain that the movement of staff is a two-way process and that any of their employees who cross into the NHS take with them skills which they might otherwise not have acquired. However, there are just a small number of private hospitals (approximately 8) engaged in basic nurse training and the majority mount only brief post-basic courses or study days. Griffith *et al.* argue that this is a very minor contribution to the education of the 6794 nurses who worked in the private sector in 1982, each of whom cost £9750 to train (1983 prices) and makes no impact at all on medical education where doctors, in 1983, cost around £100 000 to train (Griffith *et al.*, 1985, p. 55).

The basic problem for many health authorities is that they tend to lose staff to the private sector from those groups whose training is long and expensive (such as intensive care nursing or operating theatre staff) or in those areas, such as psychiatric nursing, where there are longstanding problems of recruitment. There seems little doubt that in parts of the country such as Central London, where there is a concentration of private facilities, this leads to direct and overt competition for staff. In other areas where recruitment problems arise they may be attributed to cuts in health authority budgets, frozen posts and low rates of pay as much as to competition from the private sector. The first real information on the movement of nurses between the private sector and the NHS is likely to come from a study currently being undertaken in the Medical Care Research Unit at the University of Sheffield.

The effects on NHS waiting lists

Another common debate about the impact of private medicine in Britain centres upon its effects on NHS waiting lists and waiting times. One assumption has been that the private sector must inevitably assist the NHS by taking some patients off its waiting lists and shortening the queue for treatment for other patients. The reality, in fact, is far more complex. First of all, not all the patients who find their way into the private sector were ever on an NHS waiting list. An indeterminate number will have been deterred from ever seeking treatment in the public sector by their assumptions about the length of waiting times and will have elected for the private sector from the start.

Second, a certain proportion of private patients are from overseas and would not have been an NHS responsibility at all. Williams *et al.* (1985) have calculated that 13.6 per cent of all operations undertaken in private hospitals in 1981 were performed on overseas patients while Griffiths *et al.* suggest that the figure for London may be as high as 25–30 per cent (1985, p. 50).

Third, it is likely that the increase in private practice since 1980 may have reduced the amount of consultant time available to NHS patients and may have contributed to the lengthening rather than the shortening of waiting lists. The number of patients waiting for treatment in the NHS, which had remained steady at around 500 000 from 1948 to the early 1970s, went up dramatically during the next decade to three-quarters of a million by the early 1980s. The decline after 1982–3 to the 1985 level of 680 000 has been attributed, only in part, to an increase in clinical activity and may largely be explained by the decrease in industrial action after 1982 (which disrupted normal working) and, more importantly, by the directive from the Secretary of State in 1984 that health authorities should weed out patients from the list who no longer required surgery (College of Health, 1985, pp. 2–3). What is of more significance to patients, however, is that although waiting lists may appear to be contracting, waiting times for hospital appointments have been increasing. A BMA survey in 1984 revealed a very substantial lengthening of waiting times in all major specialities and it was clear that districts reporting decreases were 'far outweighed by districts showing increases' (*Guardian*, 17 Sept. 1984).

The most significant point to make about waiting lists is that they are artefacts which will reflect consultant preferences as well as medical need. Hospital doctors have the discretion to decide who shall and who shall not join the list and there have been regular reports that waiting lists in some specialities are maintained at an artificially high level in order to create a demand for private practice and to protect the private incomes of the consultants concerned. There is no reason to believe that the situation has changed markedly since 1972 when the Expenditure Committee of the House of Commons observed that 'a minority of consultants tended to do little or nothing to reduce their waiting lists, or might even be tempted to let them build up' (HMSO, 1972, p. xix). Although many doctors react with outrage at such a suggestion there is enough anecdotal evidence to suggest that it is not entirely inaccurate and some members of the medical profession will acknowledge that such practices occur, though they may not condone them. It may be no coincidence that the five specialities which the College of Health lists as having the longest waiting lists nationally – general surgery, trauma and orthopaedics, ear, nose and throat, gynaecology and opthalmology – were also those which the Royal Commission on the National Health Service reported as having the smallest proportions of staff holding whole-time NHS appointments (College of Health, 1985, p. 3; Royal Commission on the National Health Service, 1979, p. 430). In other words, the specialities with the longest waiting lists may also be those which offer the greatest opportunity for private practice.

However, there is no doubt that, if this problem does not defy investigation altogether in the present climate, it is very difficult to quantify. Two investigations of the subject have turned up neutral or inconclusive findings. Firstly, a DHSS

Working Party in 1981 on waiting times for orthopaedic services, while not denying the existence of the problem, remarked that:

> We have been presented with no evidence to support the view that long waiting lists exist to bolster private practice or that private practice materially affects the time which National Health Service patients have to wait for treatment, but a small spill-over effect where waiting lists are long is inevitable. (DHSS, 1981, p. 28)

Unfortunately there was no attempt to define the nature of this 'spill-over effect' or its extent, but the Working Party were reasonably confident that because of the small number of private beds available in England, at that time, private practice was unlikely to have a major overall impact. The Report concluded that: 'private practice has so far contributed little either to the shortening of waiting lists and the reduction of waiting times on the one hand or to their lengthening on the other' (ibid., p. 75).

A similar finding resulted from the study by Williams *et al.* (1985) of in-patient clinical activity in the private sector. Although their overall conclusion was that 'the level of private sector activity has little immediate effect, favourable or unfavourable, on NHS waiting times' (p. 62), they did adduce some evidence to demonstrate a link between long waiting times and higher than average operation rates in the private sector. While they described the evidence as 'weak' they demonstrated that 'in RHAs where there is a larger than average private sector operation rate there are longer than average NHS waiting times' (ibid.). There are a number of reasons why this might have been so but the alternatives considered by Williams *et al.* included the possibility that some consultants were contributing to lengthening NHS waiting lists by substituting private work for NHS work and that patients were more likely to opt for private treatment where waiting times were lengthy.

The cumulative evidence about the relationship between private practice and NHS waiting lists, therefore, suggests either that the growth of private medicine has had no effect on

waiting times or waiting lists in the NHS because it accounts
for such a small proportion of clinical activity or that it has
had a deleterious but marginal effect. There is no evidence to
suggest that the private sector has succeeded in reducing NHS
waiting lists, except in specific cases where NHS patients have
been 'contracted out' to the private sector on a one-off basis to
clear a particular backlog. In 1985, for example, Bath District
Health Authority contracted with King Edward VII Hospital
to undertake orthopaedic surgery on a group of elderly patients
and with the Bath Clinic to carry out surgery on 120 children
waiting for ENT operations. According to press reports, however, these latter operations cost 10 per cent more than they
would have done in the NHS and were performed by the NHS
consultant from whose NHS waiting list they had been removed! (*Guardian*, 5 Jan. 1985).

Additional burdens on NHS staff

A further issue which must be examined when calculating the
losses to the NHS and its patients of the growth of private
medicine is the effect, especially on NHS staff, of the changes
in consultants' contracts and of the ways in which consultant
staff determine their priorities and allocate their time. The
report from the House of Commons Expenditure Committee
examined in some detail the harmful effects which private
practice could have upon junior hospital doctors and nursing
staff in the public sector. Not only were junior doctors being
asked to contravene their contractual obligations to the NHS
by assisting at operations in the private sector but they were
also shouldering a heavy burden while their senior colleagues
were absent from their NHS duties. Nursing staff also felt that
they carried extra responsibility and had more demanding
workloads when consultant staff were away from the wards
undertaking private practice. Although there is no direct
evidence on this issue there is no reason to suppose that the
problem has lessened since 1972 and it may, indeed, have
grown after 1980 as the volume of private practice has increased. One junior hospital doctor, for example, recently
commented, 'My consultant frequently phones up from Harley Street to ask me to take his clinic because he has been

delayed. But I can't say anything because one day I'll need a reference from him' (*Observer*, 18 May 1986), while Sir Douglas Black, former President of the Royal College of Physicians and of the BMA, observed, 'At every hospital one knows, there are one or two doctors skimping on their public work for the sake of their private patients' (ibid.).

Not only may consultant staff doing private practice create extra work for their NHS colleagues but they may actively oppose the recruitment of other consultant staff to share the burden. Sharing the burden, of course, invariably means that any new consultant staff will also share the private work. As one surgeon commented, 'An extra consultant in a district such as this with four consultant surgeons would effectively reduce the amount of private practice each consultant could do by 20 per cent' (*The Health Service Journal*, 17 July 1986). The incentive to do private practice, therefore, tends to carry with it the disincentive to increase NHS medical manpower to cope with any resulting deficits.

It is clear that the consultant who works in the private sector may not only create additional (and often unremunerated) work for his NHS colleages but he creates an additional burden for himself. If it is true, as the medical profession often claims, that most consultants with a private practice not only meet their contractual obligations to the NHS in full but frequently exceed them, the extra work they undertake will eat into their leisure time to a significant degree. The spectre of the overworked surgeon can be of no more comfort to NHS and private patients alike than the spectre of the overworked airline pilot flying for more hours than is safe or desirable. The difference is that airline passengers are protected by rigid safety regulations whereas the patient relies on the doctor's judgement of how his skills are being affected by fatigue. The pursuit of profit may have pushed some doctors beyond the bounds of what are acceptable working hours and may be damaging to both public and private patients.

Subsidising pay beds

A good deal of recent evidence suggests that other losses have been incurred by the NHS – this time in relation to the use of pay beds. Here there are three separate but related issues: first, the income to health authorities from pay bed charges has been reduced because of declining numbers and occupancy, part of which can be attributable to competition from the private sector. That is, increasing numbers of consultants have preferred to admit their private patients to the private sector rather than to NHS pay beds. Second, the NHS – through administrative weaknesses, inadequate procedures and sometimes deceit – has failed to identify all the private patients using its facilities and has therefore failed to charge them. Third, DHAs have been required to fix pay-bed charges at levels which do not always reflect the type of treatment which the private patients using them receive. These three problems will be considered in turn:

First of all, the numbers of pay beds in NHS hospitals in the UK decreased from 5334 in 1974 to 3293 in 1983 and levels of occupancy fell from 48.3 per cent to 40 per cent over the same period (in England). In Wales and Scotland average occupancy fell from around 30 per cent to 13.8 per cent and 21.8 per cent respectively. Part of the reason for this decline can be attributed to competition from the private sector during this decade. The reduction in private patient income to health authorities which this decline has caused is difficult to calculate at the national level but a recent study in Wessex gives approximate figures for that region (Higgins, 1987). Seven of the districts in Wessex estimated that they were losing between £60 000 and £240 000 p.a. (at current prices) as a result of private sector expansion in their area, though two of them at least were able to reduce some of their losses by selling services (pathology, pharmaceutical services, laundry, etc.) to the private sector at economic rates. The losses may well be as great, if not greater, in other parts of the country and any further growth in the private sector can be expected to eat into the £61 million which the Government claimed to be raising in pay bed charges in 1986.

Second, DHSS auditors have discovered that – largely through administrative inadequacies (but sometimes through abuse) – DHAs were failing to identify private patients in NHS hospitals (both in-patients and out-patients) and failing to charge them accordingly. As a result of a confidential inquiry into practices in 37 districts the Minister of Health wrote to all Health Authority chairmen in December 1984 asking them to review their arrangements for collecting private patient income. His letter touched upon the need to establish adequate systems of financial control, the need to ensure the identification of private patients at different points in the system and the need to obtain from them an undertaking to pay the appropriate charges. Districts which did not already have designated private patients officers, whose responsibility it was to monitor transactions with private patients, were exhorted to employ one (quoted in Griffith et al., 1985, p. 52). Having been unsuccessful in securing the publication of the Auditor's confidential reports the shadow Social Services Secretary, Michael Meacher, revealed some of his own findings in a press release on 11 March 1985. This listed 10 charges including evidence of abuse and fraud in 7 districts, consultants failing to hand over fees due to the authorities in 6 districts and a complete failure to identify all the private patients in 14 districts. Other errors had meant that private patients were not being charged for diagnostic tests and the use of NHS equipment and under-charging was also discovered in some authorities. In several districts consultants were accused of delaying, for long periods, payments due to health authorities for the treatment of patients in pay beds. Later, in March 1985, Sir Gordon Downey, the Comptroller and Auditor General, took the serious step of qualifying the 1983–4 NHS accounts because he remained unhappy about the persistent failure of authorities to follow departmental guidelines on private patient income and to set up adequate monitoring facilities (Griffith et al., 1985, p. 52).

The third set of problems relating to pay beds has been examined in detail in a report from the National Audit Office on the level of charges for private resident patients in the NHS, issued in 1986. Since 1968 pay bed charges have been fixed nationally and are intended to reflect average costs per day. Fixed daily rates have been determined for 8 different classes of hospital and remain the same (within these bands) whether the private patient is having major surgery or minor investigations. In 1984–5 10 health authorities made representations to the National Audit Office arguing that the fixed rates did not reflect the actual costs of treatment and that they were losing between £30 000 and £376 000 p.a. as a result. In a survey of 3 Regions the National Audit Office discovered that the proportion of private patients undergoing major surgery (and in most cases 'intermediate' surgery) was greater than that for NHS patients. At the same time the proportion of minor operations undergone by private patients was less than that for NHS patients (National Audit Office, 1986, p. 8). This meant that the pay bed charge (which assumed comparability between the two sets of patients) did not reflect the much higher real costs which the private patients incurred. In addition, because private patients had, on average, shorter lengths of stay, health authorities did not have the opportunity to retrieve the costs over a period of time. The concerns of one district that consultants were admitting patients to NHS pay beds for the most expensive part of their stay and discharging them to the private sector for the least expensive appear to have widespread relevance. Finally, the report concludes with the comment that:

> with the increasing sophistication of medical techniques, and the advances made in recent years in surgery, there is a strong possibility that the range of cost between the least and most expensive operations is widening. In these circumstances NAO consider it must be open to question whether an average daily charge can equitably reflect the extremes of the range of treatment costs involved. (ibid., p. 10)

In January 1987, it was announced that as from April that year districts would be allowed to fix their own pay bed charges, at levels which would allow them to cover costs, if they did not wish to continue to charge the rates set by the DHSS.

In the ways outlined above, the NHS has lost valuable pay bed income – sometimes as a result of its own inefficiency, sometimes because of central government policies, sometimes because of the activities of the private sector and sometimes because of consultants' admission policies. Where patients use pay beds for expensive treatment and the private sector for less costly techniques they (and their insurance companies) may benefit – but at the expense of the NHS.

When the Royal Commission on the NHS published its Report in 1979 it commented that: 'We have reached no conclusions about the overall balance of advantage or disadvantage to the NHS of the existence of a private sector . . . but it is clear that whichever way it lies it is small as matters now stand' (Royal Commission on the National Health Service, 1979, p. 291).

Although in the late 1980s the private sector in Britain is still small (in terms of bed numbers, health insurance cover, etc.) there has been considerable growth since 1979. It may remain the case that any damaging effects of the private sector on the NHS, especially outside London and the South where facilities are concentrated, are rather marginal. They are important nevertheless, not only for their practical implications but because of the broader issues they raise about public/private relationships. The Royal Commission's observation that it was inhibited in its investigations by the lack of hard data on the effects of private practice remains pertinent but the growing evidence which is accumulating, not least in the National Audit Office, has enabled us to begin to calculate the losses which the NHS may now be suffering.

6. Trends and Issues in the Private Sector

The developments which have been described in earlier chapters throw up a whole series of issues which require further analysis. Some of these, such as the implications of a two-tier health service, have been debated extensively elsewhere while others have attracted much less attention. This chapter looks at some of the key dilemmas posed for health services and health policy in Britain if the private sector – especially the for-profit sector – continues to grow. It draws upon comparative evidence, both cross-national and historical, to highlight some of the future options and possible trends. At the heart of the debate lies the tension between the two basic models of health care distribution – one based upon market principles and the other upon the principle of equity.

Is Small Beautiful?

It has become increasingly clear, in the research for this book, that one of the most important features distinguishing the private sector from the NHS is size and in particular the size of hospitals. Size was a factor in the debate about private medicine as far back as the 1940s and formed a crucial part of Bevan's arguments in favour of a National Health Service and in favour of retaining private practice (if there were to be any) within the public sector. The question of size has a number of elements. On the one hand, small hospitals appear to be popular with patients because they are said to be friendly and intimate and the patient feels like a 'person' rather than a 'number'. Nursing and ancillary staff may prefer them because they permit greater flexibility, are less hierarchical and allow for greater individual responsibility. On the other hand, it has been argued that small hospitals can be unsafe for complex medical procedures because they lack the necessary support services, the range of qualified staff and resident medical cover. During a period in which the public sector has been closing down its small cottage hospitals and concentrating its resources in large district general hospitals, the private sector has been opening its own 'cottage hospitals' to provide for a range of needs.

For many years the typical private hospital had 30–40 beds. In 1979, for example, the average number of beds in a Nuffield Hospital was 34 and only one Nuffield Hospital had more than 70 beds and two had more than 60 beds. Between 1979 and 1985 many of the existing Nuffield Hospitals were extended and the average number of beds went up to 42. During this same period the average number of beds per hospital for the private sector as a whole went up from 44 to 50, with the independent for-profit hospitals having the smallest average (31 beds) and the American for-profit groups the largest (80 beds) (Association of Independent Hospitals, 1985a). Even with this significant increase the average private hospital, with its 50 beds, remains very small.

As Laing has pointed out, attitudes to hospital size vary from company to company in the private sector with AMI, for example, favouring hospitals of around 100 beds, regardless of their location, on the grounds that 'the quality of care and range of services they wish to offer are uneconomic below a certain size' (Laing, 1985, p. 15). BUPA Hospitals has also gone for larger than average hospitals for the same reasons while HCA has tailored the size of its hospitals to suit their locations. At the other end of the scale Nationwide Hospitals has opted for small 'mini-hospitals' of 20–30 beds. Laing's summary of the situation highlights the conflicts which occur in determining the most appropriate hospital size:

Trade-offs between small and large hospitals in the independent sector are precisely analagous [*sic*] to those that are increasingly recognised in the public sector as NHS authorities try to restructure their acute services. Quality and supply economies dictate concentration in large centres while access and convenience (whether for doctors or their patients) dictate dispersal in small units. (ibid.)

The debate about optimum hospital size in the NHS has been somewhat tortured. When the Service came into existence in the 1940s Bevan argued passionately in favour of the larger hospital. In 1946, during the Second Reading of the National Health Service Bill, he maintained that the existing hospitals were 'too small – very much too small' (*Hansard*, 30 Apr. 1946, col. 44). At that time 70 per cent of them had less than 100 beds and 30 per cent had less than 30 beds. 'No-one can possibly pretend', he argued, 'that hospitals so small can provide general hospital treatment . . . Everybody knows that if a hospital is to be efficient it must provide a number of specialised services' (ibid.). He held this view even though he recognised that some people wished to preserve the small hospitals on the grounds of their 'localism and intimacy'.

Bevan insisted that the way forward was to aim for hospital units of 1000 beds, not necessarily in the same building but in a group, so as to permit an appropriate concentration of services and an adequate range of specialties. Although he rejected the notion of bigness for bigness' sake he was concerned about poor standards in the small hospitals as well as their over-ambitiousness: 'Many of the cottage hospitals strive to give a service that they are not able to give. It very often happens that a cottage hospital harbours ambitions to the hurt of the patients because they strive to reach a status that they can never reach' (ibid., col. 48). Despite some opposition, therefore, the view which came to predominate in the 1940s was that the smaller hospitals should be taken into public ownership not only for ideological reasons but also because of the need to group hospitals into larger, more efficient, units to overcome the problems of isolation and poor standards which were prevalent in some of the cottage hospitals.

The matter did not rest there, however, and after a decade of modest activity in hospital building and planning it was raised again in 1962 in a document known as 'The Hospital Plan' (Ministry of Health, 1962). The Plan included a number of recommendations on bed norms (as a result of which bed numbers per thousand population were expected to fall) and on new hospital building. Most importantly, the Hospital Plan introduced the concept of district general hospitals (DGHs). The new DGH would have between 600 and 800 beds and would serve a population of 100 000 to 150 000. It was anticipated that it would provide in-patient and out-patient facilities in all the common specialties and would also draw in services for the mentally ill and for the elderly. Economies of scale were expected to result from the concentration of these resources in larger units but there was also an emphasis upon technical and medical excellence. A later report (the Bonham-Carter Report) on the functions of the DGH recommended that hospitals should be even bigger and that they should typically provide 1200–1800 beds for a population of 250 000–300 000 (DHSS, 1969). Although the Bonham-Carter Report was never fully accepted these two documents together did lead to changes in hospital organisation and – despite local opposition – to the closure of many small hospitals.

Judy Allsop has argued that they were both conceived with the service providers in mind rather than the patients (Allsop, 1984, p. 56). The Bonham-Carter Report recommended that no consultant should work on his own and without frequent contact with colleagues in the same specialties. It argued that for each acute specialty there should be at least two consultants with the appropriate support staff (Watkin, 1978, pp. 66–7). Klein has also suggested that not only did the interests of the medical establishment predominate in the drawing up of the Hospital Plan, but other important priorities, including the 'accessibility for patients or the effect or hospital size on staff morale or recruitment' were ignored (Klein, 1983, p. 74). It should not be assumed, however, that what is good for the medical profession is necessarily bad for the patient, especially where centralisation means higher standards of care, greater expertise, a wider variety of available services, the most effective use of resources and so on.

Nevertheless, it was not long before the commitment to very large hospitals began to weaken and professional and public opinion turned away from the centralisation of hospital facilities in favour of smaller hospitals. The 1970s Labour Government began to talk again about the need for 'community hospitals' and for 'nucleus hospitals' around which decentralised services might be grouped. The Royal Commission on the National Health Service maintained that the disadvantages of large hospitals – their impersonality and the physical distances between them – were becoming evident: 'We believe that increasingly the human aspects of hospital size, such as good communications, building up group loyalties and good industrial relations will be seen to be important for both patients and staff'. (Royal Commission on the National Health Service, 1979, p. 135). Despite this change of heart, however, the new DGHs which had been planned and started in the 1960s were now reaching completion and it was too late, in many areas, to embark upon a radical re-think of hospital design. In many cases the cumbersome process of capital planning in the NHS meant that hospital building was often a decade behind current thinking about service delivery.

The new private hospitals which came on stream in the late 1970s therefore satisfied a demand which the public sector recognised but which the NHS had been unable to satisfy. This was the demand for acute medical and surgical care in small, local hospitals where flexibility and informality prevailed. The private sector has the considerable advantage over the NHS that it can select the particular specialities which it will offer and, unlike the public sector, it does not have to take all comers. Not only is this financially beneficial but it means that the private hospital can remain small and specialised. It can also provide the intimate environment which some patients appear to desire and for which they are prepared to pay. Hospitals which are not constrained by public expenditure rules and priorities may also use their resources more imaginatively and those, such as the American for-profit hospitals, which can sustain losses over the short to medium term, may provide facilities and equipment which would be way beyond the reach of NHS hospitals of a similar size.

On the negative side, the small hospitals have all the disadvantages which Bevan enumerated in the 1940s and more besides. They can become not only geographically but professionally isolated. Unless the hospitals specialise there is the possibility that staff will see too few patients with any particular diagnosis to maintain their professional knowledge and skills. There is a danger that small hospitals will become over-ambitious and attempt too wide a range of procedures, with insufficient support services and expertise. Small private hospitals – even those which see high technology as a crucial element in the competitive market – cannot generally afford the equipment and technical support available in the average DGH. Most important of all, they cannot provide the out-of-hours medical cover of the standard, and to the extent, available in the NHS.

It is interesting to note that American for-profit hospitals in the USA have, as they have grown larger, been subject to the same criticisms as are made of NHS hospitals. Patients complain that the hospitals are too anonymous and lack a 'personal touch' (Griffith *et al.*, 1985, p. 37). This is further evidence that it may be size rather than the fee-paying element which really sets the private sector in Britain apart from the NHS.

The real choice, in both sectors, lies between giving people what they want and giving people what the medical profession maintains is good for them. The private sector has aimed to satisfy the first requirement while the NHS has concentrated upon the latter. Choosing between the two is a matter of personal preference and professional judgement. Although the NHS may move some way towards more 'user-friendly' hospitals and learn lessons from the private sector it cannot, because of its present commitment to comprehensive high quality coverage, satisfy some of the needs which are met in the small, specialist hospitals. The private sector, on the other hand, cannot – at its current level of development – aspire to provide all the services and facilities available in a DGH. Most private patients in Britain today must balance convenience, flexibility and intimacy against safety, technical and medical excellence and comprehensive care.

Two Tiers or Many?

Many of the critics of private medicine have argued that its greatest effect, in Britain and elsewhere, is to create a two-tier health service which provides preferential treatment for the rich and a residual, stigmatised and low quality service for the poor (see, for example, C1S, no date; Griffith *et al.*, 1985; Himmelstein and Woolhandler, 1984; Iliffe, 1983; Politics of Health Group, no date; Thunhurst, 1982). The evidence collected in previous chapters of this book indicates that, although this generalisation is not incorrect, it oversimplifies a very complex pattern of benefits and losses and changing responsibilities. Before looking at the way in which the distributional map is being redrawn this section examines the effects in other countries of the development of private medicine within and outside public health services.

The American experience

Some of the greatest contrasts between public and private health care have been reflected in the development of health services in the USA in the last 50 years. For some time the USA has been held up as the model of where Britain could and might go in the future if the 'mixed' financing and provision of health services were to become more extensive. In a series of articles Paul Torrens has spelled out the lessons for Britain of going down this road. While acknowledging some of the beneficial effects of private health insurance in the American context Torrens has emphasised its negative features.

First of all, private sector growth has favoured the increased utilisation of high technology facilities at the expense of preventive medicine and non-technological solutions to ill health. 'The American people', he argues, 'have the highest rates of operative surgery and one of the highest rates of hospital admission in the world, but much of it is unnecessary and dangerous' (1980, p. 29).

Aaron and Schwartz show that the USA, in the late 1970s, did around 10 times more coronary artery by-pass operations than Britain. However in more than 60 per cent of American patients surgery did not increase life expectancy, though it did reduce pain. One side of the argument here is that Britain was doing fewer operations than was justified but also that the Americans were doing more. One American cardiologist, in an interview with Aaron and Schwartz, commented that:

neurial aspect of surgery in this country makes it
urgeons to pursue the recruitment of patients
ted in Aaron and Schwartz, 1984, p. 67).
ures to invest in high-technology equip-
ly to its apparent over-use in clinical
under-utilisation and inefficient use
ught more equipment than they actu-
ostic or treatment purposes (see Gray,
ner *et al.*, have shown that, in 1979, the USA
canners per million population compared with
Germany, 1.7 in Sweden and only 1 per million in
(Heidenheimer *et al.*, 1983, p. 84). Despite a heavy
stment in sophisticated technology in the USA and what
some critics would argue was under-investment in such equipment in the NHS, the outcomes are somewhat better in
Britain. According to Aaron and Schwartz, 'Crude indicators
of health status put Britain almost or slightly ahead of the
United States' (Aaron and Schwartz, 1984, p. 12).

Health care costs in the USA have risen dramatically with
both an increased dependence on high cost services and
increased administrative costs where widely differing types of
insurance cover apply. Torrens estimates that the cost of
administering private schemes for individual subscribers is
more than twice that of the public programme Medicaid, at
around 8–12 per cent. A significant proportion (20–30 per
cent) of subscription income in private schemes goes on
advertising, sales and administrative expenses (ibid., p. 30).

A further consequence of the growth of commercialism in
health care is what Torrens has described as the 'encouragement of the entrepreneurial spirit among providers' and a
'gradual growth of a mentality among hospitals and doctors
that health care is a business more than a huminatarian
effort'. It has become increasingly clear, both in Britain and
America, he maintains, that 'health insurance is not just a
neutral, value-free administrative mechanism for paying bills;
depending on how it is organised and administered, it affects
everything it touches, both the organisations and the people
who operate them and the values that motivate them' (ibid.,
p. 30). Health insurance in the USA, he concludes, has helped
to create a two-class health system with an expansion of

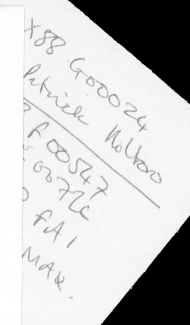

private sector facilities for the 'haves' (the insured population) and contracting and under-funded public hospitals for the 'have-nots' (the uninsured or poorly insured). The outcome has been a widening rather than a narrowing of differentials in health care treatment and outcomes across different social groups.

Himmelstein and Woolhandler, similarly, have argued that the reliance upon private medicine in the USA has led not only to great inequalities in care and failures in prevention but also to the direct refusal of care – the extent of which they describe as 'staggering'. A Harris Poll in 1982 showed that over a million families were refused care and there is evidence that the problem is common and increasing (Himmelstein and Woolhandler, 1984, pp. 392–3). Other sources show that ill health is the cause of one in four of all personal bankruptcies in the USA (*Guardian*, 13 Nov. 1979). In 1985 Katherine Swartz estimated that 35 million people in the United States (15 per cent of the population) had no insurance and a further 5–18 per cent of under 65 year olds were underinsured (Gray, 1986, p. 117).

Elsewhere Torrens has argued that the two class system consists of a private sector which deals increasingly with short-term acute illnesses and a public sector which is left to cater for long-term chronic disability. The distinction becomes clearly visible with 'the bright, cheery, well-equipped private hospital with its middle-class patients coming and going after treatment for short-term problems, and the older, drearier, less well-equipped public hospital, with poorer, more chronically ill and socially distressed patients coming and staying' (Torrens, 1982, p. 29). Evidence also suggests that for-profit investor-owned hospitals are more likely to provide facilities which could enhance their image and increase profits such as ultrasound, CT scanning and diagnostic radioisotopes. The public hospitals on the other hand are more likely to provide facilities such as accident and emergency rooms, hospice care and health promotion services which are likely to be money losers (Gray, 1986, pp. 107–9).

Furthermore, American experience shows that the unco-ordinated movement into the market by private hospitals and insurance companies could lead to fragmentation of the rela-

tively unified social planning process which Britain has tried
to achieve since the 1940s.

In many respects America represents the 'worst case' when
looking at the potential effects of private medicine on the
distribution of health care goods. For many years it has been
very low in the list of international league tables in its willingness to accept public responsibility for health care. Conversely, almost every developed country, including a number
of socialist societies, has a greater private input into the health
care 'mix' than does Britain and everywhere the disadvantages are to be seen – high administrative costs, a tendency to
provide unnecessary treatment where payment is based on
fee-for-item of service, excessive hospitalisation, treatment
orientation rather than prevention, concentration of facilities
in urban areas and privileges for patients who can pay direct
(or extra) for medical care.

Despite their ideological commitment to publicly provided
comprehensive services, free at the point of receipt, several
socialist countries contain significant (if unofficial) elements of
private practice. In some cases private practice is overt and
organised. In Russia, for example, private medicine is available to distinguished members of the Party and is also prac-
tised at spas and holiday resorts where patients are away from
home. In both Poland and Russia groups of doctors have
organised themselves into private co-operatives where patients
pay fees for their treatment (Roemer, 1984, p. 200). Charges for
drugs, dentures, spectacles and surgical appliances are common.
In other countries such as Czechoslovakia and Hungary, where
private medicine is officially denounced, the practice of giving
'gifts' and 'tips' to doctors is widespread, especially amongst
older patients and those living in country areas. Not only is it
a mark of respect, but patients may secure for themselves
longer and more convenient consultations with their GPs and
earlier admission to hospital.

The heterogeneity of the private sector in Britain

The simple notion that the coexistence of public and private
medicine leads inexorably to a clearly defined 'two-tier' or
'two-class' system is inaccurate in three respects. First, the

distribution of functions between the public and private sectors differs from country to country and will determine the nature of the two sectors. In Britain, for example, a significant proportion of private sector work (around 22 per cent) is involved with the termination of pregnancies. It would be wrong to categorise all patients using the private sector for this purpose as necessarily rich or privileged. Costs are relatively low and finite, they are not covered by insurance and the main advantage purchased in this case is normally one of speed of access. The fact that abortions can be done in three locations – charitable clinics, commercial clinics and the NHS – also complicates the notion of a two-tier system. Similarly, private nursing homes and rest homes now accommodate a large proportion of low income people whose costs are met by the social security system. Where the private sector accounts for a much larger share of health care provision, however, as in the USA, the dichotomy between public and private may be more marked.

Second, the idea that the private sector in health always provides good care for the rich while the public sector provides bad care for the poor is not reflected in recent developments in Britain. Because there is no clear separation between the two sectors in terms of medical staffing the quality of medical treatment in the two sectors may be closely comparable. In many cases the patient in the private sector will see the same consultant as he/she would have seen in the NHS. What the private patient in Britain purchases is quicker consultations, more convenient admission dates, privacy and so on. These advantages, however, must be set against the drawbacks of receiving treatment in a small hospital (described earlier) and the possibility that excessive medical intervention and unnecessary treatment may take place. At the same time, there is no guarantee that the private patient will receive value for money or that resources will not be wasted on high technology equipment which is not needed and on administrative costs. Without more data we cannot test the assumption that private necessarily means better. As Alan Maynard has pointed out: 'There is no evidence of a scientific nature about the relative clinical and economic attributes of public and private provision' (1983, p. 28). We should beware, he advises, of the liberal advocates of private medicine who argue that the private sector is both qualitatively superior and more efficient and that it should be enlarged. Such writers, he suggests, 'have much in common with Hans Christian Anderson: their views are fictional and the implications of such advice may be grim' (ibid.).

Third, the private sector in Britain is a very heterogeneous grouping of institutions which vary considerably in size, ownership and objectives. At one end of the spectrum there are the aggressive and ambitious profit-oriented foreign-owned corporations while, at the other, there are the small, religious-owned homes or hospices which struggle financially and which aim to provide a humanitarian service. Similarly, the patients who use the private sector differ in their backgrounds and expectations. It would be misleading to imply that the private sector and its patients are a single tier of a two-tier system with a single set of interests. Just as a variety of social groups may use the private sector, so the NHS serves poor and non-poor alike. Because the private sector is relatively small and specialised the vast majority of the British population have all their health needs met in the public sector while a small minority move between the two sectors as their requirements change. The situation is unlike that in other countries where patients would opt for (or be forced into) one sector exclusively.

Although a much clearer dichotomy could emerge in Britain if private health insurance grew and the private hospital network became more extensive, the two 'tiers' or 'classes' in medicine are, at present, relatively under-developed. Rather than a rigid and structured relationship between public and private medicine, what we see is considerable fluidity with responsibilities shifting between different provider groups and benefits and losses flowing between different groups of patients and different geographical areas. In a very general sense we may argue that private sector growth has led to a shift (albeit somewhat marginal) away from public, collective responsibility for health care towards a situation in which employers take an increasing financial responsibility for the health of their workforce and in which patients themselves display a willingness to make extra payments for services purchased outside the public sector.

BUPA's view in the 1970s that what we were seeing was the development of an 'embryonic occupational health service' may prove to be of considerable significance, over the longer term. As a growing proportion of the users of private health services have insurance cover and as an increasing number of them are subscribers to occupational, rather than individual, schemes we may see a private sector which is orientated more towards the demands of employers. In this situation the relationship between employers and insurance companies becomes critical. The sensitivity of employers to price increases and subscription costs can create a volatility in the marketplace which significantly shapes the nature of services. One of the most important changes in health care provision, therefore, may be the shift in the burden of responsibility from state to employer and an extension of occupational welfare.

To a certain degree the years since 1979 have also seen an overall shift from non-profit to for-profit medicine with the changing pattern of ownership of private hospitals, the growth of private practice resulting from changes in consultants' contracts and the movement of commercial companies into the insurance market. In 1979, for example, the not-for-profit hospitals owned 71 per cent of private acute beds with the for-profit groups owning the rest (29 per cent). By 1986 the for-profit hospitals had increased their share of the bed numbers to 51.5 per cent (Association of Independent Hospitals, 1986). These changes have been accompanied by marginal shifts from public to private health care financing. As Laing (1985) has demonstrated, although in some specialties such as maternity care and the long-term care of mentally ill and mentally handicapped people, the public sector both finances and supplies 97–99 per cent of all services, in other specialties such as elective surgery there is a greater variation. In 1981, for example, 86.8 per cent of elective surgery (excluding termination of pregnancy) was publicly financed and publicly supplied while 9.2 per cent was privately financed and privately supplied. The remaining 4.1 per cent was financed and supplied on a mixed basis. The proportion of services privately financed and supplied in 1984 would, Laing suggested, have been 'substantially greater' than three years earlier (Laing, 1985, p. 6). The other important change has been that as British health care providers have slowed down their expansion into the private market the number of American providers has increased, adding a new ingredient to the public/private mix in British health care.

Finally, although the complex of contemporary health services in Britain is multi-tiered rather than two tiered, a number of trends can be discerned which consistently favour some social groups and areas at the expense of others. What is striking is that, with a few exceptions (related to age and sex), the benefits are distributed in the private sector along very similar lines to those in the public sector. Assuming that private health insurance cover and access to private hospital facilities are 'benefits' (with the qualifications noted earlier) and that the lack of these opportunities is a 'loss' we can identify the following patterns:

London and the South are more likely to benefit than the North of England, Wales and Scotland.

The working population are more likely to benefit than the unemployed.

The middle aged are more likely to benefit than the young and old.

Women are more likely to benefit than men.

Social Classes I and II are much more likely to benefit than Classes IV and V and the rich are more likely to benefit than the poor.

Married men and women are more likely to benefit than their single counterparts.

In certain circumstances it could also be argued that the healthy are more likely to benefit than the sick.

The complexity and fluidity of these developments demonstrate that the existence of private medicine alongside the NHS does not create two separate but homogeneous classes of patient. Instead what it does is to replicate the patterns of privilege and disadvantage to be found in the public sector. Private medicine does not create a new privileged class but benefits the same privileged groups who already gain most from the NHS.

Consumers and the Health Care Market

The advocates of private medicine have argued that one of its greatest contributions has been the extension of choice in a free market and the strengthening of consumer sovereignty. In fact, there is very little information in Britain on how health care consumers behave in the private market and whether the conventional expectations about rational decision-making are indeed applicable. The argument has been that one of the attractions of private medicine is the ability to choose not just the time and place of treatment but also who should deliver that care. The private sector itself, for example (both hospitals and insurance companies), has emphasised that its patients have the advantage of choosing both their consultant and the hospital in which they wish to be treated. In practice these choices are very much constrained. The typical private patient does not refer him/herself directly for hospital treatment and is channelled via his/her general practitioner. Through lack of information, the patient is unlikely to choose from a range of suitable consultants and will be strongly influenced by the recommendation of the general practitioner. Although some patients will have been informed by family and friends, past patients and by word of mouth, the majority are likely to accept the advice of the GP about the most suitable person. Medical staff are not permitted to advertise and the average first-time patient is unlikely to know which consultant staff work in which specialties (especially outside their locality) and which of them do private practice. Having chosen a consultant, the patient is unlikely then to have much choice of hospital. Most consultants do their private practice on a limited number of sites or perhaps only one. In practice, the private patient may choose the hospital or choose the consultant but not both. If they select the hospital of their choice they may have to accept the one consultant in the appropriate specialty (if any) who does his private practice there. If they select the consultant of their choice they may have to undergo treatment in the hospital chosen by him rather than by them.

The private patient in Britain is also disadvantaged in any attempt to anticipate the costs of treatment or to discriminate between competing suppliers. The only information which is readily available to patients about charges relates to the hotel costs of hospital treatment. These rates, however, are a poor guide to total costs and represent only a proportion of the fees which a hospital will charge. Additional fees are raised through itemised billing for ancillary services, drugs, theatre time, medical treatment and so on. As a number of patients have complained, it is only *after* treatment (when it is too late) that they have any real idea of the costs involved and of whether they can afford to pay for what they have consumed. The private patient does not normally seek out 'estimates' from different providers before choosing the treatment to suit his/her needs. Although some companies have addressed this problem and are now introducing fixed charges for common procedures, the average patient is still unable to shop around to ensure that he/she gets the best value for money. Competitiveness, commercialism and secrecy in the industry mean that precise costs and charges remain secrets which are closely guarded not only from other suppliers but also from potential consumers.

In the absence of any detailed information about private patient behaviour in the acute sector it is interesting to note the conclusions of the Committee of Enquiry into Unnecessary Dental Treatment where the debate has been analogous, though less complex. The Committee demonstrated that individuals requiring dental treatment are not well informed about the choices before them, about the questions they need to ask to secure the best treatment or about the range of services available to them in different dental surgeries. They do not appear to 'shop around' for the 'best buy' and they display a good deal of what would be called in the commercial world 'brand loyalty'. As the Committee remarked, previous surveys have demonstrated that people 'show a marked loyalty to a particular dentist and return to him over and over again' (DHSS, 1986, p. 62). Although patients are not required to register with a dentist in the same way they register with a GP the research does show that 'they do regard

the dentist as "their" dentist' (ibid.), and over half the patients who had been having dental treatment in the previous
five years had been going to the same dentist. The Committee
advised that this was strongly to be recommended as it
appeared to reduce the incidence of unnecessary treatment.

In her study of patients and their doctors Ann Cartwright
also found that, in practice, few patients actually 'shop-
around' for a GP even though they have the freedom to do so.
Of her sample 40 per cent said that they had 'inherited' their
GP when he took over from their previous doctor and they had
not bothered to changed. Another 24 per cent had chosen him
because he was accessible and only 22 per cent had made their
choice on the basis of a recommendation. Cartwright talks
about 'the casual way in which many people apparently select
their doctor' and the fact that few of them enquire about his
qualifications, whether his practice is single-handed or whether he
runs an appointment system (1967, pp. 18–22). 'Most people
either go to the nearest one or accept the doctor who moves
into a practice when their doctor retires or dies' (ibid., p. 21).
Few of the patients in this study, then, displayed the charac-
teristics of the acute consumer and few of them exercised their
right to make informed choices or to change their doctor –
even when they were dissatisfied with him.

There has been considerable debate in Britain since the
1960s about the nature of the health care market and about
the appropriateness of regarding medicine as a consumer
good. In a Fabian Lecture in 1966 Richard Titmuss repudi-
ated the views of radical right economists who advocated the
extension of free market principles in the provision of health
services and maintained that medical care was qualitatively
different from any other goods which could be bought and sold
in the market. His argument hinged upon the problems of
uncertainty and unpredictability. Consumers could not know
how much medical care they would need in advance, they
could not always learn from previous episodes of illness, they
could not assess the value of the medical care they consumed
and they could not return it to the seller if they were dissatisfied. Their ability to accumulate knowledge in order to make
rational choices was limited by the technical nature of the
information, by its unavailability and by the inequality of the

doctor-patient relationship. There was a tendency to assume that the doctor 'knew best'. Titmuss rejected the idea that medical care was a personal consumption good indistinguishable in principle from other goods' and that a private market in medicine should be substituted for collective provision and the pooling of risks (Titmuss, 1976, pp. 145–7).

Nevertheless, the private sector has drawn upon a range of opinion polls in recent years to demonstrate that consumers *do* want a choice between public and private suppliers, that they do wish to purchase medical care in the private market and that – even if they do not plan to use the private sector themselves – they want others to have the opportunity of doing so. In 1982, for example, 73 per cent of respondents in an NOP poll commissioned by BUPA felt that people should be allowed to pay for private medicine. In 1983, in a similar poll, 81 per cent said that private health insurance should not be abolished, 62 per cent said that private hospitals should not be taken over by the state and 69 per cent felt that doctors should not be banned from having private patients (quoted in Grant, 1985, p. 140). However, the 1984 British Social Attitudes Survey which was concerned with the same issues provoked different responses when the questions were posed in a different way. Only 20 per cent of this sample felt that private treatment should be encouraged to expand and 64 per cent opposed the principle of a two-tier health service in which the NHS would be available only to those on lower incomes and under which the better off would take out insurance to pay for their health care. The groups most opposed to a two-tier service were Social Classes I and II and Conservative and Alliance voters (Bosanquet, 1984, pp. 83–8). Judge *et al.* have suggested that the correct interpretation of public opinion surveys should be that there is a 'pluralist tolerance of a mixed economy' (1983, p. 487) and that permissive attitudes about the privatization of welfare coexist with support for public spending on services such as health (ibid., p. 475).

It is clear that, for a variety of reasons, the consumer in the health care market is often in a weak position to exercise a free choice and to make a rational selection between competing alternative providers or goods. At the point where a consumer needs medical treatment he may be at his most distressed and dependent. If the healthy man faces so many obstacles in 'playing the market' how much more difficult is the process for the man who is sick. As Kingman Brewster put it: 'The trouble is that the patient, when he thinks something is wrong with him, is not an economic man. He is a fearful, ignorant, helpless, miserable creature. He does want health almost at *any* price' (Brewster, 1979, p. 720). In this weakened state the consumer is at the mercy of monopolistic providers (doctors) who may seek either to protect his interests or their own. The doctor may choose to provide a good quality service at a realistic price (and will probably do so) but, equally, he can prescribe unsuitable or unnecessary treatment at an exorbitant cost. The patient requests the doctor's assistance precisely because he is unable to diagnose his own illness or to treat himself. He must take it on trust that the remedy offered is both the best and the cheapest. Because of his mental and physical vulnerability and because of the fundamental inequality of the doctor-patient relationship during periods of sickness the consumer in the health care market is perhaps less able to protect his own interests and assert his rights than any other consumer in any other setting. As Culyer has remarked:

> The robust individualism of the marketeers betrays a naive faith in the capacity of individuals to resolve their own problems. . . . What is clear is that the marketeers' image of a prototypical consumer shopping around for the best quality care at the least price, and getting it, is not a phenomenon that is anywhere actually going to be observed. (1982, pp. 38–9)

It is an irony that in most societies committed to free market principles in medicine it has been recognised that the only way to protect the consumer's interest is through an extensive network of regulations and controls. The USA, for example, home of free market medicine, has far tighter controls on private sector developments and private practice than anything operating in Britain. Indeed cross-national comparisons would suggest that the regulatory environment in health care is toughest where the free market is strongest. The price of consumer sovereignty, then, may be growing control over the suppliers and providers. Rudolf Klein has concluded that: 'To make the consumer sovereign may, paradoxically, involve a very strong dose of government intervention designed to redress the imbalances in the health care market: imbalances which are particularly marked in that market, though not necessarily unique to it' (Klein, 1982, p. 100). Marmor and Christianson have argued that where governments have intervened in the private market it has been in order to protect individual rights to medical care and, in particular, to remedy the failure to provide patients with adequate 'consumer information' (1982, p. 42).

It may well be that the lack of regulations governing the private sector in Britain has been an important factor in the decision of American hospital corporations to move into the market. Once in Britain they have been able to extend their operations with the minimum of interference from planning authorities or from DHAs (who are responsible for the registration of private facilities). The contradictory nature of the guidance on private sector developments, the minimal restrictions on siting, standards of care and charges have meant an easy run for American entrepreneurs in all but a handful of cases (see Higgins, 1983; Higgins 1984 a and b). The consumer in the British market, therefore, may not only be unfree but also unprotected to a very large degree. We may conclude, as does Abel-Smith, that 'there are few fields of consumer expenditure where the consumer is as ill-equipped to exercise his theoretical sovereignty as in health services' (1976, p. 48). Little has changed since one of Bevan's fellow Labour MPs remarked, in the debate on the Second Reading of the National Health Service Bill in 1946, that 'free choice when applied to medicine is simply a catch phrase which will not bear serious analysis' (Hansard, 30 Apr. 1946, col. 85).

Doctors, Patients and Money

There is a good deal of evidence, not only from contemporary Britain but also from other countries and from the pre-war experience, that the existence of a financial relationship between doctor and patient changes the transaction between them. There is some question, however, whether it changes it for better or for worse.

Klein and Day, for example, imply that doctors work more efficiently in the private sector where they are paid on a fee-for-item of service basis and where money changes hands between patient and doctor. It is paradoxical, they argue, that NHS consultants in the private sector suddenly discover that they can work perfectly well without the support of the junior doctors whom they insist upon in the NHS. In a hospital which may have only as many beds as one ward in the NHS and few comparable facilities, they are able to give a service which satisfies patients and which patients wish to buy. Even though many of the procedures carried out in the private sector are simpler than those done in the NHS this contrasting behaviour does, Klein and Day argue, call into question the ever increasing demands of the medical profession to have 'more complex and expensively equipped hospitals at their disposal'. 'In the private sector', they go on, 'consultants seem to discover a flexibility, a readiness to make do with less technological back-up, an ability to use resources efficiently, which they do not show in the NHS' (Klein and Day, 1985, p. 1293). It is an open question whether this willingness is, in fact, to the advantage of patients in the private sector. Making do with less may mean making do with something less good. It can also be argued that NHS consultants survive with the simplicity of the private sector precisely because they also have the technology of the NHS at their disposal for diagnostic facilities and pathology tests and they continue to benefit from the advice of NHS colleagues. They also know that in a real emergency they can admit their private patients to the NHS.

Nevertheless, there is an argument that the introduction of cash in the doctor-patient relationship may improve the performance of the doctor and may improve the quality of the relationship – at least as far as the patient is concerned. As we argued in the last chapter, the status of the patient may be changed from one of supplicant (grateful for anything from the 'free' service) to one of consumer. The private patient may buy the right to be heard – a right which the NHS patient does not always feel able to enforce. However, it may be that these benefits to the patient only exist so long as the private sector remains small and competitive. When the public monopoly (the NHS) is contrasted with a private monopoly or private dominance of the medical market (as in pre-war Britain or the USA) the position of the fee-paying patient may be less advantageous.

As we saw in Chapter 1 the limitations of fee-for-service medicine in Britain before 1948 were often overwhelming for the patient and inconvenient for the doctor. There were the problems of actually collecting the fees, the difficulties and embarrassment of bad debts (not to mention the financial hardship for the patients themselves), the sheer complexity of administering the system and the somewhat distasteful association with 'trade'. The business office of the modern private hospital may relieve many of those pressures upon the doctor and may avoid the discomfort of patients who are unsure when and how to hand over the money. The fact that three-quarters of all in-patients pay for their care through insurance policies also reduces the difficulties for patients. The number of patients sitting on the edge of their chairs, opening and shutting their purses, not knowing whether to slide the money across the desk or to press it into the doctor's hand (like the woman in Forsyth's example) is thereby minimised, but the problem does not altogether disappear.

In the USA the financial relationship between doctor and patient has had a number of undesirable consequences. Some writers have argued that private medicine may lead to 'moral hazard' by encouraging patients to over-consume and by encouraging doctors to over-provide.

> Once they have paid their premiums patients may take the view that they want to 'get their money's worth' and consume more health care than they otherwise would; and the doctor, knowing that either a large company or the government is paying, may advise unnecessary treatment and inflate his bills. (Green, 1986, p. 114)

Where there is a financial incentive for doctors to prescribe treatment (and sometimes unnecessary treatment) the relationship is often characterised by suspicion rather than trust. In the public opinion polls which take place from time to time, asking respondents to rank occupational groups such as solicitors, doctors, policemen, etc. in terms of status, reliability and trustworthiness, doctors in Britain come out consistently well and doctors in America come out consistently badly.

Another outcome of this set of attitudes is that Americans, who are in any case a litigious nation, are much more likely to sue their doctors for malpractice (and much more likely to win substantial awards). In 1981 there were 45 awards to patients of more than $1 million (compared with only 4 in 1976) and, over the same period, the average award increased to $840 396 from $192 344. Awards were highest in California and New York but Arizona, Florida, Illinois and Pennsylvania were also said to be good for lawyers but bad for doctors. The specialties with the highest malpractice rates were orthopaedic surgery, anaesthesia and general surgery. Obstetricians and gynaecologists and general practitioners also had higher than average rates. Unlike Britain there are comparatively few channels through which the American patient can pursue a complaint against his doctor so that, as one writer put it, 'either he can reach for his gun or file a suit' (quoted in Hawkins, 1985, p. 247).

The so-called 'malpractice crisis' which has arisen in the USA is cyclical and is exacerbated by a number of factors. The costs of treatment are high and the dissatisfied patient is inclined to sue. In order to protect himself the doctor will take out malpractice insurance (which in some states and some specialties now costs an average of $100 000 p.a.). Juries make higher and higher awards, insurance premiums rise, doctors charge more for their services (so as to pay the new premiums), thereby increasing the incentive for patients to recoup their losses by suing the doctor – and the process begins again. The vested interests of lawyers in the process has been regarded with some scepticism and in medical malpractice cases they have earned for themselves the description of 'ambulance chasers'.

Another consequence of malpractice suits has been the growth of 'defensive medicine'. Doctors will undertake unnecessary treatment as a means of increasing their incomes but will also order unnecessary tests and X-rays so as to avoid charges of negligence and ensure that no stones can be said to have been left unturned by anxious patients or over-eager lawyers. According to Hawkins, defensive medicine probably accounts for caesarian sections being four times more common in the USA than in Europe (ibid., p. 254) and it also accounts for the reluctance of the medical profession to take 'brain dead' people off respirators. The American Medical Association discovered in 1977 that 75 per cent of its members ordered unnecessary X-rays and tests and in 1984 it was estimated that defensive medicine added $15.1 billion to America's medical bill (Hawkins, p. 251).

Alford has also argued that medical priorities in America, determined by professional power and profit orientation, have distorted student training with the result that there is excessive specialisation. Figures quoted by Heidenheimer *et al.* (now rather dated) show that only 23 per cent of American doctors are in general practice compared with 48 per cent in England (Heidenheimer et al.; 1983, p. 68). Alford maintains that such a level of specialisation results in fragmented care and is 'not particularly responsive to the human problems motivating much patient concern'. In particular he argues, it 'contradicts the physician's claim that fee-for-service practice allows for the closest doctor-patient relationship' (1975, p. 197). The free market principles which operate not only in the payment of doctors but in their geographical location and choice of specialty do not ensure that manpower resources are used most effectively or that they are used to the benefit of patients. In 1974 Senator Edward Kennedy was moved to ask why Massachusetts, with a population of 5 million, had the same number of neurosurgeons as England, with its population of 40 million, and twice the number of operations. 'Could it be', he asked, 'because we have a Parkinson's Law for surgery, which says that the amount of surgery performed in America expands to fill the time of the surgeons available to do it?' (quoted in Heidenheimer *et al.*, 1983, pp. 67–8). Similarly Abel-Smith has argued that the high rate of appendectomies in West Germany and of tonsillectomies in California can be explained more by the operation of the market and fee-for- service payment than by patient needs or demands (1976, pp. 62–3). Cross-national data suggests that there is a distinct social class gradient in surgery rates, especially for operations

– such as hysterectomies – which can be palliative or pro-phylactic. Even in Britain, McPherson has argued that the hysterectomy rate among women in the highest social classes is more than twice as high as for other social classes and he speculates that 'when private surgery is much more wide-spread the positive class gradients exhibited by hysterectomy will appear for some of the other operations. We have to ask ourselves then', he goes on, 'whether it is appropriate that surgery should behave as a luxury' (McPherson, 1982, p. 13). Nevertheless paying patients in Britain do appear to value the extra time and consideration they buy from their doctor in private practice and the advantages which they secure from the financial relationship.

Generally speaking, the balance of evidence from other countries would seem to suggest that health care systems which are heavily reliant upon fee-for-service payments rather than salaries or capitation fees do disadvantage patients. They provide too many incentives for unnecessary tests and treat-ment, undermine the trust of patients in their doctors, divert scarce resources and may result in expensive and stressful litigation.

The problem is not a new one and little has changed since the turn of the century Britain when George Bernard Shaw commented:

> That any sane nation, having observed that you could provide for the supply of bread by giving bakers a pecuniary interest in baking for you, should go on to give a surgeon a pecuniary interest in cutting off your leg, is enough to make one despair of political humanity. But that is precisely what we have done. And the more appalling the mutilation, the more the mutilator is paid. He who corrects the ingrowing toe-nail receives a few shillings: he who cuts your inside out receives hundreds of guineas, except when he does it to a poor person for practice! (Shaw, 1946, p. 7)

The Problem of Equity

The growth of the private market in health care in Britain, especially since 1979, has breached the fundamental principle of health service distribution established after World War II, that services should be allocated according to need rather than to demand or ability to pay. The principle of equity requires that individuals in similar states of need should be treated similarly. They should be afforded equal access to treatment, even though equality of take-up and of outcome cannot be guaranteed. The strength of commitment to this principle, in theory if not always in practice, in the post-war NHS has been very striking and popular support for the NHS has been consistently high. Rudolf Klein has commented that, in political debate since the 1940s, 'Nothing is more remarkable than the shared assumption that the health service should be both free and comprehensive – and that it should be based on the principle of the collective provision of services and the pooling of financial risks through the public financing of the service' (1983, pp. 26–7). For many years, he goes on, 'the NHS ranked next to the monarchy as an unchallenged landmark in the political landscape of Britain' (ibid., p. 32).

Why did this particular social institution display such resilience? Why did it remain, for so long, above political debate? Why did the principle of equity continue to be such a central value and how far is that principle undermined by private sector growth?

It was clear, from the publication of the Beveridge Report in 1942, that the main aim of British social policy after the war would be to modify the play of market forces, to ensure that the costs of social change would not lie where they fell. Much of the debate focused upon the social services as 'shock absorbers' which would provide a cushion against the hardships engendered by persisting social inequalities. In all this, the NHS was to be the jewel in the post-war Labour Government's crown – attracting all-party support and popular acclaim. So it has turned out to be, the one public service set apart, politically untouchable for so long. This was due, in part, to dissatisfaction with pre-war health services where money was often a barrier to access and where the geographical distribution of services was grossly inequitable. As Taylor-Gooby has argued, the strength and popular appeal of the NHS has also been due to the fact that it caters for the 'deserving', unlike other benefits which have a negative image, such as unemployment benefit. It is a 'universal' service available to, and used by, the whole population rather than selected, stigmatised groups (1985, pp. 32–3). It was more obvious with the NHS than with any of the other public services that – from the moment of conception – everyone was a potential consumer.

It is clear, however, that support for the NHS has also been based upon altruism as well as upon self-interest and that commitment to the NHS is emotional as well as rational. As Robert Sugden put it: 'The welfare state and the NHS in particular is a source of deep and genuine national pride for many British people. There is something very comforting in the belief that the NHS is not merely another nationalised industry but an embodiment of people's regard for the needs of others' (1983, p. 13). For many people, therefore, health care was special, it was different from other public goods and services and its distribution had to be governed by criteria other than those operating in the marketplace.

Norman Daniels has looked at these common sense arguments and has attempted to analyse them within a more systematic framework. In his view not only is health care 'special' but it is almost universally regarded as such. Even in countries like the USA with profoundly inegalitarian health care systems there is a firm belief that health services should be distributed more equally than other goods (including food). Health care is special because it is designed to satisfy those human needs which contribute to 'normal species functioning'. Disease and disability which restrict normal functioning limit an individual's opportunity to develop his/her skills and talents to achieve 'life plans' or goals. The role of health services is, as far as possible, to 'correct for the effects of the 'natural lottery''' (Daniels, 1985, pp. 1–35).

But there are more obvious reasons for suggesting that health care is special.

Some health care, in a direct and simple way, for example reduces pain and suffering – and no fancy analysis of opportunity is needed to show why people value reducing them. Similarly, disease reminds us of the fragility of life and the limits of human existence – and the solidarity we show with the ill by caring for them has come to have deep religious and moral significance in many cultures. (ibid., p. 49)

It is important to note, Daniels continues, that health care is not homogeneous and that it serves different purposes for different people. For some it postpones death or reduces pain and suffering, while for others it has a more positive role in improving the quality of life. While other services and consumer goods may serve this last function Daniels concludes that: 'The *way* in which quality is improved by health care seems critical to our estimate of its importance' (ibid., p. 49).

Although Daniels' analysis does not help us to explain why different countries accord different priorities to meeting health care needs and why the principle of equity is stronger in the distributional systems of some countries than others, it does help us to understand why, in Britain, health services have been regarded as a 'special' public good.

There is little doubt that the introduction of a market in health threatens a distributional system based on equity. In Britain it has done this in two ways, first by setting up alternative health care institutions where access is determined almost exclusively by ability to pay and, second, by reducing the capacity of the public sector (if only marginally) to respond to health care needs in an equitable fashion. It draws resources from the NHS in an unplanned and haphazard way which distorts priorites and makes equal treatment for equal needs more difficult to attain. It is important to recognise, however, that the principle of equity is concerned with the question of who *should* have access to services and who *should* use them rather than with the question of who does use them. It may be that a shift towards market principles and away from the equity model has surprisingly little effect on health outcomes.

It is a striking fact that although the principles of distribution in public and private medicine are diametrically opposed the end results may be indistinguishable. Even though access to the public sector is determined by medical need and access to the private sector is broadly determined by ability to pay, the result in terms of the *actual use* of health services is remarkably similar. As we saw in the Chapter 5, 22–3 per cent of Social Classes I and II have private health insurance compared with only 1 per cent Classes IV and V. In looking at out-patient attendances and in-patient stays it was clear that not only did Classes I and II have higher rates of use of private facilities than other social classes but that their use of private health care was disproportionate in relation to morbidity. Put simply, the healthier patients got most private health care. Within the public service, despite its very different ethos and despite different entry criteria the outcome has been almost exactly the same. As Julian Le Grand demonstrated in 1982, 'public expenditure per person reporting illness is greater the higher the social group' (1982, p. 26). Just as in the private sector, the NHS favours the better off even though they are healthier than the worst off in our society. The Black Report on inequalities in health drew similar conclusions, arguing that class differentials in the use of health services derived from the interaction of social and ecological factors. Access to NHS resources was restricted by their unavailability in some locations, by long waiting times, and by shortage of space as well as by barriers facing the less articulate and the less mobile (Townsend and Davidson, 1982, p. 89).

It is paradoxical then, that although critics will condemn private medicine because it discriminates in favour of the better off and support the NHS because it is said to treat everyone equally, the outcome under both systems may actually be the same in terms of the use of services and, arguably, in terms of health and morbidity. The conclusion must be, as the Black Report argued, that factors other than the need for medical care determine who gets what and how that affects health. We may even go as far as Victor Fuchs in arguing that: 'Differences in health levels . . . are not related to differences in quantity and quality of medical care' (1974, p. 6). If this is so, the breach in the principle of equity as a distributional criterion in Britain – as a result of growth in the private sector – may affront the nation's conscience more than it damages the nation's health.

Conclusions

Although the private market in health care in Britain remains small and specialised its existence has raised a number of important issues. The rapid growth of the private sector since 1979 has posed a series of challenges and brought into sharp relief the different attitudes which exist towards the financing and provision of health services under conditions of economic and social change. In this sense, private sector developments have provided a valuable stimulus to our thinking about health service delivery. They provide a point of comparison against which to evaluate forty years of a universal and publicly-financed NHS. This concluding chapter has three main aims: first, to summarise and analyse the changes which have taken place in the private market; second, to examine the lessons for the NHS; and third, to look at some of the moral arguments involved in the provision of health care.

The Significance of Changes in the Private Market

In looking at the changes which have taken place in the private market, especially since 1979, a number of broad trends are discernible.

The expansion of for-profit medicine

First, there has been a very substantial shift (in both Britain and America) from not-for-profit health services to for-profit services. This is particularly evident in the hospital sector, but similar changes are also taking place in the insurance market. As earlier chapters have shown, for-profit hospital corporations have increased their share of the British market from 29 per cent to 51.5 per cent in just seven years (1979–86). The main casualties of these changes have been the small

religious-owned hospitals which have been unable to survive
in the new competitive market. Over a similar period the
commercial insurance companies have expanded their market
share from less than 2 per cent to 8.5 per cent.

The Americans in Britain

The second and related change has been in the ownership of
private hospitals in Britain. In 1979 American groups owned
just 2 per cent of all private beds outside the NHS and by 1986
they owned 22.5 per cent. They owned nearly half of all the
for-profit beds but none of the beds in charitable institutions.
The American hospitals were newer, larger and more sophisticated than the average private hospital and they were able to
offer a wide range of services to patients. Similarly the majority of new entrants to the insurance market were American-
owned commercial companies.

The significance of these changes should not be underestimated. The traditional market leaders in hospitals and
insurance in Britain, Nuffield and BUPA, have begun to lose
the initiative to these American-owned corporations which have
different attitudes to marketing, cost-control and patient services. The size and power of the American corporations has
enabled them to invest resources in private medicine on a
scale unprecedented in Britain. Their wealth has also insu-
lated them from the vagaries of the market which have
knocked Nuffield and BUPA more severely. The virtual
monopoly which the British companies enjoyed until 1979 has
now been shaken and it is increasingly the Americans who
have made the running. This has resulted in deep divisions
within the private sector. We are looking now not just at
competition between the NHS and private suppliers but at
fierce territorial battles within the private sector itself. The
way in which the private market in Britain develops in the
future will increasingly be determined by the interests of the
American corporations.

Medicine as a business

The third major change discussed in the book has been the
transition from private medicine as a cottage industry to

private medicine as a business enterprise. The renewed emphasis on profit-seeking has become evident in a number of ways. At the institutional level it is clear that the American corporations have none of the sensitivities about making profits from ill health which are often felt in Britain. In their view, health care is a product which can legitimately be bought and sold like any other product. The market is left to determine the extent of success or failure.

At the individual level, NHS consultants have shown a much greater interest in private practice since their contractual position changed in 1980. The vast majority of them now choose to supplement their NHS salaries by income raised through treating private patients. The extent and scope of private practice in the 1980s was considerably more extensive than it had been a decade earlier. American experience has shown, however, that there comes a point (and it may be some way off in Britain) where the profit-seeking interests of the hospitals begin to conflict with the profit-seeking behaviour of doctors. In America it has increasingly been the hospital corporations which have called the shots and, as Wohl put it in 1984, it is the grey flannel suit and not the white coat which is now in control of the nation's health care (pp. 80–81). The status of most British doctors, who are employed by the NHS but who may practise in the private sector, has so far afforded them considerable protection against the power of the business community. This may not continue, however, if the private sector continues to expand or if the contractual position of doctors should change.

The growth of employer-financed care

The fourth trend, described in earlier chapters, has been the small but significant shift in health care financing and provision from the state and from individuals to employers. In 1975, 40 per cent of private hospital bills were settled by patients themselves. By 1985 this proportion had fallen to just 25 per cent and 75 per cent of all bills were paid by insurance companies (Grant, 1985, p. 65). The main growth in the insurance market was in company purchase or employee purchase schemes rather than in individual schemes. Although the individual subscriber continued to pay part of the premium in many cases, the General Household Survey showed that 45 per cent of all insurance policies in 1982 were paid for in whole or in part by employers (see Laing, 1985, p. 24).

If Britain were to imitate American experiences this transfer of responsibility to employers would become enormously important. The escalation of health care costs in the USA has meant a growing burden for employers. As a result they have become much more critical of the insurance market and the way it operates. They have played an increasingly central role in the battle to control costs and are now equal partners in the health care enterprise. If insurance cover in Britain remains at its present level (less than 10 per cent of the population) the role of the employer in health care financing will be relatively small. If it should increase substantially, the British employer, like his American counterpart, will acquire a growing interest in controlling the ways in which health services are delivered and funded.

The trends outlined in this book, then, demonstrate that in 1987 the plurality of financiers and suppliers of health care was much greater than at any time since 1946. Within the private sector itself there was increasing diversification and competition, a movement away from charitable provision in health care and a growing emphasis upon profits.

The Lessons for the NHS

The operations of the private market in Britain, especially in the hospital sector, have drawn attention to a number of weaknesses in the public service. They have also shown ways in which the NHS might improve its services to the public. Although levels of satisfaction with the NHS are generally high, a number of criticisms crop up repeatedly in patient surveys. It has been attention to these details which has allowed the private sector to score some of its greatest successes.

Meeting the demands of patients

Of all the factors which encourage people to 'go private', waiting times and admission arrangements appear to be the most important. BUPA has argued, for example, that it is not so much *earlier* admission which attracts people to the private sector but *planned* admission dates which can be fixed well in advance. The Consumers' Association survey, quoted in Chapter 5, showed that only 31 per cent of NHS patients were given a choice of hospital admission date compared with 80 per cent of private patients (Consumers' Association, 1986, pp. 322–3). Although it may be considerably easier to provide a choice of dates in the private sector where there are relatively few patients requiring a limited range of treatments (most of it 'cold' surgery which can be planned in advance), there seems to be no reason why the 31 per cent figure for the NHS should not be considerably improved. The use of new technology has created opportunities for streamlining booking procedures and could be put to good use on behalf of patients. Not only would this improve consumer satisfaction in the NHS but it would almost certainly reduce the numbers of people failing to keep appointments and lead to more effective use of resources.

The Consumers' Association survey also underlined the potential for improved time-keeping in the NHS: 95 per cent of private patients were seen on time by consultants, compared with only 63 per cent of NHS patients. This large difference is indefensible and better administrative procedures in the NHS and the co-operation of medical staff could ensure a much better service for NHS patients. A more recent survey in 1987 showed that 'waiting around' was one of the two major complaints in the NHS (the other being 'poor food') and that the middle class were especially intolerant of being kept waiting (*The Health Service Journal*, 2 Apr. 1987, pp. 382–3).

Another preoccupation which drives people into the private sector, but which is less easily attainable in the NHS, is privacy. As the Consumers' Association survey discovered, 85 per cent of patients in the private sector are in single rooms and 85 per cent of patients in the NHS are not. However, the significance of privacy may have been exaggerated. The majority of NHS patients are now in small wards and only 13 per cent of the sample in the Consumers' Association survey complained that they disliked sharing (1986, pp. 322–3). An equally small number (11 per cent) surveyed by OPCS for the

Royal Commission on the National Health Service, expressed a preference for single rooms, while 60 per cent actually preferred to be in small wards (DHSS, 1979, p. 131). Although the NHS would have difficulty satisfying all those patients who would prefer a single room, it could be made clearer to those who do that this option is sometimes available and would be a high priority if the patient's medical condition demanded it. A single room in the NHS would be unlikely to provide the same amenities as one in the private sector, with a television, en-suite bathroom and so on, but it could offer privacy and quiet. Other areas of dissatisfaction within the NHS, such as early waking times, and brusque and uninformative reception procedures, could be remedied at little cost and in ways which would considerably enhance patient satisfaction.

Finally, a complaint which features in almost all patient surveys is that of poor communication. Patients want to be told what is happening to them and why. Most want to be told their diagnosis and prognosis and want time to discuss their feelings with caring staff. Time to talk may be more readily available in the private sector and it is a commodity which patients are clearly willing to buy. Nevertheless it would not be impossible, within the NHS, to give patients what the Royal College of Nursing maintains they want: 'the right information, in the right way at the right time' (Royal Commission on the National Health Service, 1979, p. 130).

Improving the image of the NHS

Despite a widespread commitment to the NHS in Britain there is, nevertheless, a view that it is an underfunded, bureaucratic institution which – except in emergencies – responds only slowly to patients' needs. There seems to be little doubt that some patients are attracted to the private sector because it offers a smart, glossy and well-packaged alternative. As we noted earlier, many private hospitals genuinely *are* different in important respects. Almost half of them have been built within the last 10 years, whereas 70 per cent of NHS hospitals pre-date 1914 and only 10 per cent of them have been built since 1948 (*The Health Service Journal*, 9 Apr. 1987, p. 412). The private sector really does have an advantage over the NHS in the appearance of its small, modern hospitals conveniently located for doctors and patients.

The crucial difference between a private hospital and an NHS hospital, of course, is that the former benefits financially from admitting patients whereas the latter does not. It may be that poor physical conditions have been allowed to persist in the NHS as a form of rationing through deterrence. Even if this is regarded as an acceptable and legitimate means of controlling scarce resources (which is questionable) there is a case for improving services to the patients who do eventually find their way into the system.

Private hospitals in Britain and America have demonstrated the value of attractive and informative reception facilities. For them, first impressions are a matter of some commercial importance. In contrast, as Tony Hall (1974) argued in his book *The Point of Entry*, the public sector is notoriously bad at receiving clients or patients and may place both physical and psychological barriers between them and the services they require. It is often the least skilled and most junior member of staff who sits at the reception desk and who makes important rationing decisions about the use of professional time and access to services. Robert Bessell's comments about social work agencies are also relevant in the NHS:

> Possibly the most important single factor which determines the public image [of a social work agency] is the way in which the agency receives its prospective clients and it is no exaggeration to say that, in many cases, what happens before the client sees the social worker will not only determine the outcome of the interview but whether the client will even be admitted to see a social worker and if he does whether he will return. (quoted in Hall, 1974, p. 31)

The NHS as a public agency available to all citizens on a 24-hour basis faces particular problems at 'the point of entry' in its relationships with the people it meets. Nevertheless, it is a service to which every taxpayer contributes and all those using it are entitled to a sensitive and courteous reception. For anxious patients and relatives first impressions may be vital in providing the comfort and reassurance they need. The NHS can learn from the private sector that modern, inexpensive (even 'cosmetic') changes in reception areas can considerably enhance the image of the organisation and lead to greater consumer satisfaction.

The marketing techniques of the private sector may also be relevant to the NHS – not in the sense that the NHS may wish to sell more services to more people, but in terms of providing better information about the facilities and treatments which do exist. As we observed earlier, some patients in taking the decision to go private are ill-informed about NHS provision and its availability. The private sector flourishes to a degree through lack of public confidence in the NHS. Where resources are restricted and waiting times are long this attitude may be justifiable. Where it is not, the NHS could do considerably more (at little cost) to advise and inform the public about its services, its facilities and achievements. At the moment the private sector wins the public relations battle almost entirely by default.

It is a short-sighted view that, as one Health Authority Chairman put it; 'concepts such as marketing, advertising and public relations might seem to be part of an alien culture, and smack of something not quite savoury' (quoted in the *The Health Service Journal*, 12 Feb. 1987, p. 188). It is important that the highly developed marketing skills which the private sector has used so successfully now be used to the benefit of NHS patients. One goal should be more and better information to enable consumers to exercise intelligent choices. Another should be to give NHS staff and patients a sense of value and worth, by creating an environment with a strong and positive image.

Regulating the private sector

The growth of the private sector in Britain has underlined some of the contradictions and weaknesses which exist in the regulation and monitoring of developments outside the NHS. The American experience has shown that 'free' markets in health are invariably much more strictly controlled markets, and cross-national comparisons illustrate the strengths and limitations of different regulatory mechanisms. Two particular points can be made by way of conclusion. The first is that the Registered Homes Act 1984 (and the legislation which preceded it) was not designed for, and is inadequate for, monitoring standards in private acute hospitals (see Higgins, 1984b). Its implementation has led to inconsistencies between districts and it omits scrutiny of procedures and practices which are characteristic of acute hospitals undertaking complex surgical procedures.

The second point is that the advice on new private hospital building from different government departments is contradictory and unhelpful (see Higgins, 1984a). One argument is that planning procedures quite properly limit the participation of interested parties (in this case DHAs) in decision-making about competing developments. However, it can also be argued that the interests of patients are best protected where measures are available to control not only the siting but also the type and content of health facilities (for example, the Certificate of Need procedure in the USA). The best means of controlling private sector developments fairly and efficiently are by no means self-evident and the experience of different countries reveals flaws in many of the possible options. In many areas outside London where there are few private hospitals it is not a pressing issue but, if private sector growth is to continue, more attention must be given not only to the control of planned developments but also to monitoring standards of care and accreditation procedures in both institutional and non-institutional settings.

Value for Money

There is, as yet, no comparative data in Britain on the costs and benefits of public and private acute health services. In evaluating the relative merits of public and private medicine, therefore, the best that can be achieved is a comparison of broadly different *systems* on a cross-national basis.

Comparisons between public and private markets in health illustrate two important points about their respective costs.

First of all, the NHS has been remarkably effective in controlling the costs which have plagued those health care systems with larger private sectors. However, it has done so at the expense of under-investment in services which patients want and which would be of benefit to them, such as total hip replacements, renal dialysis and coronary artery surgery (Aaron and Schwartz, 1984). The second is that fee-for-service medicine tends to lead to waste, over-supply, unnecessary treatment and (in America at least) to defensive medicine. Expenditure and costs are often higher than in the public sector but the outcome in many cases is no better (see for example, Culyer, 1982; Aaron and Schwartz, 1984). Despite these differences patient satisfaction with both systems is generally high.

It is clear that, in Britain, the private sector acts as a 'safety valve' absorbing some of the excess demand which the NHS cannot meet (Aaron and Schwartz, 1984, pp. 105–7; Cairns, 1986, p. 165). Nevertheless, as we argued in Chapter 5, there is no evidence that the private sector relieves the burden on the NHS by reducing waiting lists (except where specific groups of patients are contracted out to the private sector). Indeed, there is anecdotal evidence to the contrary. The present arrangements create incentives for NHS doctors to add to their waiting lists in order to boost their private practice (HMSO, 1972; Culyer, 1982; Aaron and Schwartz, 1984). However, waiting list figures can be used to support an infinite variety of different (and contradictory) arguments. In practice the NHS list can easily be manipulated and is more a reflection of clinical practices and consultant preferences that patient demand. Other measures of private sector impact are potentially more valuable.

On balance, the evidence suggests that public systems of care (such as the NHS) may be relatively cost-effective and moderately successful in controlling costs but at the price of under-investment in important facilities and services. Private systems, on the other hand, are often characterised by waste, for which patients (or their insurers) have to pay in the form of higher prices, over-provision of services and under-occupancy of beds.

Morality and the Market

For many observers, the ultimate test of the private market in
health care is not its cost-effectiveness or its effects on NHS
waiting lists but its success or failure in meeting certain moral
criteria about justice, fairness and equity. Questions of value,
whether explicitly or not, are at the heart of most debates
about private medicine and, in Britain particularly, antipathy
towards profit-seeking in health services has a long history.
The evidence in this book suggests that positive lessons can be
learned from an examination of approaches and techniques in
the private sector. Nevertheless, the conclusion must be that
the growth of for-profit medicine in Britain has weakened the
commitment to equal access to health services for all, irrespective of age, gender, race, class or ability to pay. It has challenged the notion that 'health is different' and rejected the
claim that the distribution of health services should take place
beyond the play of market forces.

The American experience has highlighted vividly the dangers inherent in a health care system where a commitment to
profit-making becomes an over-riding priority. At its worst,
the private market creates a setting in which caring for the
poorest and sickest becomes just a residual function after the
fit, the better off and the 'best risks' have received attention.
The NHS in Britain is so large and the private sector so small
that the corruption of moral values on a grand scale may not
occur. Nevertheless, private sector growth has already been
divisive both socially and geographically and it has exacerbated existing inequalities in access to health care. It has also
drawn the vast majority of NHS consultants into a system
which emphasises medicine for profit. Moreover, it has
created a change in the moral climate of health service provision which many supporters of the NHS find distasteful. As
Plant has argued, there is a tendency for markets to undermine the neutrality of professional judgements and to encourage self-interested decision-making. In his view, 'There
may well be a place for markets in a humane society but they
must be kept in their place because they encourage some
forms of human behaviour rather than others, viz egotism

over altruism, and rational calculation of advantage over trust' (1984, p. 13). Even where the doctor renders his services honestly and conscientiously, the nature of the market is such that socially undesirable outcomes may result. As we have seen, the private market in health is organised around a distributional system which allocates resources to the healthiest rather than to the sickest in our society. In Plant's words the market:

> does not secure social justice, whether understood in terms of need, desert, performance or anything else; it does not secure a fair worth of liberty; it does not secure equality. The market is neutral and amoral. Success depends upon luck as much as on anything else, the luck of birth, of upbringing, of education, of being in the right place at the right time, and certainly not upon merit or desert. (ibid., p. 13)

The creation of the NHS in 1946 was a recognition that some needs could not be left to the market for their satisfaction. It was a collective agreement that the chances of obtaining medical treatment should not be left to luck, birth, upbringing, education or being in the right place at the right time as they had been before the war. It signified that the risks were to be pooled and shared between healthy and sick, rich and poor. Payment for treatment was to be made, for the most part, when people were healthy and in work and able to pay their taxes rather than when they were unhealthy, out of work and financially vulnerable. It established that treatment would be allocated to each according to his needs and not according to his merit, worth or ability to pay. It was to be rationed (where this was necessary) through waiting lists, waiting times, appointment systems and professional judgement rather than by charges. The growth of the private market in health care in Britain, especially the for-profit sector, provides a fundamental challenge to these principles and expectations. It is not governed by morality or notions of social justice. It provides a choice to those who are inhibited or constrained by the egalitarianism of the NHS, but in doing so it widens the gulf between the rich and the poor and between the healthy and the sick. The price of further expansion in the market will be increasing inequality and social divisiveness. Many would argue that it is too high a price to pay.

Bibliography

Aaron, Henry J. and Schwartz, William B. (1984) *The Painful Prescription: Rationing Hospital Care* (Brookings Institution, Washington DC).

Abel-Smith, Brian (1964) *The Hospitals 1800–1948* (Heinemann, London).

Abel-Smith, Brian (1976) *Value For Money in the Health Services* (Heinemann, London).

Adam Smith Institute (1985) *Omega Health Policy* (London).

Alford, Robert R. (1975) *Health Care Politics* (University of Chicago Press, Chicago).

Alleway, Lynn (1985) 'The Cost of Rewards from a Token Economy', *Health and Social Service Journal*, 15 August 1985.

Allsop, Judy (1984) *Health Policy and the National Health Service* (Longman, London).

Ashton, John (1983) 'Chalybeate private hospital: a case study in opposition', *Medicine in Society*, vol. 9, no. 4, Winter 1983–4.

Association of Independent Hospitals (1985a) *Survey of Acute Hospitals in the Independent Sector* (London).

Association of Independent Hospitals (1985b) *Nursing Home Beds, AIH Estimates* (London).

Association of Independent Hospitals (1986) *AIH Acute Hospital Survey: Ownership Summary*, December.

Balfour Lynn, Stanley (1982) *Times Health Supplement*, 6 August 1982.

Bosanquet, Nick (1984) 'Social policy and the welfare state' in Jowell, R. and Airey C. (eds) *British Social Attitudes: the 1984 Report* (Gower, Aldershot).

Brewster, Kingman (1979) 'Health at any price?', *Journal of the Royal Society of Medicine*, vol. 72, October 1979.

Brown, Pauline (1983) 'Insurers and hospitals decide: it's time for more talks', *Independent Medical Care*, April 1983.

Brown, Pauline (1983a) 'HCA's goal – to be a Number One in the United Kingdom', *Independent Medical Care;* June 1983.

Bryant, Sir Arthur (1968) *A History of the British United Provident Association: B.U.P.A. 1947–68* (BUPA, London).

BUPA (1981) 'Union leaders out of touch with members', *Press Release*, 18 June 1981.

BUPA (1982) 'Local Government union obstructs members' wishes', *Press Release*, 26 January 1982.

BUPA (1985) *Independent Health Care in Britain: the Facts* (BUPA, London).

Burleson, Gene (1984) 'Management budgeting and the use of resources: a private sector view', *Hospital and Health Services Review*, May 1984.

Butcher, Tony and Randall, Ed (1981) 'The politics of pay beds: Labour Party policy and legislation', *Policy and Politics*, vol. 9, no. 3.

Cairns, John A. (1986) 'Demand for abortion services in the private sector and excess demand in the public sector' in Culyer, A.J. and Jönsson, B. (eds) *Public and Private Health Services* (Blackwell, Oxford).

Calder, A. (1969) *The Peoples War* (Cape, London).

Cartwright, Ann (1976) *Patients and Their Doctors* (RKP, London).

Castle, Barbara (1980) *The Castle Diaries 1974–76* (Weidenfeld & Nicolson, London).

CIS (no date) *NHS: Condition Critical*, C.I.S. Report (Counter Information Services, London).

Clarke, Lynda; Farrell, Christine and Beaumont, Berry (1983) *Camden Abortion Study: the Views and Experiences of Women Having NHS and Private Treatment* (British Pregnancy Advisory Service, Solihull).

College of Health (1985) *Guide to Hospital Waiting Lists 1985* (College of Health, London).

Consumers' Association (1986) 'Private medical insurance', *Which?*, July.

Cooke, Claudia (1985) 'A private alternative?', *BMA News Review*, vol. 11, no. 10, October 1985.

Crossman, Richard (1977) *The Diaries of a Cabinet Minister, vol. 3, 1968–70* (Hamish Hamilton and Cape, London).

Culyer, A.S. (1982) 'The NHS and the market: images and realities', in McLachlan, Gordon and Maynard, Alan (eds) *The Public/Private Mix for Health* (Nuffield Provincial Hospitals Trust, London).

Culyer A.S. and Jönsson B. (1986) *Public and Private Health Services* (Blackwell, Oxford).

Cunningham, Robert (1982) *The Healing Mission and the Business Ethic* (Pluribus Press, London).

Daniels, Norman (1985) *Just Health Care* (Cambridge University Press, Cambridge).

Davies, Peter (1985) 'Buddy can you spare a hospital?', *Hospital and Health Service Journal*, 8 August 1985.

Davies, Peter (1987) 'Private sector is bedding in', *The Health Service Journal*, 9 April 1987.

DHSS (1969) *Report of the Committee on the Functions of the District General Hospital* (Chairman: Sir Desmond Bonham-Carter) (HMSO, London).

DHSS (1973) *Private Practice in National Health Service Hospitals*, Cmnd 5270 (HMSO, London).

DHSS (1977) *Common Waiting Lists for NHS and Private Patients in NHS Hospitals*, Cmnd 6828 (HMSO, London).

DHSS (1978) *Health Services Board Annual Report, 1977* (HMSO, London).

DHSS (1978) *Personnel Memorandum: Pay and Conditions of Service Contracts of Consultants and Other Senior Hospital Medical and Dental Staff*, PM (79) 11 (DHSS, London).

DHSS (1980) *Health Services Board Annual Report* (HMSO, London).

DHSS (1980) *Health Services Development. Health Services Act 1980: Private*

Practice in Health Service Hospitals and Control of Private Hospital Developments. Amenity Beds, HC (80) 10; (DHSS, London).

DHSS (1981) *Orthopaedic Services: Waiting Time for Out-Patient Appointments and In-Patient Treatment* (HMSO, London).

DHSS (1986) *Report of the Committee of Enquiry into Unnecessary Dental Treatment* (HMSO, London).

Dobson, Frank (no date) *Monitoring Consultants' Commitment to the NHS: a Report of Two Surveys* (Unpublished report).

Dobson, Frank (1985) Letter to Chairman of the Public Accounts Committee, reproduced in *Medicine in Society*, vol. 11, no. 2, Summer 1985.

Donnelley, Clare (1985) *Diagnosis: Healthy or Ailing? the State of Private Health Care in Scotland*, unpublished undergraduate dissertation (Department of Social Administration, University of Edinburgh).

Drummond, Margaret (1983) 'How private medicine stopped being just a perk', *The Times*, 17 June 1983.

Eckstein, Harry (1958) *The English Health Service: Its Origins, Structure and Achievements* (Harvard University Press, Cambridge, Massachusetts).

Ekaterini, S. (1981) *Investor-Owned Hospitals and Their Role in Changing Health Care* (F and S Press, New York).

Family (1981) 'Clinic-Air, a patient's package to beat over-charging claims', vol 3, no. 1, April 1981.

Fightback (no date) *Going Private: The Case Against Private Medicine* (Fightback and the Politics of Health Group, London).

Foot, Michael (1975) *Aneurin Bevan 1945–1960* (Paladin, London).

Forsyth, Gordon (1966) *Doctors and State Medicine* (Pitman, London).

Forsyth, Gordon (1982) 'The semantics of health care policy and the inevitability of regulation' in McLachlan and Maynard (eds) (1982). *The Public/Private Mix for Health* (Nuffield Provincial Hospitals Trust, London).

Foster, Geoffrey (1985) 'Gene Burleson picks AMI's primary target', *Management Today*, December 1985.

Fraser, Derek (1984) *The Evolution of the British Welfare State*, 2nd edn (Macmillan, London).

Fuchs, Victor (1974) *Who shall Live?* (Basic Books, New York).

Gilbert, Neil (1984) 'Welfare for profit: moral, empirical and theoretical perspectives', *Journal of Social Policy*, vol. 13, pt 1.

Grant, Clive (1985) *Private Health Care in the UK: Review*, Economist Intelligence Unit, Special Report no. 207 (London).

Gray, Bradford H. (ed.) (1983) *The New Health Care For-Profit* (National Academy Press, Washington DC).

Gray, Bradford H. (ed.) (1986) *For-Profit Enterprise in Health Care* (National Academy Press, Washington DC).

Green, David (1986) *Challenge to the NHS* (Institute of Economic Affairs, London).

Griffith, Ben; Rayner, Geof and Mohan, John (1985) *Commercial Medicine in London* (Greater London Council).

Guillebaud Report (1956) *Committee of Enquiry into the Cost of the National Health Service*, Cmnd 663 (HMSO, London).

Hadley, J. (1982) *More Medical Care: Better Health?* (The Urban Institute Press, Washington DC).

Hall, Anthony S. (1974) *The Point of Entry* (Allen & Unwin, London).

Halpern, Stephen (1986) 'Lessons from over the Atlantic', *Health and Social Service Journal*, 13 February 1986.

Hawkins, Clifford (1985) *Mishap or Malpractice?* (Blackwell Scientific, *Publications*; Oxford).

Heidenheimer, Arnold J; Heclo, Hugh and Teich Adams, Carolyn (1983) *Comparative Public Policy*, 2nd edn (Macmillan, London).

Higgins, Joan (1983) 'Collaboration with the private sector: problems for District Health Authorities', *Public Administration*, vol. 16, Summer 1983.

Higgins, Joan (1984a) 'The public control of private health care', *Public Administration*, vol. 17, Summer 1984.

Higgins, Joan (1984b) 'The limits of legislation', *Health and Social Service Journal*, 21 June 1984.

Higgins, Joan (1987) *Private Medicine and Pay Bed Income*, Occasional Paper (Dept. of Sociology and Social Administration, University of Southampton).

Himmelstein, David V; Woodhandler, Steffie (1984) 'Pitfalls of private medicine: health care in the USA', *The Lançet*, 18 August 1984.

Horne, David (1983) 'The contracting NHS', *The Health Services*, 1 July 1983.

Horne, David (1984) 'A survey of patients in the private sector', *Hospital and Health Services Review*, March 1984.

House of Commons (1972) *Fourth Report from the Expenditure Committee, Session 1971–72, National Health Service Facilities for Private Patients* (HMSO, London).

Howard, Anthony (ed.) (1979) *The Crossman Diaries – Selections from the Diaries of a Cabinet Minister 1964–70, Richard Crossman* (Magnum, London).

Illich, Ivan (1976) *Limits to Medicine* (Penguin, Harmondsworth).

Illife, Steve (1983) *The NHS: a Picture of Health?* (Lawrence & Wishart, London).

Illman, John (1978) 'Private care on the never-never', *General Practice*, 15 December 1978.

Jewkes, John and Jewkes, Sylvia (1961); *The Genesis of the British National Health Service* (Blackwell, Oxford).

Judge, Ken; Smith, Jillian and Taylor-Gooby, Peter (1983) 'Public opinion and the privatization of welfare', *Journal of Social Policy*, vol. 12, no. 4.

Klein, Rudolf (1982) 'Private practice and public policy: regulating the frontiers', in McLachlan, Gordon and Maynard, Alan (eds) *The Public/ Private Mix for Health* (Nuffield Provincial Hospitals Trust, London).

Klein, Rudolf (1983) *The Politics of the National Health Service* (Longman, London).

Klein, Rudolf and Day, Patricia (1985) 'Towards a new health care system?', *British Medical Journal*, vol. 291, 2 November 1985.

Kolde, E.J. (1975) *The Multinational Company* (Lexington Books, Lexington, Massachusetts).

Laing, William (1985) *Private Health Care 1985* (Office of Health Economics, London).

Lee, Jennie (1980) *My Life with Nye* (Cape, London).

Lee, Michael (1978) *Private and National Health Services* (Policy Studies Institute, London).

Lee, Michael (1980) 'Charting the growth of the private health provident associations', *Medeconomics*, 11 April 1980.

Lees, Dennis (1961) *Health Through Choice*, Hobart Paper 14 (Institute of Economic Affairs, London).

Le Grand, Julian (1982) *The Strategy of Equality* (Allen & Unwin, London).

Levi, Peta (1983) 'When your GP goes private', *The Times*, 17 June 1983.

Lewis, E.B. (1981) 'Private practice', *British Medical Journal*, vol. 282, 7 March 1981.

Lindsey, Almont (1962) *Socialized Medicine in England and Wales: the National Health Services, 1948–1961* (University of North Carolina Press, Chapel Hill).

McKinlay, John B. (1985) *Issues in the Political Economy of Health Care*, (Tavistock, London).

McLachlan, Gordon and Maynard, Alan (eds) (1982) *The Public/Private Mix for Health* (Nuffield Provincial Hospitals Trust, London).

McPherson, Klim (1982) 'Opting to operate', *Times Health Supplement*, 12 March 1982.

Marmor, Theodore R. and Christianson, Jan B. (1982) *Health Care Policy: A Political Economy Approach* (Sage, London).

Marsh, Peter (1986) 'Paying for test tube babies', *Financial Times*, 22 January 1986.

Martin, J.P. and Williams, Sheila (1959) 'The effects of imposing prescription charges', *The Lancet*, 3 January 1959.

Mayer, T.C. (1975) 'Scrap the pay beds now and improve our medicine', *Pulse*, vol. 30, no. 18, 10 June 1975.

Maynard, Alan (1983) 'Privatising the National Health Service', *Radical Community Medicine*, no. 18, Autumn.

Medicine in Society (1983) 'Problems in the private sector', vol. 9, no. 1.

Mencher, Samuel (1967) *Private Practice in Britain*, Occasional Papers on Social Administration, no. 24 (G. Bell, London).

Ministry of Health (1944) *A National Health Service*, White Paper, Ministry of Health, Cmd 6502 (HMSO, London).

Ministry of Health (1946) *NHS Bill: Summary of the Proposed New Service*, Cmd 6761 (HMS0, London).

Ministry of Health (1947) *Report of the Chief Medical Officer, 1945*; Cmd 7119 (HMSO, London).

Ministry of Health (1962) *National Health Service: A Hospital Plan for England and Wales*, Cmnd 1604 (HMSO, London).

Mohan, John (1984) *Spatial Aspects and Planning Implications of Private Hospital Developments in South-East England 1976–84*, Occasional paper (Department of Geography, Birkbeck College, London).

Moore, Judith; Phipps, Kathy and Marcer, Don (1985) 'Why do people seek treatment by alternative medicine?', *British Medical Journal*, 5 January 1985.

Morone, James A. (1985) 'The unruly rise of medical capitalism', *Hastings Center Report*, vol. 15, no. 4.

National Audit Office (1986) *Report by the Comptroller and Auditor General: National Health Service: Level of Charges for Private Resident Patients* (HMSO, London).

National Health Service Consultants' Association (with NHS Unlimited) (1984) *Thinking of Going Private?* (London).

Navarro, Vicente (1978) *Class Struggles, the State and Medicine* (Martin Robertson, Oxford).

NHS Unlimited (1983) *The Conservatives, the National Health Service and Private Medicine*, Memorandum 6, April 1983 (London).

Nicholl, J.P.; Williams, B.T.; Thomas, K.J. and Knowelden, J. (1984) 'Contribution of the private sector to elective surgery in England and Wales', *The Lancet*, 14 July 1984.

Noble, Anthony D. (1985) 'Changing trends in gynaecological surgical workload', *British Medical Journal*, vol. 290, 12 January 1985.

Open University (1985) *Caring for Health: Dilemmas and Prospects (Open University Press, Milton Keynes)*.

Palmer, Rachel (1977) 'Come to Britain for health and holidays campaign', *General Practitioner*, 16 September 1977.

Pater, John E. (1981) *The Making of the National Health Service* (King Edward's Hospital Fund for London, London).

Plant, Raymond (1984) *Equality, Markets and the State*, Fabian Tract 494, (Fabian Society, London).

Platt, Sir Robert (1963) *Doctor and Patient: Ethics, Morale and Government* (Nuffield Provincial Hospitals Trust, London).

Poullier, Jean-Pierre (1986) 'Levels and trends in the public/private mix of the industrialized countries' health systems' in Culyer, A.J. and Jönsson B. (eds) *Public and Private Health Services* (Blackwell, Oxford).

Rathwell, T.; Sics, A and Williams, S. (1985) *Towards a New Understanding* (Nuffield Centre for Health Service Studies, University of Leeds).

Rayner, Geof (1982) 'Overpriced and over here?', *Health and Social Service Journal*, 9 December 1982.

Rayner, Geof (1984) 'Assessing the evidence', *Health and Social Service Journal*, 26 April 1984.

Rayner, Geof (1986) 'Private hospital treatment' in Harrison, A. and Gretton, J. (eds) *Health Care UK, 1986* (Policy Journals, London).

Reagle, Alina (1983) 'The joy of having your own room', *The Times*, 17 June 1983.

Relman, Arnold S. (1983) 'The new medical-industrial complex', *New England Journal of Medicine*, vol. 303, no. 17.

Robb, Douglas and Brown, Peter (1984) *BUPA 1968–1983: A Continuing History* (BUPA, London).

RIPA (1984) Unpublished survey of collaboration between public and independent sectors of health care.

Roemer, Milton, I. (1984) 'Private medical practice: obstacle to health for all', *World Health Forum*, vol. 5, no. 3.

Royal Commission on the National Health Service (1979) *Report*, Cmnd 7615 (HMSO, London).

Rutherford, Andrew (1986) *Growing Out of Crime* (Penguin, Harmondsworth).

Ryan, Michael (1975) 'Hospital pay beds: a study in ideology and constraint', *Social and Economic Administration*, vol. 9, no. 3.

Salmon, J. Warren (1985) 'Organising medical care for profit' in McKinlay, John B. (ed.) *Issues in the Political Economy of Health Care* (Tavistock, London).

Shaw, George Bernard (1946) *The Doctor's Dilemma* (Penguin, Harmondsworth).

Sherlock, Douglas, (1984) 'The psychiatric hospital industry: industry overview', *Stock Research: Health Services* (Solomon Brothers, New York).

Social Trends 1986 no. 16 (HMSO, London).

Starr, P. (1982) *The Social Transformation of American Medicine* (Basic Books, New York).

Stopford, John M. and Turner Louis (1985) *Britain and the Multinationals* (Wiley, Chichester).

Sugden, Robert (1983) *Who Cares?*, Occasional Paper 67 (Institute of Economic Affairs, London).

Taylor-Gooby, Peter (1985) *Public Opinion, Ideology and State Welfare* (RKP, London).

Thunhurst, Colin (1982) *It Makes You Sick: The Politics of the NHS* (Pluto Press, London).

Timbs, Olivia (1985) 'From perk to automatic benefit', *Financial Times*, 13 February 1985.

Timmins, Nicholas (1985) 'US group buys GP service', *The Times*, 31 July 1985.

Titmuss, Richard (1973) *The Gift Relationship* (Penguin, Harmondsworth).

Titmuss, Richard (1976) *Commitment to Welfare*, 2nd edn (Allen & Unwin, London).

Torrens, Paul R. (1980) 'Health insurance in the United States: implications for the United Kingdom', *The Lancet*, 5 January 1980.

Torrens, Paul R. (1982) 'Some potential hazards of unplanned expansion of private health insurance in Britain', *The Lancet*, 2 January 1982.

Townsend, Peter and Davidson, Nick (1982) *Inequalities in Health* (Penguin, Harmondsworth).

Watkin, Brian (1978) *The National Health Service: The First Phase 1948–1974 and After* (Allen & Unwin, London).

White, Geoff (1983) 'Has the private health perk reached its peak?' *Personnel Management*, August.

Widgery, David (1979) *Health in Danger* (Macmillan, London).

Williams, B.T.; Nicholl, J.P.; Thomas, K.J. and Knowelden, J.; (1984) 'Analysis of the work of independent acute hospitals in England and Wales, 1981', *British Medical Journal*, 18 August 1984.

Williams, Brian; Nicholl, Jonathan; Thomas, Kate and Knowelden, John (1985) *A Study of the Relationship Between the Private Sector of Health Care and the NHS in England and Wales: Short Stay Clinical Activity* (Department of Community Medicine, University of Sheffield).

Wohl, Stanley (1984) *The Medical Industrial Complex* (Harmony Books, New York).

Wood, Lisa (1986) 'Spiralling costs cause diversions', *Financial Times*, 22 January 1986.

Index